# Strategic Management, Regulatory Challenges, and Global Governance of MedTech

Ricardo Marcão
*ISLA Santarém, Portugal*

Vasco Ribeiro Santos
*Instituto Politécnico de Tomar, Portugal*

Stéphanie Monteiro
*Institute for Systems and Robotics, Portugal*

IGI Global Scientific Publishing
Publishing Tomorrow's Research Today

| | |
|---|---|
| Vice President of Editorial | Melissa Wagner |
| Managing Editor of Acquisitions | Mikaela Felty |
| Managing Editor of Book Development | Jocelynn Hessler |
| Production Manager | Mike Brehm |
| Cover Design | Phillip Shickler |

Published in the United States of America by
IGI Global Scientific Publishing
701 East Chocolate Avenue
Hershey, PA, 17033, USA
Tel: 717-533-8845
Fax: 717-533-7115
Website: https://www.igi-global.com E-mail: cust@igi-global.com



Library of Congress Cataloging-in-Publication Data

LCCN: 2025010077 (CIP Data Pending)
ISBN13: 9798337312057
Isbn13Softcover: 9798337312064
EISBN13: 9798337312071

British Cataloguing in Publication Data
A Cataloguing in Publication record for this book is available from the British Library.

# Table of Contents

# Detailed Table of Contents

Patent evergreening is a strategy used by pharmaceutical companies to extend their market exclusivity through minor modifications of existing drugs, often without significant therapeutic advancements. This practice raises concerns about access to affordable medicines, particularly in developing countries like India, where high drug prices impact public health. A comparative analysis with the European Union (EU) reveals that while India relies on patent law restrictions, the EU employs competition law under Article 102 of the Treaty on the Functioning of the European Union (TFEU) to regulate evergreening. Cases such as AstraZeneca v. European Commission demonstrate the EU's effects-based approach to curbing anti-competitive patent strategies. This study highlights the gaps in India's regulatory framework, emphasizing the need for greater coordination between the Indian Patent Office (IPO) and the Competition Commission of India (CCI), and adopting an effects-based approach are crucial to preventing evergreening while ensuring both innovation and consumer welfare.



This chapter examines the moderating influence of regulatory barriers on the relationship among risk management and new product development in the Eastern Africa. Conducting a investigation on a sample of 390 participants, exploratory factor analysis (EFA) check data suitability according to Kaiser-Meyer-Olkin(KMO) measure of sampling adequacy. Second, Confirmatory factor analysis (CFA) is used to assess the overall accuracy of measurement model in defining the constructs. Based on the data obtained, structural equation modeling using AMOS software is used to analyze the relations among risk management styles on the one hand, and regulatory barriers and product development outcomes on the other. This paper's evidence manifests that the kind influence of risk management strengthens product development capacities; nevertheless, this is moderated by several regulatory constraints. Much as there are advantages such as augmented marketplace access, regulation poses assortment of quandaries that slows down innovation and new products launch therefore governments need to master challenges.

combined with targeted innovation strategies, guiding leaders to effectively navigate regulatory demands and competitive pressures.

# Preface

In recent years, the MedTech industry has emerged as a critical pillar in the advancement of global healthcare systems. From AI-driven diagnostics to implantable medical devices, and from ethical debates to cybersecurity concerns, the sector has seen a rapid transformation – one that demands not only technical innovation, but also strategic foresight, regulatory adaptability, and strong leadership.

This book, Strategic Management, Regulatory Challenges, and Global Governance of MedTech, brings together a diverse set of interdisciplinary perspectives to explore the evolving landscape of medical technology. It is the result of collaborative efforts by scholars and practitioners from various geographies and domains, unified by a common goal: to better understand the dynamics shaping the future of MedTech at the intersection of innovation, ethics, regulation, and strategy.

The ten chapters presented herein reflect this richness. Beginning with a bioethical lens on artificial intelligence in emergency contexts, the volume proceeds to explore corporate responsibility, patent strategies, and leadership challenges in regions as distinct as the Horn of Africa and Western markets. Issues such as cybersecurity in implantable devices, virtual reality applications in Alzheimer's care, and privacy-preserving AI models for clinical settings are addressed not only with academic rigor, but also with practical insight.

The chapters offer more than theoretical reflection – they also provide actionable models and frameworks. Whether it's a strategic roadmap for managing organizational behavior in MedTech firms or an adaptive approach to regulatory compliance, this book equips its readers with tools to engage critically with current challenges and anticipate future trends.

This work would not have been possible without the dedication of our contributors, whose expertise and commitment to advancing the field of MedTech are deeply appreciated. We also extend our gratitude to the editorial and scientific committees who supported this publication, and to the institutions and professionals who continue to push boundaries in healthcare innovation.

It is our hope that this volume will serve as both a resource and a catalyst – informing policy, guiding leadership, and inspiring future research in the dynamic and vital field of medical technology.

Ricardo Marcão, Vasco Santos, Stéphanie Monteiro

# Acknowledgment

This book is the result of collaboration, resilience, and a shared belief in the transformative potential of medical technology. We are deeply grateful to all the contributors whose chapters brought depth, innovation, and critical reflection to this work. Their expertise and dedication have been essential to shaping this volume.

We also thank the peer reviewers and the editorial team at IGI Global, whose insights and support were vital throughout the publication process. Their professionalism ensured that each chapter met the highest standards of academic rigor.

To our fellow researchers and academic colleagues – thank you for the continued exchange of ideas, for the shared challenges, and for pushing the boundaries of what we can achieve together. Your curiosity and critical thinking inspire us daily.

To our students, past and present, thank you for reminding us of the power of questioning, learning, and growing. Your energy and commitment to knowledge give meaning to our work as educators and researchers.

Above all, we dedicate this work to our families.

To our families, for their unwavering belief in the value of education.

To ISLA Santarém – Instituto Politécnico, for all support.

This book is, in many ways, a tribute to those who stand beside us – at home, in academia, and in life.

Ricardo Marcão, Vasco Santos, Stéphanie Monteiro

Chapter 1

# Artificial Intelligence in Emergency Services: A Bioethical Perspective

**Filipa Soares**
https://orcid.org/0009-0004-6863-1068
*Polythecnic Institute of Santarém, Portugal*

**David Padeiro**
*Polythecnic Institute of Santarém, Portugal*

**Marta Correia Sampaio**
https://orcid.org/0000-0003-0004-601X
*Polythecnic Institute of Santarém, Portugal*

**Gonçalo Rodrigues Brás**
*Polythecnic Institute of Santarém*

**Ricardo Marcão**
https://orcid.org/0000-0003-3277-3078
*ISLA Santarém, Portugal*

**Vasco Santos**
*Polytechnic Instuitute of Tomar, Portugal & ISLA Santarém, Portugal & GOVCOPP, Portugal & CITUR, Portugal*

## ABSTRACT

*Artificial intelligence (AI) is a field of computing that has been increasingly applied in healthcare services, demonstrating significant potential to enhance both the delivery of care to populations and the management of human resources. This study is based on a literature review and aims to evaluate whether the use of AI in emergency services might challenge bioethical principles in healthcare, as well as to assess its potential to*

DOI: 10.4018/979-8-3373-1205-7.ch001

*improve and streamline patient triage. Online databases and grey literature providing open-access documents from the last five years were consulted in December 2024 and January 2025. This process resulted in a total of 20 documents, which were analyzed and form the basis of this review article. Articles were deemed relevant for inclusion if their abstracts or conclusions demonstrated a correlation between the identified keywords and the objectives outlined in this study.*

## INTRODUCTION

In recent years, there has been an exponential growth in the use of Artificial Intelligence (AI) across numerous development areas, with the healthcare sector significantly benefiting from this trend. Technological advancements in health-related research have demonstrated that AI is a growth tool for ensuring the quality of care and improving the overall quality of life for patients. However, its application in this sector raises questions related to bioethical principles that healthcare professionals adhere to and cannot overlook. Non-compliance with ethical principles in AI usage impacts daily life, creating administrative entropy within services, rendering health outcomes ineffective and insufficient (Ning et al., 2024).

AI is a branch of computer science that enables computing systems to become smarter and drive rapid and significant technological advancements. Essentially, it is a computerized replication of how the human brain generates knowledge and reasoning (Mahato, 2022), but without the internal and external biological influences to which humans are subject.

Currently, much attention has been focused on the development of the Chat Generative Pre-trained Transformer (ChatGPT, or GPT-4) and other chatbots powered by large language models (LLMs), which have captured the interest of the general public, researchers, and other stakeholders in Generative AI (GenAI) technology, whose growth is occurring at a breathtaking pace (https://generativeai.net). The main distinction of GenAI compared to general AI lies in its ability to generate realistic content, that's like what would be provided by a human.

GenAI is a powerful technology with potential applications in healthcare and other fields. The use of AI in emergency service contexts offers benefits such as reducing waiting times (Rajput et al., 2023) and enabling improved patient triage (Hamadeh, 2024; Núñez et al., 2024).

This work is based on a review of the available literature and aims to understand whether the use of AI in emergency services (ES) might challenge bioethical principles in healthcare and whether AI could assist in improving and streamlining patient triage.

Literature Review

In recent years, there has been an exponential increase in the use of AI globally.

According to Singh et al. (2023), AI is a research field that combines computer science, engineering, and other disciplines to produce behaviors that, for humans, would require intellectual capacity.

Advances in AI technologies and their application in healthcare facilities have the potential to enhance citizens health by making patient care more personalized, accurate, and predictive (Bajwa et al., 2021). The use of AI and machine learning algorithms in ES has seen significant growth, demonstrating benefits such as reduced waiting times and improved diagnostic accuracy (Rajput et al., 2023).

According to Hamadeh (2024) and Núnez et al. (2024), AI can enhance triage processes, predict critical outcomes, and assist in reorganizing human resources more efficiently.

An emergency service is a healthcare system or structure designed to provide immediate assistance to individuals with medical conditions or clinical situations requiring rapid intervention (Garg, 2024) to prevent health deterioration, alleviate suffering, or preserve life.

With the introduction of OpenAI's new models, specifically the OpenAI o1-Preview, the goal is for these AIs to "spend more time thinking before they respond. They can reason through complex tasks and solve harder problems than previous models in science, coding, and math" (https://openai.com/index/introducing-openai-o1-preview/). Compared to ChatGPT, particularly in healthcare contexts, these newer models demonstrate an enhanced capacity for "reasoning" in areas such as genetic diseases, treatment of complex conditions, support for health research (Temsah et al., 2024), and problem-solving.

It is worth noting that OpenAI aims for these models to more closely resemble human reasoning and learning processes: "We trained these models to spend more time thinking through problems before they respond, much like a person would. Through training, they learn to refine their thinking process, try different strategies, and recognize their mistakes" (https://openai.com/index/introducing-openai-o1-preview/).

Temsah et al. (2024) highlight that the tandem optimization of large language models (LLMs) for use in healthcare contexts can enhance effectiveness and accuracy. However, it also presents challenges, including ethical issues, disparities in access, and technological limitations.

Hamadeh (2024) and Núnez et al. (2024) highlight that the implementation of AI in emergency services encounters multiple barriers, particularly ethical ones. Bioethics, as defined by Tornini et al. (2023), is the discipline that examines ethical considerations in relation to advancements and applications in biology and medicine.

While AI presents a powerful tool for enhancing and optimizing healthcare processes, its full potential and real-world impacts remain largely uncharted. Ethical concerns surrounding AI demand careful attention and proactive management due to the multidisciplinary nature and wide-ranging implications of these technologies (Singh et al., 2023).

Discussions on the ethical implications of AI in healthcare aim to ensure that AI systems adhere to fundamental ethical principles: autonomy, beneficence, non-maleficence, and justice. These principles serve as the foundation for ethical AI development (Singh et al., 2023). Elias (2024) further asserts that, in addition to these four principles, explainability and compliance with human rights legislation are fundamental guarantees for the ethical implementation of AI.

Singh et al. (2023) emphasize the importance of respecting patient rights, ensuring informed consent, and addressing potential legal responsibilities. AI algorithms must be designed to be as transparent and interpretable as possible to prevent ethical dilemmas in healthcare applications. The same author also argues that the successful integration of AI into healthcare depends on balancing technological advancements with ethical considerations, allowing AI to reinforce human values rather than undermine them. As AI technology evolves, bioethical principles must also be adapted to address new challenges posed by its rapid development (Elias et al., 2024).

To mitigate ethical risks associated with AI, Elias (2024) advocates for the involvement of bioethicists and multidisciplinary teams throughout the development process. Engaging experts in ethics and related fields at an early stage significantly reduces the likelihood of ethical violations in AI applications for healthcare.

In the context of global health AI research, the capacity of organizations such as Research Ethics Committees (RECs) to intervene varies considerably across different regions. This disparity stems from diverse ethical and legal frameworks among countries, impacting the effectiveness and governance of AI research and development. Achieving ethical equity in AI-driven health research requires close international cooperation and regulatory harmonization (Shaw et al., 2024).

Tijs (2024) argues that an entrepreneurial vision, alongside a clear distinction between local and global ethical approaches to AI, is essential for its responsible development and application. These ethical considerations are often shaped by the social and environmental contexts in which AI technologies are created.

To ensure the safe and effective integration of AI into healthcare, it is imperative to address issues related to the professional-patient relationship, data protection, ethical standards, and transparency in decision-making processes_(Celik et al., 2024).

Moreover, the role of the State as a regulatory authority is crucial in ensuring compliance with legal frameworks governing AI usage. This responsibility must also encompass the application of bioethical principles related to consent, autonomy, and privacy in the treatment of patient data, even when the patients may be vulnerable due to the use of new technologies (Nunes et al., 2022).

The same author also refers to the social responsibility of everyone to limit and preserve the use of new technologies as a means of dignifying the human being. Innovations should be regulated so that "technology is for people and not people for technology" (Nunes et al., 2022).

Santos et al. (2024) notes that while AI has the potential to personalize healthcare, it is imperative that its application in this area does not replace the human element, which is essential in caregiving.

Gomes et al. (2024) reports that holding AI responsible for making choices, a function inherently tied to human behavior, can be extremely dangerous because human rationality is laden with experiences and sensitivities that machines cannot replicate.

The development of AI-based algorithms for patient triage shows great potential to improve healthcare delivery and patient outcomes (Guzzi, 2023).

In ES, one of the most important goals is to quickly identify which patients will benefit from faster care (Feretzakis et al., 2022) and which ones do not face an immediate life-threatening risk.

In Portugal, the degree of urgency and acceptable waiting time for care is determined by the Manchester Triage Scale, which assigns a color to each patient based on the severity of their symptoms in hospital triage.

According to the Portuguese Triage Group (https://www.grupoportuguestriagem.pt/grupo-portugues-triagem/protocolo-triagem-manchester/), the Manchester Triage Scale was developed in the United Kingdom in 1994 and is widely used in several countries. Its purpose is to standardize how to prioritize patient care in ES, ensuring that those in more critical conditions receive faster treatment. The colors included in the scale, listed in order of increasing severity, are: blue (considered non-urgent with a potential waiting time of up to 240 minutes), green (considered low urgency with a potential waiting time of up to 120 minutes), yellow (considered urgent with a potential waiting time of up to 60 minutes), orange (considered very urgent with a potential waiting time of up to 10 minutes), and red (considered emergent and requiring immediate care).

The use of AI in emergency contexts presents benefits for the services themselves, particularly in reducing waiting times (Rajput et al., 2023), and can lead to improved patient triage (Hamadeh, 2024; Núñez et al., 2024).

According to Guzzi et al. (2023), the common triage methods used in emergency services are based on the analysis of each patient by the triage nurse, which can be subjective and lead to errors. The author further notes a significant increase in interest in developing AI algorithms for patient triage. Guzzi et al. (2023) also argues that introducing computer science, such as AI, into the triage processes will benefit healthcare professionals by improving efficiency and accuracy, enabling them to assign the correct level of urgency to patients. They also indicate that AI can optimize resource allocation.

Similarly, Magalhães et al. (2024) states that the use of AI contributes to a quicker response and greater accuracy in classifying patients, especially in high-traffic settings, showing effectiveness in detecting critical situations requiring immediate interventions.

Kachman et al. (2024), aligning with other scholars, emphasizes that the use of AI in emergency services has improved diagnostics and optimized triage for critically ill patients. They further mention that this tool has facilitated the management of routine tasks, freeing healthcare professionals to perform more complex interventions on patients.

## METHODS

This literature review was conducted using the PRISMA method (Preferred Reporting Items for Systematic Reviews and Meta-Analyses). This methodology allows for consistent and transparent review of existing literature (Liberati et al., 2009). The PICOS model (Participants, Interventions, Comparators, Outcomes, and Study Design) was used to facilitate the inclusion criteria considered during the information search (Saaiq & Ashraf, 2017).

In December 2024 and January 2025, reliable digital libraries and grey literature (Hopewell et al., 2007) were consulted to extract open-access documents (with the exception of one limited-access document), full-text, published in the last 5 years, regardless of the language in which they were written.

Reliable digital libraries refer to well-established and recognized repositories of academic and scientific information. Grey literature includes unpublished materials (Hopewell et al., 2007). The search in digital libraries was performed using the following search inputs: ("artificial intelligence" OR "AI") AND ("emergency service"), ("artificial intelligence" OR "AI")

AND ("bioethics" OR "bioethical"). For grey literature, the query was placed in the search fields of Google and AI tools.

Articles were considered relevant for inclusion in this review if their abstract or conclusions referenced a relationship between the identified keywords and the objectives outlined for this review (Figure 1). A total of 20 documents were analyzed and consulted for this literature review, which are listed in the bibliography.

The content of the analyzed scientific articles is summarized in Table 1, and their organization by subject is presented in Table 2.

*Figure 1. Workflow for document identification*

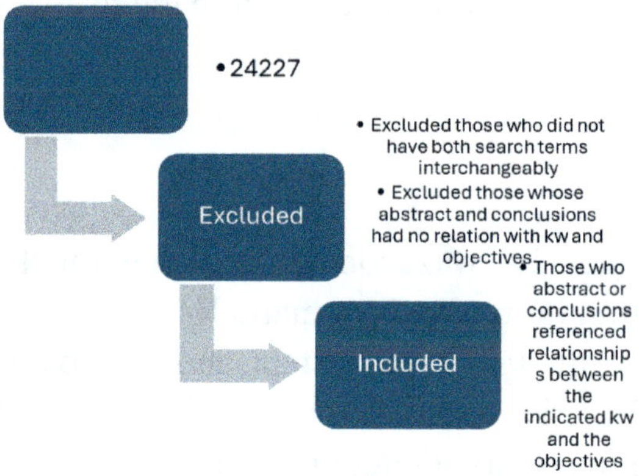

*Table 1. Scientific articles content*

| Author(s), year, title | Content |
|---|---|
| **Bajwa et al. (2021)., Artificial intelligence in healthcare: transforming the practice of medicine** | Potential of AI in Healthcare and How to Make Its Use More Effective, Safe, and Reliable |
| **Çelik & Kaya (2024). Sağlık Hizmetlerinde Yapay Zeka ve Etik: Bir Bibliyometrik Analiz** | Ethical Dimensions of AI in Healthcare to Ensure Data Security and Increase Transparency in AI Decision-Making Processes |
| **Elias et al. (2024). Inteligência artificial em saúde e implicações bioéticas: uma revisão sistemática** | Identifying the Use of AI in Healthcare and Its Bioethical Implications Through a Systematic Literature Review Based on PRISMA Guidelines |
| **Feretzakis et al. (2022). Using Machine Learning Techniques to Predict Hospital Admission at the Emergency Department** | Determining an Algorithm Using Machine Learning Techniques to Assist in Clinical Decision-Making in the Emergency Context |
| **Guzzi et al. (2023). A novel Network Science Algorithm for Improving Triage of Patients.** | Development of an Algorithm for Patient Triage Based on Patient Data Analysis to Make Decisions Regarding Their Prioritization Using AI |
| **Gomes et al. (2024). Desafios do uso da inteligência artificial nos diagnósticos de saúde: uma revisão integrativa** | Accountability of AI for Choices and Functions Performed by Humans and the Impact on Diagnoses |
| **Hamadeh (2024). Artificial intelligence in emergency medicine: a narrative review** | The Evolution of AI Applications in Emergency Services and Their Potentialities Without Undermining Ethical Principles |
| **Kachman et al. (2024). How artificial intelligence could transform emergency care.** | Transformative Potential Benefits of AI Without Undermining Ethical Principles |
| **Khalifa et al. (2024) Advancing clinical decision support: The role of artificial intelligence across six domains** | Impact of AI Use on Patient Outcomes and Healthcare Service Efficiency |
| **Magalhães et al. (2024). The Use of Artificial Intelligence in Patient Triage in Emergency Departments: an Integrative Review.** | Benefits of Using AI in Emergency Services Without Undermining Ethical Guidelines |

continued on following page

*Table 1. Continued*

| Author(s), year, title | Content |
|---|---|
| **Ning et al. (2024). Generative artificial intelligence and ethical considerations in health care: a scoping review and ethics checklist.** | Ethical Discussion on the Use of AI |
| **Nunes et al. (2022). Desafios bioéticos do uso da inteligência artificial em hospitais** | Advantages and Possible Bioethical Challenges of Using Artificial Intelligence in Hospitals |
| **Núnez et al. (2024). Envisioning the Future of Emergency Management focused on Artificial Intelligence.** | Integration of AI in Emergency Services |
| **Ragavi et al. (2021). Impact of Artificial Intelligence in the field of Health Care** | Impacts of AI on the Healthcare Sector |
| **Rajput et al. (2023). Artificial intelligence for emergency medical care** | AI in Emergency Services |
| **Santos & Alves Lopes (2024). A inteligência artificial nas ciências da saúde: oportunidades, desafios e perspetivas futuras** | Impact and Implications of AI in Health Sciences |
| **Shaw et al. (2024). Research ethics and artificial intelligence for global health: perspectives from the global forum on bioethics in research.** | Challenges and Strategies for Promoting Ethics in Health Research Using AI |
| **Singh et al. (2023). AI Ethics in Healthcare - A Survey** | Challenges Arising from the Relationship Between AI and Healthcare |
| **Temsah et al. (2024). OpenAI o1-Preview vs. ChatGPT in Healthcare: A New Frontier in Medical AI Reasoning.** | Comparison of OpenAI o1-Preview with ChatGPT in the Healthcare Context |
| **Tijs (2024). The ethics of artificial intelligence systems in healthcare and medicine: from a local to a global perspective, and back.** | AI Systems in Healthcare and Medicine |

*Table 2. Subjects identified*

| Subjects | Quantity |
|---|---|
| **Bioethics in AI** | 8 |
| **AI in Emergency Services** | 5 |
| **AI in Healthcare** | 7 |
| **Total** | 20 |

## RESULTS

Observing the articles obtained through the research conducted based on the applied methodology, it is evident that there is a close relationship between the concepts of AI, Emergency Services (SU), and bioethics, with bioethics being referenced by several authors. Table 2 resulted from the synthesis of the articles, presenting them grouped by major themes, aligned with the established keywords.

## DISCUSSION

Healthcare worldwide has witnessed a significant transformation with the use of AI. The programming language used in these AI systems, combined with their automated self-learning capabilities, has shown the ability to address healthcare-related issues globally, with applications across all sectors (Ragavi et al., 2021).

The integration of artificial intelligence (AI) into emergency services (ES) represents a transformative advancement in healthcare, with the potential to enhance efficiency, improve diagnostic accuracy, and expedite the referral of critical cases. AI-driven healthcare systems have demonstrated exceptional capabilities in processing and analyzing vast amounts of data inputted by healthcare professionals into databases, particularly results from complementary diagnostic and therapeutic methods (CDTM), such as laboratory tests and imaging exams, with remarkable precision.

By incorporating CDTM results for each patient into an AI system, the order of medical attention could be dynamically adjusted. In cases classified as non-urgent, patients might be redirected to primary healthcare services while hospital examination results remain accessible for physician review, ensuring continuity of care. Khalifa et al. (2024) argues that AI enhances healthcare by improving diagnostic accuracy, predicting clinical outcomes, and optimizing healthcare workflows. Additionally, it benefits medical professionals by providing remote access to patient data while preserving human decision-making in treatment choices. Furthermore, AI can facilitate the development of personalized treatment plans tailored to individual patient needs by leveraging insights derived from health database analysis.

However, the author also highlights key challenges associated with AI implementation, particularly concerning patient data privacy and ethical considerations. A critical concern is the reliance on extensive patient data, which raises issues regarding the protection of sensitive information and compliance with regulatory frameworks such as the General Data Protection Regulation (GDPR) in the European Union (EU). It is crucial to ensure that data is handled transparently and used solely for purposes authorized by the patients, ensuring privacy protection and maintaining trust, using informed and clear consent. Health institutions must adopt a multidisciplinary strategy when implementing AI in their systems.

There may be fear about the potential replacement of healthcare professionals by AI tools, but from an ethical perspective, AI should only serve as a complementary tool to the healthcare professional's work, not as a replacement.

Also, accountability for diagnostic errors must be considered: should the doctor or the AI development team be held responsible?

As Portugal is an EU member state, AI usage guidelines must align with those outlined in European Commission regulations, always ensuring principles of transparency, equity, security, and respect for human rights.

The doctor-patient relationship may be affected when AI is used: it is essential to educate patients on understanding AI-generated results and inform them that the doctor or other healthcare professionals will always be available to clarify any doubts, maintaining empathy and trust.

The National Health Plan 2030 (PNS-2030, "https://pns.dgs.pt/pns-2021-2030") for Portugal acknowledges and validates the increased use of technology systems, especially telemedicine, which aligns with the massive use of technological tools by various age groups in the Portuguese population. This use of available technologies also allows more isolated populations to access non-urgent healthcare, such as teleconsultations with doctors/nurses or chats with artificial intelligences for symptom assessment. It is important to ensure that technology is accessible to all populations, "leaving no one behind," regardless of their socio-economic context.

The ethical discussion about AI usage in healthcare should involve a multidisciplinary team to maximize the benefits of AI, minimize risks, and ensure it is used in a fair and human-centered manner.

Protecting fundamental principles such as autonomy, beneficence, non-maleficence, and justice is essential to ensure that AI implementation does not compromise human rights, equitable access to care, transparency in processes, and the protection of patient data. The balance between technological innovation and the preservation of ethical values should be the cornerstone of any AI integration in emergency services.

In the case of Portugal, AI could be used to manage the Urgent Patient Guidance Center (CODU), directing patients to the emergency services with the shortest waiting times, even if it's not at their reference hospital. With the organization of the Portuguese national health system into Local Health Units since January 1, 2024 (DL nº 102/2023, 17 november), which includes various health structures, obtaining patient clinical documentation has become simpler.

Although AI can reduce operational costs in the long run, its initial implementation requires significant investments, which could create inequalities between hospitals or healthcare systems with differing resources.

AI could also assist managers, especially human resources managers, in understanding which areas need staffing reinforcement. The severe shortage of healthcare professionals is widely reported daily, and it is challenging to formulate a rapid and effective response, as would be desirable.

## CONCLUSION

The transformative potential of artificial intelligence (AI) in the healthcare sector is undeniable. The findings of this review demonstrate that AI can enhance various aspects of medical care, from improving diagnostic accuracy to optimizing the classification of patients based on urgency levels. Its implementation in healthcare services has proven to be a valuable asset for professionals, delivering tangible benefits in ensuring higher quality care and increasing efficiency, particularly in time-sensitive areas such as emergency and urgent care.

However, like any technological system, AI is not without limitations and challenges. One of the most pressing concerns identified in this review is the ethical dimension of AI integration in healthcare. It is imperative to uphold core ethical principles—autonomy, beneficence, non-maleficence, and justice—to ensure that AI-driven solutions align with human values, professional integrity, and equitable patient care. Additionally, transparency, explainability, and compliance with human rights legislation must be central to AI development to foster trust and accountability.

At the hospital management level, AI tools offer substantial benefits by streamlining administrative processes, enhancing resource allocation, and reducing patient wait times. These improvements significantly contribute to the overall efficiency and quality of healthcare services, positively impacting all stakeholders, from medical professionals to patients. AI also plays a crucial role in managing human resources within healthcare systems, assisting in workload distribution and decision-making to enhance operational effectiveness, particularly in emergency response scenarios.

Beyond its clinical and administrative applications, AI has become an indispensable tool for medical research and innovation. By leveraging advanced data analysis, predictive modeling, and simulations, AI accelerates the discovery of new drugs and therapies, driving medical progress and expanding treatment possibilities. In emergency services, AI-powered predictive analytics enhance risk assessment, enabling proactive responses to medical crises and optimizing triage and resource distribution.

The successful integration of AI in healthcare depends not only on technological advancements but also on the establishment of robust regulatory frameworks and ethical guidelines that ensure responsible and fair implementation. Maximizing the benefits of AI while minimizing potential risks requires a steadfast commitment to transparency, fairness, and ethical safeguards. AI should be developed and deployed as a tool that complements human expertise rather than replacing it, ensuring that medical decision-making remains under human oversight.

Ultimately, a multidisciplinary approach involving bioethicists, medical professionals, policymakers, and AI developers is necessary to shape AI's future in healthcare. Only through collaborative governance, continuous evaluation, and adherence to ethical principles can AI truly enhance medical practice while maintaining its alignment with human dignity and patient-centered care. The future of AI in healthcare must prioritize equity, safety, and efficiency, ensuring that technological advancements serve both professionals and patients in a fair, ethical, and transparent manner.

## REFERENCES


Bajwa, J., Munir, U., Nori, A., & Williams, B. (2021). Artificial intelligence in healthcare: Transforming the practice of medicine. *Future Healthcare Journal*, *8*(2), e188–e194. DOI: 10.7861/fhj.2021-0095 PMID: 34286183

Çelik, Ö., & Kaya, E. (2024). *Sağlık Hizmetlerinde Yapay Zeka ve Etik: Bir Bibliyometrik Analiz.* Süleyman Demirel Üniversitesi Vizyoner Dergisi., DOI: 10.21076/vizyoner.1455659

Elias, M. A., Faversani, L. A., Moreira, J. A. V., Masiero, A. V., & da Cunha, N. V. (2024). Inteligência artificial em saúde e implicações bioéticas: uma revisão sistemática. Revista Bioética, 31, e3542PT. https://doi.org/DOI: 10.1590/1983-803420233542EN

European Commission. (2018). Artificial Intelligence for Europe. in *Communication from the commission to the european parliament, the european council, the council, the european economic and social committee and the committee of the regions* [Report]. https://eur-lex.europa.eu/legal-content/EN/TXT/PDF/?uri=CELEX:52018DC0237 item

Feretzakis, G., Karlis, G., Loupelis, E., Kalles, D., Chatzikyriakou, R., Trakas, N., Karakou, E., Sakagianni, A., Tzelves, L., Petropoulou, S., Tika, A., Dalainas, I., & Kaldis, V. (2022). Using Machine Learning Techniques to Predict Hospital Admission at the Emergency Department. *Journal of Critical Care Medicine*, *8*(2), 107–116. DOI: 10.2478/jccm-2022-0003 PMID: 35950158

Garg, A. (2024). Emergency Services. In: Handbook on Hospital Planning & Designing. Springer, Singapore. https://doi.org/DOI: 10.1007/978-981-99-9001-6_12

Gomes, G., Paixão, H., & Luiza, M. (2024). Desafios do uso da inteligência artificial nos diagnósticos de saúde: Uma revisão integrativa. *Cadernos Ibero-americanos de Direito Sanitario = Cuadernos Iberoamericanos de Derecho Sanitario*, *13*(2), 11–18. DOI: 10.17566/ciads.v13i2.1241

Guzzi, P. H., Defilippo, A., & Veltri, P. (2023). A novel Network Science Algorithm for Improving Triage of Patients. https://doi.org/https://doi.org/10.48550/arXiv.2310.05996Focustolearnmore DOI: 10.1109/BIBM58861.2023.10385396

Hamadeh, W. A. (2024). Artificial intelligence in emergency medicine: A narrative review. *International Journal of Scientific Research, 13*(09), 1–5. Advance online publication. DOI: 10.36106/ijsr/9024151

Hopewell, S., McDonald, S., Clarke, M. J., & Egger, M. (2007). Grey literature in meta-analyses of randomized trials of health care interventions. In *Cochrane Database of Systematic Reviews* (Issue 2). John Wiley and Sons Ltd. https://doi.org/DOI: 10.1002/14651858.MR000010.pub3

Kachman, M. M., Brennan, I., Oskvarek, J. J., Waseem, T., & Pines, J. M. (2024). How artificial intelligence could transform emergency care. *The American Journal of Emergency Medicine*, *81*, 40–46. DOI: 10.1016/j.ajem.2024.04.024 PMID: 38663302

Khalifa, M., Albadawy, M., & Iqbal, U. (2024). Advancing clinical decision support: The role of artificial intelligence across six domains. In *Computer Methods and Programs in Biomedicine Update* (Vol. 5). Elsevier B.V., DOI: 10.1016/j.cmpbup.2024.100142

Liberati, A., Altman, D. G., Tetzlaff, J., Mulrow, C., Gøtzsche, P. C., Ioannidis, J. P. A., Clarke, M., Devereaux, P. J., Kleijnen, J., & Moher, D. (2009). The PRISMA statement for reporting systematic reviews and meta-analyses of studies that evaluate health care interventions: Explanation and elaboration. In *PLoS Medicine* (Vol. 6, Issue 7). https://doi.org/DOI: 10.1371/journal.pmed.1000100

Magalhães, M. E. A., Silva, C. V. L., da, , Oliveira, H. M., de, , Lima, A. B. R., de, , Flores, M. T. S., Leite, I. F., Silva, G. A., da, , Faria, I. A. F. K., de, , Cruz, A. N., da, , & Costa, J. H. (2024). The Use of Artificial Intelligence in Patient Triage in Emergency Departments: An Integrative Review. *Revista de Gestão Social e Ambiental*, *18*(12), e010260. DOI: 10.24857/rgsa.v18n12-052

Mahato, R. (2022). "Artificial intelligence, what is it?" *in Outcomes of Best Practices in Classroom*. India. L' Ordine Nuovo Publication. pp. 197-202

Ning, Y., Teixayavong, S., Shang, Y., Savulescu, J., Nagaraj, V., Miao, D., Mertens, M., Ting, D. S. W., Ong, J. C. L., Liu, M., Cao, J., Dunn, M., Vaughan, R., Ong, M. E. H., Sung, J. J.-Y., Topol, E. J., & Liu, N. (2024, November). Generative artificial intelligence and ethical considerations in health care: A scoping review and ethics checklist. *The Lancet. Digital Health, 6*(11), e848–e856. Advance online publication. DOI: 10.1016/S2589-7500(24)00143-2 PMID: 39294061

Nunes, H. da C., Guimarães, R. M. C., & Dadalto, L. (2022). Desafios bioéticos do uso da inteligência artificial em hospitais. *Revista Bioética, 30*(1), 82–93. DOI: 10.1590/1983-80422022301509pt

Núnez, A.-G., Quiroz-Palma, P., Carmen Penadés, M., Parra, O., & Alvear, O. (2024). *Envisioning the Future of Emergency Management focused on Artificial Intelligence*.

Page, M. J., McKenzie, J. E., Bossuyt, P. M., Boutron, I., Hoffmann, T. C., Mulrow, C. D., Shamseer, L., Tetzlaff, J. M., Akl, E. A., Brennan, S. E., Chou, R., Glanville, J., Grimshaw, J. M., Hróbjartsson, A., Lalu, M. M., Li, T., Loder, E. W., Mayo-Wilson, E., McDonald, S., & Moher, D. (2021). The PRISMA 2020 statement: An updated guideline for reporting systematic reviews. *BMJ (Clinical Research Ed.), 372*(71), n71. Advance online publication. DOI: 10.1136/bmj.n71 PMID: 33782057

Presidência do Conselho de Ministros. (2023). "Decreto-Lei n.º 102/2023". *Diário da República,* 1ª série, 215 (novembro): 4-20. https://diariodarepublica.pt/dr/detalhe/decreto-lei/102-2023-223906278

Ragavi, V., Santha Sheela, A. C., & Narayanan Kannaiyan, G. (2021). Impact of Artificial Intelligence in the field of Health Care. *Journal of Physics: Conference Series, 1831*(1), 012006. Advance online publication. DOI: 10.1088/1742-6596/1831/1/012006

Rajput, S., Sharma, P. K., & Malviya, R. (2023). Artificial intelligence for emergency medical care. In *Health Care Science*. John Wiley and Sons Inc., DOI: 10.1002/hcs2.72

Saaiq, M., & Ashraf, B. (2017). *Modifying "Pico" Question into "Picos" Model for More Robust and Reproducible Presentation of the Methodology Employed in A Scientific Study*. www.wjps.ir

Santos, H., & Alves Lopes, A. (2024). A inteligência artificial nas ciências da saúde: Oportunidades, desafios e perspetivas futuras. *Revista Científica Internacional RevSALUS*, *6*(1), 1–9. DOI: 10.51126/revsalus.v6i1.653

Shaw, J., Ali, J., Atuire, C. A., Cheah, P. Y., Español, A. G., Gichoya, J. W., Hunt, A., Jjingo, D., Littler, K., Paolotti, D., & Vayena, E. (2024). Research ethics and artificial intelligence for global health: Perspectives from the global forum on bioethics in research. *BMC Medical Ethics*, *25*(1), 46. Advance online publication. DOI: 10.1186/s12910-024-01044-w PMID: 38637857

Singh, B., Rahim, M. A. B. U., Hussain, S., Rizwan, M. A., & Zhao, J. (2023, October 1). AI Ethics in Healthcare - A Survey. IEEE Xplore. DOI: 10.1109/QRS-C60940.2023.00086

Temsah, M.-H., Jamal, A., Alhasan, K., Temsah, A. A., & Malki, K. H. (2024). OpenAI o1-Preview vs. ChatGPT in Healthcare: A New Frontier in Medical AI Reasoning. *Cureus*. Advance online publication. DOI: 10.7759/cureus.70640 PMID: 39359332

Tornini, V. A., Politi, S. P., Bruce, L., & Latham, S. R. (2023). Maximizing biomedical research impacts through bioethical considerations. *Disease Models & Mechanisms*, *16*(4), dmm050046. Advance online publication. DOI: 10.1242/dmm.050046 PMID: 37092345

Vandemeulebroucke, T. (2024). The ethics of artificial intelligence systems in healthcare and medicine: From a local to a global perspective, and back. *Pflügers Archiv*. Advance online publication. DOI: 10.1007/s00424-024-02984-3 PMID: 38969841

# Chapter 2
# Corporate Social Responsibility in the Medical Device Industry


**Ruquiatu Bari Seidi**
*ISLA Santarém, Portugal*

**Ricardo Marcão**
https://orcid.org/0000-0003-3277-3078
*ISLA Santarém, Portugal*

**Vasco Ribeiro Santos**
https://orcid.org/0000-0002-3535-9377
*Polytechnic University of Tomar, Portugal & ISLA Santarém, Portugal & GOVCOPP, Portugal & CITUR, Portugal*

**Stéphanie Monteiro**
*Institute for Systems and Robotics, Portugal*

**Filipa Martinho**
*ISLA Santarém, Portugal*

**Isabel Reis**
https://orcid.org/0000-0002-2008-9124
*ISLA Santarém, Portugal*


## ABSTRACT


*Corporate Social Responsibility (CSR) in the medical device industry emphasizes ethical practices, sustainability, and societal impact. It encompasses ensuring product safety, promoting transparency, and engaging in community initiatives. Companies balance profit with social good, addressing challenges like access to healthcare and environmental sustainability, while fostering trust among stakeholders. CSR drives in-*



DOI: 10.4018/979-8-3373-1205-7.ch002

*novation, accountability, and long-term value creation, benefiting both society and businesses.*

## 1. INTRODUCTION

Corporate Social Responsibility (CSR) in the medical device sector is becoming increasingly significant as companies strive to strike a balance between innovation, ethical considerations, and the social impact of their organizational activities. As the healthcare landscape evolves at a rapid pace, primarily due to groundbreaking technological advancements, medical device manufacturers find themselves facing a dual responsibility. They must not only focus on creating safe and effective products that enhance patient outcomes but also take into account the broader implications of their operations. This includes considering the effects on public health, environmental sustainability, and the overall well-being of communities. Manufacturers are now expected to engage in practices that not only comply with regulations but also promote social good, addressing issues such as waste management, resource conservation, and equitable access to healthcare solutions. (Wickert, 2021)

CSR plays a crucial and essential role in building trust and fostering loyalty among consumers, significantly boosting brand reputation in an increasingly competitive market landscape, and adeptly meeting complex and evolving regulatory requirements. By embedding CSR deeply into their core strategic frameworks and day-to-day operational practices, medical device companies can contribute meaningfully to the advancement and enhancement of healthcare systems while thoroughly fulfilling their ethical responsibilities to society at large. This commitment not only enhances corporate integrity but also cultivates long-term relationships with stakeholders. (Student, 2023)

This thoughtful and strategic approach not only drives significant innovation in the dynamic field of medical devices but also actively fosters a strong culture of accountability and genuine care that resonates deeply with an extensive array of stakeholders—including patients, healthcare professionals, regulatory bodies, and local communities. By prioritizing and embracing corporate social responsibility (CSR), these forward-thinking companies can effectively align their business goals with the essential and pressing needs of society, thereby creating meaningful positive change and significantly enhancing the overall quality of life for individuals and communities all around the globe. Through this critical alignment, they ensure that their meaningful advancements not only serve their own interests but also contribute significantly to a healthier and more sustainable future for everyone involved, paying utmost attention to the greater good. In doing so, they pave the way for a more holistic approach to healthcare innovation, which values integrity, empathy, and ethical considerations in tandem with progress and profitability. (Kim, 2023)

## 2. ORIGIN AND EVOLUTION

The concept of Corporate Social Responsibility (CSR) is significantly more nuanced and deeply rooted in historical context than it may appear at first glance. While CSR might initially seem to be a modern innovation tailored for today's business environment, its foundational principles and values actually trace back to the social, economic, and ethical movements of the 18th and 19th centuries. These early efforts, which include the stirring cooperative movement and the philanthropic initiatives undertaken by pioneering companies and visionary individuals, laid the essential groundwork for what we now recognize as CSR in contemporary society. These actions and initiatives reflected an early awareness and understanding of the critical importance of corporate goodwill, ethical accountability, and community-focused practices within the rapidly evolving modern business landscape. The recognition of these values was crucial in fostering trust and building lasting relationships between businesses and the communities they serve. (Lazzini et al., 2023)(Kaittani, 2023)

However, it wasn't until the latter half of the 20th century that Corporate Social Responsibility (CSR) began to gain significant and widespread momentum and recognition across various industries around the globe. This noteworthy shift was driven by several interconnected factors that played vital roles: mounting pressure from civil society groups, the rapid globalization of economies, and an increasing awareness of pressing environmental challenges that needed addressing. As technology and communication advanced at an unprecedented pace, societal expectations of businesses and corporations evolved significantly as well. Companies were no longer perceived as isolated profit-driven entities solely focused on their bottom lines but instead were viewed as integral parts of a larger societal framework that bore responsibilities to a diverse range of stakeholders, including employees, customers, suppliers, and local communities. (Costa & Fonseca, 2022)(Hasan et al.2022)

This significant transformation ultimately led to a profound redefinition of the role that businesses play in contemporary society. Beyond merely generating profit, companies were expected to take on greater responsibilities, engage ethically in their practices, and, most importantly, contribute positively to the communities and environments in which they operate. This shift in expectations encouraged businesses to increasingly commit to ideals of transparency, accountability, and meaningful involvement in their respective communities. As a direct result of these evolving standards, many organizations began to thoroughly reevaluate their business strategies, actively aligning their operations with ethical principles. This alignment aimed to achieve a vital balance between profitability and the broader imperatives of societal welfare and environmental sustainability. (Sjödin et al.2022)(Murray et al., 2023)

By thoughtfully integrating Corporate Social Responsibility (CSR) into their fundamental core strategies, companies have the opportunity to not only enhance their public image and reputation in the eyes of consumers and stakeholders but also to make tangible contributions to global progress and development in a meaningful way. This significant shift underscores the vital and important idea that responsible corporate stewardship is genuinely essential for achieving sustainable growth, fostering resilience, and ensuring long-term success in today's highly competitive marketplace. CSR has indeed become a crucial and indispensable part of how modern businesses engage and interact with the world around them, reflecting a deep-seated commitment to creating significant, meaningful, and lasting impacts for both society and the environment at large. This ultimately benefits everyone involved, creating a more equitable and responsible business landscape that prioritizes ethical considerations alongside profit-making endeavors. In doing so, companies are not just fulfilling moral obligations but are also positioning themselves as forward-thinking leaders committed to innovation and sustainability. (Avotra et al.2021)(Han, 2024) (Matsutani et al.2022)

## 3. CHARACTERISTICS OF CORPORATE SOCIAL RESPONSIBILITY

Reviewing the definitions of Corporate Social Responsibility (CSR), one can observe that there are several critical factors intrinsically associated with socially responsible behavior. Firstly, it is imperative that a company must make a profit to ensure its sustainability and growth. However, beyond merely generating profits, it also has an obligation to respect the people working for the company and is expected to take active measures to protect both people and the environment. This responsibility is a response to the social regulation imposed on the company, manifested in the form of taxes, inspection services, and the presence of various organizations that grade and evaluate companies based on their social performance. For this regulation to be effective, corporations have to diligently bear the obligations of paying taxes, show respect for the rights of their workers, and fulfill their own commitments outlined in social contracts. (Rolls, 2024)(Antonacopoulou and Georgiadou2021)(Addo, 2024)

We can observe that within the CSR documents issued by multinational companies, the protection of consumer rights is frequently highlighted and takes precedence. Companies are becoming increasingly adept at explaining how many of their decisions flow directly from the core values that significantly motivate their actions and corporate strategies. Thus, we can argue convincingly that a company endeavors to follow various missions and adopt an approach that clearly specifies its overarching mission and objectives. In efforts to showcase their commitment to these principles, many companies have launched a formal statement of their values. The number of companies choosing to publicly share their values has seen a steady increase over time. At the present moment, an impressive 65 percent of the 500 largest U.S. companies have formal statements detailing their non-financial objectives, showcasing a growing trend towards transparency and accountability in corporate practices. (Mysaka et al.2021)(Pelikánová & Rubáček, 2022)

## 3.1. Voluntariness

One of the most significant and notable characteristics of Corporate Social Responsibility (CSR) is its inherently voluntary nature, which distinctly sets it apart from many other business obligations that companies typically encounter in the course of their operations and strategic planning. This aspect of CSR emphasizes the freedom businesses have in choosing how deeply they want to engage with social issues and environmental challenges, without being strictly bound by legal compulsion. Companies that choose to adopt and implement social responsibility practices generally do so in innovative and creative ways that extend well beyond the bare minimum requirements that are mandated by law and regulations, demonstrating their desire to truly make a difference: they may initiate programs that enrich community life, invest in sustainable technologies, or support charitable endeavors that inspire and uplift those in need. (Ucaryilmaz Deibel, 2022)

This proactive and thoughtful approach not only demonstrates a genuine and unwavering commitment to ethics but also showcases a deep and abiding concern for social welfare and sustainability, striking at the heart of their core values. It reflects their dedication to these vital principles in a manner that is both impactful and meaningful to the communities they serve. Such an approach highlights an authentic and profound concern for the broader influence of their operations on both the environment and society at large, acknowledging that their actions reverberate through the ecosystems and communities they touch. By taking these additional proactive steps, businesses can not only contribute positively to their communities at large but also enhance their reputations significantly while concurrently working to mitigate any potential negative effects they might inadvertently have on the world around them. (Khan et al., 2024) (Ahn et al., 2021)

Through these thoughtful and intentional actions, companies can foster trust, build stronger and more robust relationships with their stakeholders, and ultimately achieve a more sustainable future for all involved parties, exemplifying the interdependence of businesses and their communities. The integration of CSR initiatives into business strategies can lead to a comprehensive positive impact that resonates beyond mere profit-making, benefiting not just the organizations but also paving the way toward a more equitable and ecologically balanced world that serves the needs of current and future generations. This embrace of CSR recognizes that sustainable business practices are not merely the responsibility of a company's leaders but are rather a collective effort that requires the involvement of employees, customers, and the community, fostering a culture of accountability that is essential in today's corporate landscape. (Rinawiyanti et al.2021)

## 3.2. Holistic Approach

Corporate Social Responsibility (CSR) is fundamentally characterized by its holistic nature, which encompasses a wide array of dimensions critical for the effective and responsible conduct of business within the increasingly intricate and interconnected global framework. This extensive scope includes a multitude of essential practices, prominently featuring corporate governance, which is pivotal for establishing and maintaining trustworthy relationships with various stakeholders, such as investors, customers, employees, and community members. Furthermore, CSR significantly extends to involve rigorous environmental management practices essential for safeguarding the planet's health. It also encompasses an unwavering commitment to human rights across all business operations, the provision of safe and healthy working conditions for all employees irrespective of their roles, and the execution of comprehensive assessments regarding the economic impact on local communities and ecosystems. (Kanade et al.2024)

Additionally, it is crucial to engage actively and inclusively with local communities to foster trust and address their specific needs and concerns. By embracing a comprehensive and holistic approach, organizations can ensure that social responsibility is not viewed as an isolated initiative, but rather as an integral element interwoven throughout the overall business strategy and operations. This strategic integration facilitates a deeper, more nuanced understanding of how business decisions influence a diverse spectrum of stakeholders, including employees, customers, suppliers, and the broader community, in both immediate and long-term contexts. (Allen et al.2021)

Moreover, this approach promotes sustainable practices across all facets of operation, ensuring that businesses achieve their economic goals while simultaneously contributing positively to society, thus striving for continual economic success and stability. Adopting such an integrated perspective not only significantly enhances a company's reputation but also establishes a foundation for cultivating strong, lasting, and mutually advantageous relationships that can lead to substantial long-term benefits, including heightened customer loyalty and improved employee morale. (Moslehpour et al.2022)

Ultimately, this can culminate in a more resilient, adaptable, and forward-thinking organization, one that is adeptly positioned to confront the diverse challenges and opportunities of the future while maintaining accountability to stakeholders and society at large. (Bracci & Tallaki, 2021)

## 3.3. Sustainability

Sustainability represents a fundamental element within the broader framework of Corporate Social Responsibility (CSR), positioning itself as a guiding principle for companies to adopt more ethical operational practices. In today's complex and rapidly changing environment, businesses face growing expectations—often dictated by regulatory requirements—to engage in responsible operations that safeguard our essential natural resources for both present and future use. This responsibility highlights the importance of ensuring these resources remain accessible for future generations. (Purwanda and Achmad2022)

Engaging in sustainable methodologies involves actively promoting practices that aim to reduce a company's environmental footprint. Effective strategies may include the substantial reduction of harmful carbon emissions, the careful and efficient utilization of various precious natural resources, and the implementation of extensive recycling initiatives that permeate all operational areas. Additionally, firms have the opportunity to integrate innovative renewable energy technologies, which can lead to transformative advancements across industries, thereby facilitating a more sustainable operating model. (Ogbu et al.2023)

By fully adopting and embedding these progressive practices into their core business strategies, companies not only adhere to their ethical responsibilities but also contribute to the wellbeing of the planet. These initiatives have the potential to generate considerable positive change in their communities, showcasing a strong commitment to environmental stewardship and the welfare of both local and global populations. In this way, businesses can lay the groundwork for a more secure and sustainable future for all stakeholders involved. (Abbas et al.2023)

## 4. ADVANTAGES OF CORPORATE SOCIAL RESPONSIBILITY

Corporations, particularly those within the medical device sector, can substantially enhance their operational success by seriously committing to the principles of good corporate citizenship. Engaging in corporate social responsibility (CSR) can yield multiple significant advantages for businesses. Analyzing this phenomenon reveals several pertinent insights. (Chen and Hung2021)

Firstly, corporations that extend their contributions to society beyond mere compliance with legal obligations and tax payments often realize positive economic outcomes. This may be reflected through various indicators such as an uptick in sales, a stronger brand image, and heightened employee morale. Secondly, stakeholders—including managers, employees, and consumers—exhibit a preference for associating with organizations that actively demonstrate authentic concern for social issues and commitment to ethical values. (Wirba, 2024)

Additionally, organizations investing resources in addressing external challenges such as environmental pollution, consumer safety, and labor conditions may exert influence on governmental policies aimed at improving these critical concerns. By becoming more attuned to societal demands and proactively engaging in the resolution of social issues, corporations may inadvertently cultivate a climate that reduces the necessity for government intervention in business practices, fostering a more synergistic relationship between business entities and regulatory bodies. (Charpin et al.2021)

Every corporation ought to carefully evaluate and determine its unique characteristics, the distinct personality it embodies, and strategically identify itself with a cause or causes that resonates well with its business objectives, offerings, products, or services. In making a conscious choice to engage in practices that are beneficial for society at large, businesses have the remarkable ability to produce positive outcomes not only for their stockholders but also for the diverse differences present within the company itself. This intricate cause-and-effect relationship is something that should be fully recognized and appreciated, as it plays a critical role in the redefinition of the corporation's function and purpose in the future landscape of our business world. (Pfajfar et al., 2022)

Our society is currently looking to the business sector to step up and take a proactive lead—a role that it has attempted to fulfill in the past, albeit with somewhat limited success and impact. With the growing emphasis being placed by stockholders on the importance of social consciousness in today's market, businesses are presented with a significant opportunity to set an example that others can follow. Imagine a future where corporate social responsibility is not just an initiative but rather a fundamental characteristic and defining personality trait of every single corporation. Envision an environment and community in which each of us resides being completely free from the damaging and harmful impacts of man-made blight and despair. (Hamwi et al., 2021)

Indeed, all companies, regardless of their industry, could reap substantial benefits from increasing their levels of involvement in corporate social responsibility initiatives and practices. In particular, the device industry, along with its unique set of characteristics and challenges, stands to derive especially meaningful advantages from a renewed commitment to these values. By embracing corporate social responsibility, the device industry can position itself not only as a leader in innovation but also as a champion of positive societal change. (Rivo-López et al.2021)

## 4.1. Improvement of Reputation and Corporate Image

Corporate Social Responsibility (CSR) presents a distinctly advantageous impact on a company's reputation, which warrants a detailed analysis. The enhancement of public perception derives primarily from companies that engage authentically in socially responsible practices. These initiatives foster a view of the organization as ethical and trustworthy, which is integral to its brand identity. In competitive markets, such distinction is crucial; companies that prioritize CSR may gain an edge over competitors that neglect these values. (Ion et al.2021)(Siripipatthanakul and Sixl-Daniell2021)

The favorable reputation associated with CSR not only attracts consumers who prioritize ethical considerations, but it also cultivates a robust foundation for long-term customer loyalty. A well-regarded public image can also ease the process of entering new and innovative markets that are otherwise challenging for companies lacking a commitment to social responsibility. This opens avenues for exploring varied segments and demographics beneficial for future growth. (Senyapar, 2024)

Furthermore, a commitment to CSR facilitates the development of strategic partnerships that can unlock additional business opportunities and collaborative efforts. This multifaceted interplay emphasizes the critical role of CSR in contemporary business practices, highlighting its significant implications for the sustainability and success of enterprises moving forward. Thus, the integration of corporate ethics within business strategy emerges as a strategic necessity, yielding substantial long-term advantages rather than being merely an ethical consideration. (Alshukri et al., 2024)

## 4.2. Attraction and Retention of Talent

Employees in today's dynamic work environment are increasingly pursuing opportunities with companies that genuinely align with and share their deeply held personal values and beliefs. In this modern landscape, it has become evident that demonstrating a true commitment to corporate social responsibility (CSR) has risen to be a significant differentiator in attracting and retaining valuable talent. This is especially true among the younger generations, who are particularly inclined to emphasize sustainability and ethical business practices in their choice of employer. Organizations that actively engage in and practice social responsibility are widely perceived as more desirable employers. This perception, in turn, fosters greater employee satisfaction and enhanced engagement throughout the workforce. (Tran, 2022)

Furthermore, by cultivating a workplace culture founded on principles of responsibility, integrity, and ethics, companies can build a more dedicated and engaged team. Such a culture ultimately promotes a more positive and productive work environment. This alignment of corporate values with the personal beliefs of employees not only attracts top talent but also plays a crucial role in building loyalty and trust among staff members. This makes it essential for contemporary organizations to prioritize CSR initiatives and invest in strategies that resonate with their workforce's beliefs and values. Ensuring this integration of corporate responsibility with employee satisfaction could provide a powerful pathway towards achieving long-term success and sustainability for organizations in today's highly competitive marketplace. It can be argued that a strong commitment to these principles can act as a catalyst for innovation and improvement within the organization, resulting in benefits that extend beyond just employee retention and satisfaction, propelling the organization towards greater heights. (Obeng et al., 2024)

## 4.3. Access to New Markets

Organizations that incorporate and rigorously apply Corporate Social Responsibility (CSR) practices can significantly enhance their access to diverse and promising new markets, along with a multitude of business prospects that may not have been readily available or thoroughly examined previously. An increasing segment of investors and consumers shows a marked preference for engaging with entities that authentically uphold and prioritize social responsibility, alongside sustainable operational models. This growing inclination is becoming a pivotal element influencing strategic decision-making in contemporary businesses across various sectors, contributing meaningfully to their sustained success over time. (Metwally et al.2024)

Moreover, an emphasis on CSR can effectively address and fulfill a broad spectrum of regulatory obligations across different global markets, which are often characterized by their complexity and challenges. Such a strategic orientation not only bolsters a firm's reputation and market positioning but also streamlines the process of international expansion for those companies aspiring to extend their operations and attract new clientele. Thus, adopting CSR principles transcends mere ethical considerations; it presents a strategic advantage that can facilitate the development of valuable partnerships and foster enduring customer loyalty. (Abdul-Azeez et al.2024)

By establishing a robust and thoughtfully designed CSR framework, organizations can enhance their competitive positioning, attracting both consumers and investors who increasingly value accountability, transparency, and a meaningful societal contribution. (Ivascu et al., 2022)(Okoye et al.2024)

## 5. BENEFITS OF CORPORATE SOCIAL RESPONSIBILITY

Organizations that engage in corporate social responsibility (CSR) substantially impact the ongoing development of the communities in which they function and interact. This development manifests in various dimensions, including substantial initiatives like comprehensive educational programs aimed specifically at improving literacy rates, enhancing learning outcomes, and equipping younger populations with critical skills. Moreover, healthcare initiatives focused on improving wellness and accessibility are vital, providing necessary support for public health and ensuring individuals have access to needed medical services. Additionally, efforts in community development that seek to enhance local infrastructure—such as public transportation, housing, and recreational spaces—play a pivotal role in cultivating resilient and sustainable neighborhoods. Environmental initiatives aiming at fostering sustainability are also critical as they not only help conserve natural resources but also promote responsible consumption habits. Through such impactful investments, organizations not only contribute to establishing a solid groundwork for long-term community growth and prosperity but also enhance social well-being and harmony among residents. Thus, CSR activities emerge as an essential aspect of an organization's wider societal role, facilitating meaningful social change and overall advancement. (Khorram-Manesh et al.2021)(Haugan & Eriksson, 2021)(Phiri et al.2024)

The integration of sustainable practices across different operational sectors can substantially alleviate various risks and lower overall operational expenditures. For example, the adoption of energy efficiency initiatives and the creation of effective waste management protocols can significantly decrease the total costs incurred by businesses. Additionally, organizations that proactively address environmental and social risks are generally more equipped to adapt to forthcoming regulatory frameworks. This strategic foresight not only mitigates the risk of incurring fines and penalties but also enhances their standing within their respective industries, thereby cultivating a favorable reputation and possibly boosting customer loyalty. (Adeniran et al.2024)(Tyler et al.2024)(Agu et al.2024)

Corporate Social Responsibility (CSR) functions as a pivotal catalyst for innovation. The continual pursuit of sustainable and ethical alternatives frequently results in the emergence of diverse new products and services, the optimization of more proficient processes, and the development of groundbreaking business models. This transformation not only enhances the organization's competitive edge within the market but also unveils fresh avenues for expansion, potentially positioning the organization for leadership within its sector. As companies adopt CSR principles, they harness creativity and ingenuity, cultivating a culture that elevates environmental and social considerations alongside conventional economic objectives. (Abbas, 2024)(Alshukri et al., 2024)(Tang et al.2021)

## 6. SUCCESS CASES

The previous section discussed various categories of CSR actions that align with the business position and the development patterns of the medical device industry. The last natural question one may ask is whether such CSR activities truly generate benefits. Are they costly but ultimately ineffective? There is an increasing number of success cases and proposals for measurement through numerical indicators that can provide a positive answer to such skeptical questions. Corporate philanthropy enhances corporate reputation and legitimacy and ultimately national image. CSR works because it not only generates goodwill but also makes companies more attractive to and valuable in the eyes of our stakeholders: employees, customers, business partners, investors, and even central and local governments. I will briefly present cases tailored to each of the overlapping CSR roles of medical device enterprises. (Pallathadka and Pallathadka2022) (Orozco, 2024)(Mircescu2023)

Regarding supply chain lines, over the past few years, companies focusing on the average annual profits of the company had a higher total shareholder return; companies focused on the risk of supply chain had a lower variability in their returns; companies that made consistent profits and partnered with acceptable suppliers or declining suppliers had a lower variability in returns. With regard to compliance with standards, there are several industry success stories in this domain. For education and training, some companies have been sponsors of annual conferences for many years. Other industry members also join in supporting our field's annual conference. Some companies also play a considerable support role in healthcare education and training. (Dohmen et al.2023)

In the context of consumer awareness, several companies have been involved in educational and informational activities in this area for several years. For the post-market phase, certain cardiac stands bear witness. Regarding responsible innovation, one company launched an expanded Indications Study in the U.S. in 2005 to demonstrate the safety of minimally invasive surgical techniques that were not used as a standard therapy. Concerning employees, another model in the current field is noted. Moreover, in the field of environmental protection, some companies have long been leading. (Onu et al., 2024)

## 6.1. Patagonia

Patagonia, an outdoor apparel company, is frequently referenced as a paradigm of successful Corporate Social Responsibility (CSR) in the contemporary marketplace. The organization has methodically embraced and executed extensive sustainable practices across its operations, ensuring that every element of its business aligns with a dedication to environmental stewardship. This commitment encompasses the judicious selection of environmentally friendly materials and the equitable treatment of employees at all organizational levels. Such dedication is reflective of Patagonia's foundational principles and its deep-seated sense of social responsibility, which are intricately integrated into its brand identity. (Lu, 2023)(Luyang, 2024)

Moreover, Patagonia allocates 1% of its annual sales revenue to support a range of environmental causes aimed at the conservation and protection of natural resources. Beyond these financial contributions, the company advocates for a consumer culture that prioritizes recycling and repairing over purchasing new items. This strategy not only fosters a sustainable mindset among consumers but also significantly mitigates waste generation, while cultivating a community of environmentally conscious individuals who actively champion these essential values. Through this initiative, Patagonia serves as a compelling case study on how businesses can weave sustainability into their core operational framework. (Burzyńska, 2024)

## 6.2. Unilever

Unilever has initiated a comprehensive and ambitious program termed the "Unilever Sustainable Living Plan," which serves as a strategic framework aimed at promoting the health and well-being of billions globally. In parallel to enhancing personal health outcomes, this innovative plan aspires to achieve a considerable reduction—specifically fifty percent—in the environmental impact linked to its diverse product portfolio. Furthermore, Unilever is focused on enhancing the living standards of millions connected to its intricate value chain. This holistic strategy underscores the company's commitment to corporate social responsibility (CSR) and has been integral in lowering operational costs while effectively addressing potential operational risks. In addition, this initiative has cultivated a strong foundation of trust among consumers worldwide, thereby enhancing brand loyalty and commitment. Through these synergistic efforts, Unilever exemplifies its steadfast dedication to sustainability and social responsibility, yielding significant benefits for both the environment and global communities. (Scott, 2024)(Shaikh, 2024)

## 7. CHALLENGES OF CORPORATE SOCIAL RESPONSIBILITY

Corporate social responsibility challenges are greatly influenced by various factors such as the specific industry, the size of the company, and the country or region in which the company operates. In particular, the medical device industry faces several critical issues related to corporate social responsibility that are noteworthy. Some of the primary problems include the insufficient regulation and control imposed by both the industry itself and local government bodies. Additionally, it is important to recognize that the voluntary actions taken by companies are often selective and, in many instances, may merely serve as a façade or image campaign rather than as genuine efforts to effect positive change. There is also a significant lack of practical approaches and tools available for the assessment and implementation of corporate social responsibility initiatives, which complicates the process for many organizations. Furthermore, the integration of corporate social responsibility into the core business operations of companies remains limited and ineffectual. The existing frameworks provided by the wellness industry appear to be structured at a high level; however, they tend to focus predominantly on selected segments of the industry, leaving many areas unaddressed. This creates a disconnect and undermines the potential for a more comprehensive application of corporate social responsibility across the medical device field. (Ye & Dela, 2023)

It is generally accepted in academic and professional circles that European corporate social responsibility research is not only well documented but also stands as a leader in the field of corporate social responsibility studies. The comprehensive list of challenges faced in this domain includes, but is not limited to, the inherent difficulties that arise in communication and the assessment of the proposed corporate social responsibility performance, which often make it challenging for companies to effectively articulate their initiatives and outcomes. Additionally, there is a pressing need for a change in corporate culture, as well as the successful integration of corporate social responsibility into the very fabric of the company's operations and strategic objectives. Furthermore, the actualization of corporate social responsibility initiatives across the company's entire supply chain is crucial, as it directly impacts the overall effectiveness and credibility of these efforts. (Wolniak et al., 2021)

Moreover, companies encounter various risks as part of their risk management processes, alongside the uncertainty that is prevalent in today's fast-paced and ever-changing market landscape. This uncertainty is compounded by the high social and administrative costs associated with implementing robust corporate social responsibility practices. On the other hand, it is essential to recognize that all stakeholders involved in corporate social responsibility have their own distinct perspectives and interests. Each stakeholder group would like to assert that their viewpoints and input in corporate social responsibility reports, guidelines, and research need to be thoroughly discussed and given proper consideration. As such, it is vital to ensure that these diverse perspectives are incorporated into the discourse surrounding corporate social responsibility. (Grondys et al.2021)(Boateng et al.2022)

Despite facing various challenges and complexities, the area of corporate social responsibility continues to be in a dynamic and exciting stage of development. This field constantly evolves and adapts to meet the ever-growing demands of the challenging market environment and the changing societal expectations that arise with it. The integration of social responsibility into corporate strategies is essential for businesses aiming to thrive and maintain relevance in today's world. (Karwowski and Raulinajtys-Grzybek2021)

## 7.1. Initial Cost and Return on Investment

One significant challenge that many companies face when it comes to Corporate Social Responsibility (CSR) is the initial cost involved in such initiatives. Implementing sustainable and ethical business practices can often require substantial investments of time, money, and resources, which can easily strain the already available resources of a company. Furthermore, the return on investment may not be immediate or readily apparent, which can indeed discourage some companies from fully committing to adopting and following through with meaningful and impactful CSR initiatives. This hesitation can often stem from short-term profit-driven mindsets that tend to overlook, undervalue, and disregard the long-term benefits and advantages of responsible corporate behavior. By focusing too much on immediate financial gains, companies may inadvertently miss out on the profound positive impacts that robust CSR can generate for their brand reputation, enhance employee satisfaction, and increase customer loyalty over time. It is essential for firms to recognize that the integration of CSR into their core operations can lead to a more sustainable business model that not only fulfills social objectives but also enhances their competitiveness in the market. (Challoumis, 2024)(Khan et al., 2024)(Gupta et al., 2021)

## 7.2. Measurement and Reporting of Impact

Measuring and reporting the substantial impact of CSR initiatives, which stand for Corporate Social Responsibility initiatives, can often be an undeniably complex and multifaceted process that many organizations face and navigate through. In the contemporary business landscape, companies must comprehensively establish clear, consistent metrics and indicators in order to appropriately assess and evaluate the overall success of their various social responsibility practices and initiatives effectively. This rigorous process involves a detailed approach to developing methodologies that are both transparent and well-defined. Having such clear methods for reporting this vital data is crucial, as it significantly contributes to maintaining credibility and solid trust among the diverse range of stakeholders involved in these initiatives. Providing accurate insights and comprehensive information not only helps all stakeholders evaluate the overall effectiveness of these ongoing efforts clearly but also allows them to ascertain how these initiatives align with both the company's overarching goals and the ever-evolving expectations of the communities they serve and impact. A robust measurement and reporting framework will empower companies to not only track their progress diligently but also to adjust their strategies as needed to strengthen their CSR commitments and ensure long-term sustainability of their initiatives, fostering a deep-seated culture of accountability and social awareness within the organization. (Vázquez-Maguirre & Benito, 2022)(Niyommaneerat et al.2023)(Lee & Cho, 2022)

## 7.3. Internal Alignment and Organizational Culture

Integrating Corporate Social Responsibility (CSR) into the overall organizational culture can present numerous challenges and obstacles that must be navigated with careful planning and meticulous attention to detail. It necessitates a steadfast and unwavering commitment from top management, ensuring that leaders actively promote and embody the core values of CSR, alongside securing the genuine buy-in from all levels within the company. Achieving this desired level of integration requires not only the establishment of robust policies but also a profound and fundamental cultural shift within the organization that encompasses every facet of operations and daily routines. Changing mindsets, attitudes, and behaviors across the entire workforce is essential for CSR initiatives to be genuinely effective and sustainable in the long run. This transformative journey may require extensive training sessions, comprehensive workshops, and ongoing communication strategies that are carefully designed to engage, inform, and educate employees systematically and effectively. It is vital to ensure that every team member fully comprehends the importance of social responsibility and how it intricately aligns with the company's core values and overarching mission. Engaging employees in meaningful discussions, activities, and initiatives that relate to CSR can foster a deep sense of ownership and accountability among the workforce. By making the value of social responsibility an integral part of the daily work environment and corporate ethos, organizations can cultivate a strong culture that not only prioritizes ethical considerations and sustainable practices but also significantly enhances overall employee morale and boosts the company's reputation in the marketplace. (Kolling et al.2022)(Moslehpour et al.2022)

# 8. CONCLUSIONS

Corporate Social Responsibility (CSR) is a strategic framework that yields a diverse array of advantages for both businesses and the broader society. It extends beyond mere enhancements to corporate reputation or talent acquisition; CSR is integral to promoting sustainable community development and environmental conservation. Firms that properly embrace CSR principles are recognized as prudent leaders within their sectors, signifying their innovative capacity and their dedication to generating value ethically and sustainably. However, the successful implementation of CSR initiatives presents distinct challenges. Such initiatives often demand substantial initial investments, a comprehensive and integrated operational strategy, and a sincere commitment to transparency and sustainable practices. Despite these challenges, the long-term benefits of adopting CSR significantly exceed its hurdles. Companies that actively pursue CSR are positioned as frontrunners in the global marketplace, reaping benefits such as increased competitiveness, customer loyalty, and robust brand equity. (Oshioste et al.2023)(Cezarino et al.2022)(Vrabcová and Urbancová2021)

In a world that is becoming more aware and demanding regarding ethical practices, corporate social responsibility (CSR) has transitioned from being a mere alternative to an indispensable strategy for companies aiming to succeed while making a beneficial impact on society and the environment. Firms that distinctly acknowledge the critical significance of CSR and purposefully integrate it into their operational frameworks are considerably more equipped to tackle imminent challenges. Such firms can position themselves as innovative and responsible leaders within their industries. Indeed, CSR has evolved into a fundamental component for any enterprise aspiring to thrive in the contemporary landscape. It transcends the realm of a routine marketing tactic or a fleeting trend, serving as a genuine reflection of a company's commitment to fostering a more sustainable, ethical, and inclusive future for all stakeholders involved. By emphasizing CSR, organizations not only elevate their brand reputation but also cultivate trust and loyalty among consumers, who are increasingly prioritizing corporate transparency and environmental responsibility. (Ghobakhloo et al.2023)(Morea et al., 2021)(Carroll, 2021)

This article has systematically examined the advantages of Corporate Social Responsibility (CSR) for organizations, highlighting its favorable effects on society as well as the obstacles that must be addressed for effective implementation. The adoption of CSR initiatives enhances corporate reputation, fortifies relationships with consumers and employees, boosts competitiveness, and aids in the development of a more equitable and sustainable marketplace. Despite the presence of challengesincluding cultural resistance, initial financial investments, and the necessity for committed leadership - the long-term advantages are significant and cannot be overlooked. (Ion et al.2021)

The trajectory of corporate social responsibility (CSR) is poised to generate a heightened degree of innovation relative to previous trends, while simultaneously integrating a range of advanced technologies designed to enhance both the transparency and effectiveness of CSR efforts. This transition is occurring alongside increasing demands from a more aware and educated demographic of consumers and investors, who prioritize accountability and ethical conduct in their preferred companies. Organizations that proactively engage with these emerging dynamics and adjust to the evolving market conditions will position themselves more favorably to tackle the challenges of a more exacting global environment. Additionally, these entities will play a vital role in initiatives directed at fostering a more just, equitable, and sustainable future for all stakeholders involved. As such, it is imperative to understand that CSR transcends its role as a mere mechanism for fostering positive social change; rather, it represents a significant avenue for companies to transform into pivotal agents in the necessary social and environmental evolution demanded by our global community. (Dorstewitz & Lal, 2022)

## REFERENCES


Abbas, J. (2024). Does the nexus of corporate social responsibility and green dynamic capabilities drive firms toward green technological innovation? The moderating role of green transformational leadership. *Technological Forecasting and Social Change*, *208*, 123698. DOI: 10.1016/j.techfore.2024.123698

Abbas, J., Al-Sulaiti, K., Lorente, D. B., Shah, S. A. R., & Shahzad, U. (2023). Reset the industry redux through corporate social responsibility: The COVID-19 tourism impact on hospitality firms through business model innovation. In Economic growth and environmental quality in a post-pandemic world (pp. 177-201). Routledge.

Abdul-Azeez, O. Y., Nwabekee, U. S., Agu, E. E., & Ignatius, T. (2024). Strategic approaches to sustainability in multinational corporations: A comprehensive review. International Journal of Frontline Research in Science and Technology, 3(02), 038-054.

Addo, M. K. (Ed.). (2024). *Human rights standards and the responsibility of transnational corporations*. Brill.

Adeniran, I. A., Abhulimen, A. O., Obiki-Osafiele, A. N., Osundare, O. S., Agu, E. E., & Efunniyi, C. P. (2024). Strategic risk management in financial institutions: Ensuring robust regulatory compliance. *Finance & Accounting Research Journal*, *6*(8), 1582–1596. DOI: 10.51594/farj.v6i8.1508

Agu, E. E., Iyelolu, T. V., Idemudia, C., & Ijomah, T. I. (2024). Exploring the relationship between sustainable business practices and increased brand loyalty. *International Journal of Management & Entrepreneurship Research*, *6*(8), 2463–2475. DOI: 10.51594/ijmer.v6i8.1365

Ahn, J., Shamim, A., & Park, J. (2021). Impacts of cruise industry corporate social responsibility reputation on customers' loyalty: Mediating role of trust and identification. *International Journal of Hospitality Management*, *92*, 102706. DOI: 10.1016/j.ijhm.2020.102706

Allen, E. H., Haley, J. M., Aarons, J., & Lawrence, D. (2021). *Leveraging community expertise to advance health equity*. Urban Institute.

Alshukri, T., Seun Ojekemi, O., Öz, T., & Alzubi, A. (2024). The interplay of corporate social responsibility, innovation capability, organizational learning, and sustainable value creation: Does stakeholder engagement matter? *Sustainability (Basel)*, *16*(13), 5511. DOI: 10.3390/su16135511

Antonacopoulou, E. P., & Georgiadou, A. (2021). Leading through social distancing: The future of work, corporations and leadership from home. *Gender, Work and Organization*, *28*(2), 749–767. DOI: 10.1111/gwao.12533

Avotra, A. A. R. N., Chengang, Y., Wei, X., Ming, J., & Marcelline, T. R. S. (2021). Struggling with business corporate cynical impression? Powerful methods of CSR to enhance corporate image and consumer purchase intention. *Frontiers in Public Health*, *9*, 726727. DOI: 10.3389/fpubh.2021.726727 PMID: 34540793

Boateng, A., Ameyaw, C., & Mensah, S. (2022). Assessment of systematic risk management practices on building construction projects in Ghana. *International Journal of Construction Management*, *22*(16), 3128–3136. DOI: 10.1080/15623599.2020.1842962

Bracci, E., & Tallaki, M. (2021). Resilience capacities and management control systems in public sector organisations. *Journal of Accounting & Organizational Change*, *17*(3), 332–351. DOI: 10.1108/JAOC-10-2019-0111

Burzyńska, O. (2024). Navigating branding frontiers: De-influencing, accessibility, and anti-greenwashing at Patagonia. [Master's thesis, Malmö University]. DiVA Portal.

Carroll, A. B. (2021). Corporate social responsibility: Perspectives on the CSR construct's development and future. *Business & Society*, *60*(6), 1258–1278. DOI: 10.1177/00076503211001765

Cezarino, L. O., Liboni, L. B., Hunter, T., Pacheco, L. M., & Martins, F. P. (2022). Corporate social responsibility in emerging markets: Opportunities and challenges for sustainability integration. *Journal of Cleaner Production, 362*, 132224. DOI: 10.1016/j.jclepro.2022.132224

Challoumis, C. (2024, October). Building a sustainable economy-how ai can optimize resource allocation. In *XVI International Scientific Conference* (pp. 190-224).

Charpin, R., Powell, E. E., & Roth, A. V. (2021). The influence of perceived host country political risk on foreign subunits' supplier development strategies. *Journal of Operations Management*, *67*(3), 329–359. DOI: 10.1002/joom.1127

Chen, R. C., & Hung, S. W. (2021). Exploring the impact of corporate social responsibility on real earning management and discretionary accruals. *Corporate Social Responsibility and Environmental Management*, *28*(1), 333–351. DOI: 10.1002/csr.2052

Costa, J., & Fonseca, J. P. (2022). The impact of corporate social responsibility and innovative strategies on financial performance. *Risks*, *10*(5), 103. DOI: 10.3390/risks10050103

Dohmen, A. E., Merrick, J. R., Saunders, L. W., Stank, T. P., & Goldsby, T. J. (2023). When preemptive risk mitigation is insufficient: The effectiveness of continuity and resilience techniques during COVID-19. *Production and Operations Management*, *32*(5), 1529–1549. DOI: 10.1111/poms.13677

Dorstewitz, P., & Lal, D. (2022). Re-imagining business agency through multi-agent cross-sector coalitions: Integrating CSR frameworks. *Philosophy of Management*, *21*(1), 87–103. DOI: 10.1007/s40926-021-00180-2 PMID: 34812263

Dumitru Mircescu, G. (2023). Corporate Social Responsibility as a Strategic Tool: Impact on Stakeholder Perceptions and Organizational Performance. Case Study: The Pharma Industry. Ovidius University Annals, Series Economic Sciences, 23(1).

Ghobakhloo, M., Iranmanesh, M., Morales, M. E., Nilashi, M., & Amran, A. (2023). Actions and approaches for enabling Industry 5.0-driven sustainable industrial transformation: A strategy roadmap. *Corporate Social Responsibility and Environmental Management*, *30*(3), 1473–1494. DOI: 10.1002/csr.2431

Grondys, K., Ślusarczyk, O., Hussain, H. I., & Androniceanu, A. (2021). Risk assessment of the SME sector operations during the COVID-19 pandemic. [PubMed]. *International Journal of Environmental Research and Public Health*, *18*(8), 4183.

Gupta, H., Kumar, A., & Wasan, P. (2021). Industry 4.0, cleaner production and circular economy: An integrative framework for evaluating ethical and sustainable business performance of manufacturing organizations. *Journal of Cleaner Production*, *295*, 126253. DOI: 10.1016/j.jclepro.2021.126253

Hamwi, M., Lizarralde, I., & Legardeur, J. (2021). Demand response business model canvas: A tool for flexibility creation in the electricity markets. *Journal of Cleaner Production*, *282*, 124539. DOI: 10.1016/j.jclepro.2020.124539

Han, B. (2024). Retracted Article: Fostering sustainability: integrating social responsibility, green finance, and corporate performance. *Economic Change and Restructuring*, *57*(2), 64. DOI: 10.1007/s10644-024-09656-3

Hasan, I., Singh, S., & Kashiramka, S. (2022). Does corporate social responsibility disclosure impact firm performance? An industry-wise analysis of Indian firms. *Environment, Development and Sustainability*, *24*(8), 10141–10181. DOI: 10.1007/s10668-021-01859-2

Haugan, G., & Eriksson, M. (2021). Health promotion in health care–vital theories and research.

Ion, L. M., Vodă, A. I., Butnaru, R. C., Butnaru, G. I., & Mircea Chirita, G. (2021). Effect of pharmaceutical companies' corporate reputation on drug prescribing intents in Romania. Economic research-. *Ekonomska Istrazivanja*, *34*(1), 521–544. DOI: 10.1080/1331677X.2020.1798263

Ivascu, L., Ali, W., Khalid, R., & Raza, M. (2022). The impact of competitive strategies on performance of banking sector; the mediating role of corporate social responsibility and operational excellence. *Energies, 16*(1), 297. DOI: 10.3390/en16010297

Kaittani, N. (2023). Corporate Social Responsibility: Where did it Originate From, How has it Evolved and Why is it Important?: a literature review of the history and evolution of CSR.

Kanade, T. M., Joseph, J., Ansari, S., Varghese, M. A. M., & Savale, T. (2024). Solid waste management for environmental sustainability and human health. *Journal of Informatics Education and Research, 4*(1).

Karwowski, M., & Raulinajtys-Grzybek, M. (2021). The application of corporate social responsibility (CSR) actions for mitigation of environmental, social, corporate governance (ESG) and reputational risk in integrated reports. *Corporate Social Responsibility and Environmental Management, 28*(4), 1270–1284. DOI: 10.1002/csr.2137

Khan, T., Emon, M. M. H., & Siam, S. A. J. (2024). Impact of Green Supply Chain Practices on Sustainable Development in Bangladesh. Available at *SSRN* 4958443.

Khorram-Manesh, A., Dulebenets, M. A., & Goniewicz, K. (2021). Implementing public health strategies—the need for educational initiatives: A systematic review. *International Journal of Environmental Research and Public Health, 18*(11), 5888. DOI: 10.3390/ijerph18115888 PMID: 34070882

Kim, S. (2023). The COVID-19 pandemic and corporate social responsibility of Korean global firms: From the perspective of stakeholder theory. *Emerald Open Research, 1*(4). Advance online publication. DOI: 10.1108/EOR-04-2023-0013

Kolling, C., Ribeiro, J. L. D., & de Medeiros, J. F. (2022). Performance of the cosmetics industry from the perspective of Corporate Social Responsibility and Design for Sustainability. *Sustainable Production and Consumption, 30*, 171–185. DOI: 10.1016/j.spc.2021.12.002

Lazzini, A., Lazzini, S., & Balluchi, F. (2023). Social and moral accountability in action: the religious roots of corporate social responsibility in an Italian entrepreneurial family (1900–1950). Accounting History Review.

Lee, Y. J., & Cho, M. (2022). Socially stigmatized company's CSR efforts during the COVID-19 pandemic: The effects of CSR fit and perceived motives. *Public Relations Review*, *48*(2), 102180. DOI: 10.1016/j.pubrev.2022.102180 PMID: 35368969

Lu, R. (2023). Set it in stone: Patagonia and the evolution toward stakeholder governance in social enterprise business structures. *Columbia Journal of Law and Social Problems*, *57*(4), 1–45.

Luyang, L. (2024). Brand management from the perspective of sustainable development: Responsibility marketing and social value creation. *Academic Journal of Business & Management*, *6*(1), 15–30.

Matsutani, L., Rampasso, I. S., Serafim, M. P., Quelhas, O. L., Leal Filho, W., & Anholon, R. (2022). Critical analysis of corporate social responsibility projects developed by Brazilian companies: Providing new insights for debates. *Cleaner Engineering and Technology*, *7*, 100412. DOI: 10.1016/j.clet.2022.100412

Metwally, A. B. M., Elsharkawy, A. A. M., & Salem, M. I. (2024). The impact of corporate social responsibility on operating cash flow opacity: The moderating role of tax avoidance. *Cogent Business & Management*, *11*(1), 2390692. DOI: 10.1080/23311975.2024.2390692

Morea, D., Fortunati, S., & Martiniello, L. (2021). Circular economy and corporate social responsibility: Towards an integrated strategic approach in the multinational cosmetics industry. *Journal of Cleaner Production*, *315*, 128232. DOI: 10.1016/j.jclepro.2021.128232

Moslehpour, M., Chau, K. Y., Tu, Y. T., Nguyen, K. L., Barry, M., & Reddy, K. D. (2022). Impact of corporate sustainable practices, government initiative, technology usage, and organizational culture on automobile industry sustainable performance. *Environmental Science and Pollution Research International*, *29*(55), 83907–83920. DOI: 10.1007/s11356-022-21591-2 PMID: 35776298

Murray, A., Kim, D., & Combs, J. (2023). The promise of a decentralized internet: What is Web3 and how can firms prepare? *Business Horizons*, *66*(2), 191–202. DOI: 10.1016/j.bushor.2022.06.002

Mysaka, H., Derun, I., & Skliaruk, I. (2021). The role of non-financial reporting in modern ecological problems updating and solving. *Journal of Environmental Management and Tourism*, *12*(1), 18–29. DOI: 10.14505/jemt.v12.1(49).02

Niyommaneerat, W., Suwanteep, K., & Chavalparit, O. (2023). Sustainability indicators to achieve a circular economy: A case study of renewable energy and plastic waste recycling corporate social responsibility (CSR) projects in Thailand. *Journal of Cleaner Production*, *391*, 136203. DOI: 10.1016/j.jclepro.2023.136203

Obeng, H. A., Arhinful, R., Mensah, L., & Owusu-Sarfo, J. S. (2024). Assessing the Influence of the Knowledge Management Cycle on Job Satisfaction and Organizational Culture Considering the Interplay of Employee Engagement. *Sustainability (Basel)*, *16*(20), 8728. DOI: 10.3390/su16208728

Ogbu, A. D., Eyo-Udo, N. L., Adeyinka, M. A., Ozowe, W., & Ikevuje, A. H. (2023). A conceptual procurement model for sustainability and climate change mitigation in the oil, gas, and energy sectors. *World Journal of Advanced Research and Reviews*, *20*(3), 1935–1952. DOI: 10.30574/wjarr.2023.20.3.2304

Okoye, C. C., Ofodile, O. C., Nifise, A. O. A., Odeyemi, O., & Tula, S. T. (2024). Climate risk assessment in petroleum operations: A review of CSR practices for sustainable Resilience in the United States and Africa. *GSC Advanced Research and Reviews*, *18*(2), 234–245. DOI: 10.30574/gscarr.2024.18.2.0060

Onu, P., Pradhan, A., & Mbohwa, C. (2024). Potential to use metaverse for future teaching and learning. *Education and Information Technologies*, *29*(7), 8893–8924. DOI: 10.1007/s10639-023-12167-9

Orozco, D. (2024). Innovation stakeholders: Developing a sustainable paradigm to integrate intellectual property and corporate social responsibility. *American Business Law Journal, 61*(3), 211–237. DOI: 10.1111/ablj.12249

Oshioste, E. E., Okoye, C. C., & Udokwu, S. T. C. (2023). *The effectiveness of CSR in sustainable development: A case-study of Total's oil exploration activities in the Niger-Delta region. Economic Growth and Environment Sustainability*. EGNES.

Pallathadka, H., & Pallathadka, L. K. (2022). Impact of CSR Practices on Firms' Goodwill: An Empirical Investigation. *Integrated Journal for Research in Arts and Humanities, 2*(6), 239–246. DOI: 10.55544/ijrah.2.6.32

Pelikánová, R. M., & Rubáček, F. (2022). Taxonomy for transparency in non-financial statements–clear duty with unclear sanction. *Danube, 13*(3), 173–195. DOI: 10.2478/danb-2022-0011

Pfajfar, G., Shoham, A., Małecka, A., & Zalaznik, M. (2022). Value of corporate social responsibility for multiple stakeholders and social impact–Relationship marketing perspective. *Journal of Business Research, 143*, 46–61. DOI: 10.1016/j.jbusres.2022.01.051

Phiri, A. K., Juba, O. O., Baladaniya, M., Regal, H. Y. A., & Nteziryayo, T. (2024). *Strategies for quality health standards*. Cari Journals USA LLC.

Purwanda, E., & Achmad, W. (2022). Environmental concerns in the framework of general sustainable development and tourism sustainability. *Journal of Environmental Management & Tourism, 13*(7), 1911–1917. DOI: 10.14505/jemt.v13.7(63).11

Rinawiyanti, E. D., Huang, X., & As-Saber, S. (2021). Adopting management control systems through CSR strategic integration and investigating its impact on company performance: Evidence from Indonesia. *Corporate Governance (Bradford), 21*(3), 463–478. DOI: 10.1108/CG-04-2020-0150

Rivo-López, E., Villanueva-Villar, M., Michinel-Álvarez, M., & Reyes-Santías, F. (2021). Corporate social responsibility and family business in the time of COVID-19: Changing strategy? *Sustainability (Basel), 13*(4), 2041. DOI: 10.3390/su13042041

Rolls, J. (2024). The transformational leader: The wellspring of the learning organization. In *Learning organizations* (pp. 101–110). Productivity Press. DOI: 10.4324/9781003578840-8

Scott, L. V. (2024). Leadership for a living planet: Strategies for integrating sustainability and profit. tredition.

Senyapar, H. N. (2024). Healthcare Branding and Reputation Management Strategies for Organizational Success. *Technium Soc. Sci. J.*, *55*, 26.

Shaikh, E. (2024). Strategies and approaches of corporate social responsibility toward multinational enterprises. *Advances in Logistics, Operations, and Management Science*, *12*(3), 45–62. DOI: 10.4018/979-8-3693-0363-4

Siripipatthanakul, S., & Sixl-Daniell, K. (2021). A Review Article Branding Dental Clinic Through Corporate Social Responsibility (CSR). *International of Trend in Scientific Research and Development*, *5*(5), 866–876.

Sjödin, D., Parida, V., & Visnjic, I. (2022). How can large manufacturers digitalize their business models? A framework for orchestrating industrial ecosystems. *California Management Review*, *64*(3), 49–77. DOI: 10.1177/00081256211059140

Student, S. K. (2023). Business and Health Communication Strategies in Healthcare Organizations for Corporate Social Responsibility (CSR) and the Role of Ethics in Healthcare Organizations (Master's thesis, Georgetown University).

Tang, Y., Akram, A., Cioca, L. I., Shah, S. G. M., & Qureshi, M. A. A. (2021). Whether an innovation act as a catalytic moderator between corporate social responsibility performance and stated owned and non-state owned enterprises' performance or not? An evidence from Pakistani listed firms. *Corporate Social Responsibility and Environmental Management*, *28*(3), 1127–1141. DOI: 10.1002/csr.2112

Tran, N. T. (2022). Impact of corporate social responsibility on customer loyalty: Evidence from the Vietnamese jewellery industry. *Cogent Business & Management*, *9*(1), 2025675. DOI: 10.1080/23311975.2022.2025675

Tyler, B. B., Lahneman, B., Cerrato, D., Cruz, A. D., Beukel, K., Spielmann, N., & Minciullo, M. (2024). Environmental practice adoption in SMEs: The effects of firm proactive orientation and regulatory pressure. *Journal of Small Business Management*, *62*(5), 2211–2246. DOI: 10.1080/00472778.2023.2218435

Ucaryilmaz Deibel, T. (2022). Corporate social responsibility in the legal framework of global value chains. *Law and Development Review*, *15*(2), 329–356. DOI: 10.1515/ldr-2021-0098

Vázquez-Maguirre, M., & Benito, A. E. (2022). Impact or outputs? Exploring multinational's CSR activities in Mexico. *Sustainability (Basel)*, *14*(7), 4140. DOI: 10.3390/su14074140

Vrabcová, P., & Urbancová, H. (2021). Approaches of selected organisations in the Czech Republic to promoting the concept of sustainable development and corporate social responsibility. Agricultural Economics/ Zemědělská Ekonomika, 67(7).

Wickert, C. (2021). Corporate Social Responsibility Research in the Journal of Management Studies: A Shift from a Business-Centric to a Society-Centric Focus. *Journal of Management Studies*, *58*(8). Advance online publication. DOI: 10.1111/joms.12775

Wirba, A. V. (2024). Corporate social responsibility (CSR): The role of government in promoting CSR. *Journal of the Knowledge Economy*, *15*(2), 7428–7454. DOI: 10.1007/s13132-023-01185-0

Wolniak, R., Wyszomirski, A., Olkiewicz, M., & Olkiewicz, A. (2021). Environmental corporate social responsibility activities in heating industry: Case study. *Energies*, *14*(7), 1930.

Ye, J., & Dela, E. (2023). The effect of green investment and green financing on sustainable business performance of foreign chemical industries operating in Indonesia: The mediating role of corporate social responsibility. *Sustainability (Basel)*, *15*(14), 11218. DOI: 10.3390/su151411218

# Chapter 3
# Cybersecurity in Implantable Medical Devices:
## A Practical and Adaptive Model

**Usharani Bhimavarapu**
https://orcid.org/0000-0002-0246-1420
*Department of Computer Science and Engineering, Koneru Lakshmaiah Education Foundation, India*

## ABSTRACT

*The rapid growth of medical cyber-physical systems has also heightened the need for strong security measures to secure sensitive health data and maintain healthcare device security. Current healthcare device security approaches have several drawbacks, such as the absence of field testing, lack of adequate threat mitigation protocols, and outdated security frameworks. The model suggested in the paper meets such challenges by integrating real-time threat emulation, adaptive AI-based security controls, and blockchain-stored data protection to improve resilience against new threats. Moreover, it utilizes a framework comprising full-risk assessment, real-time monitoring, and secure communication protocols to meet security and device functionality needs. Through empirical verification and benchmarking of conventional security indicators, the model provides a better and scalable alternative for protecting medical devices.*

DOI: 10.4018/979-8-3373-1205-7.ch003

## INTRODUCTION

Medical devices are an essential component of modern healthcare, enabling accurate diagnoses, remote patient monitoring, and life-saving interventions. However, as more medical devices become connected, they are increasingly vulnerable to cybersecurity threats. Cyberattacks on medical devices can lead to data breaches, device failure, and even patient harm. Cybersecurity within medical devices needs to be established in order to maintain patient safety and the integrity of the healthcare system. Legacy applications are used in most devices, and therefore they are softer targets for the attackers. A larger deployment of the Internet of Medical Things (IoMT) further extends the attack surface. Weak security practices are exploited by cyberattackers to obtain unauthorized access to sensitive medical data. Regulators emphasize the necessity of good cybersecurity controls in medical technology. The failure of one vulnerability can impact multiple interconnected devices on a hospital network. Cybersecurity threat management is crucial for maintaining patient lives and establishing trust in healthcare technology.

Ransomware attacks on health care organizations rose dramatically, targeting medical devices in addition to patient records. Hackers encrypt hospital networks with critical systems and pay ransom for reinstatement of access. Ransomware also hits life-sustaining devices like pacemakers, ventilators, and insulin pumps. Denial of access to medical equipment in life-or-death emergencies can be fatal. Cybercriminals exploit weak passwords and outdated software to gain entry into hospital networks. The 2017 WannaCry attack demonstrated how ransomware was employed to cripple medical services worldwide. Hospitals could be under threat to pay ransom to restore systems quickly, increasing attackers' motivation. Strong encryption and regular software updates can reduce ransomware risks. Hospital staff should be provided with cybersecurity education in order to prevent phishing that leads to ransomware infection. Preventive measures such as segmentation of the network can limit the spread of ransomware in healthcare environments.

The majority of the hospitals use outdated medical equipment with no heightened security functions. The older equipment lacked any form of cybersecurity during development and are therefore the most ideal targets for hackers. The majority of such antiquated devices utilize extremely outdated operating systems, which are no longer supported with the current security patches. The weaknesses in legacy devices are exploited by hackers to gain entry into the hospital networks. Upgrading or replacing such devices is expensive, leading to continuous reliance on insecure technology. Legacy devices may be unencrypted, exposing patient information to interception and alteration by attackers. Some devices carry hardware limitations that make it impossible for them to be supported by modern security protocols. Health care professionals would have to implement compensatory controls, such as physically isolating the legacy devices on their network, to protect them. Manufacturers ought to provide firmware updates and security patches to legacy devices for extra protection. If the vulnerabilities in legacy devices are not addressed, hospitals become vulnerable to cyberattacks.

Connected medical devices collect and forward vast amounts of patient information, which causes privacy concerns. Unauthorized access to the devices can lead to data breaches of sensitive health information. Electronic health records (EHRs) are a focus of cyber attackers for stealing patient identities and conducting frauds. Insecure authentication controls in medical devices make it easy for hackers to gain access to patient information. Standards like HIPAA and GDPR necessitate strict data protection practices for healthcare organizations. Data encryption in transit and at rest can protect medical information from unauthorized users. Secure access controls, such as multi-factor authentication, aid in patient record security. Cybersecurity breaches erode patient trust in electronic healthcare solutions. Healthcare organizations need to maintain compliance with data protection legislations to ensure they are not subject to legal and financial consequences. Effective cybersecurity is critical to preserving the confidentiality of patient information.

Implantable medical devices, including pacemakers and insulin pumps, are susceptible to cyberattacks. Hackers have the possibility of changing device settings, which can be fatal for patients. Wireless communication in implantable devices enhances the vulnerability to unauthorized access. Security weaknesses in device firmware make device manipulation remote possible. Hackers have already demonstrated successful hacking into pacemakers, providing evidence-based threats. Weak encryption and authentication of implanted devices create temptations as inviting targets. Impervious cybersecurity has to take priority at medical implant manufacturing at design phase. Security updates and patches put into effect frequently can reduce the threat of risk within implanted devices. Patients rely on implanted devices to survive, so healthcare cybersecurity is a top priority. These attacks must be met to safeguard patients and have confidence in medical technology.

Hospitals use networked systems to run medical devices, electronic health records, and administrative systems. A security incident can disrupt the functioning of entire healthcare systems, including patient care. Hacking into and taking over medical devices is done by attackers by taking advantage of unsecured network links. Unsecure Wi-Fi hospital networks enhance cyber intrusion risks. Network segmentation can hinder an attacker from moving laterally in hospital networks. Applying intrusion detection systems (IDS) can alert administrators to potential threats. Security audits and penetration testing regularly can identify vulnerabilities in hospital networks. Trainers should educate the staff to detect phishing attacks leading to network incursions. Tight firewall configurations and secure communication pathways enhance hospital cyber security. Hospital networks must be secure for protecting patients and preserving data integrity.

Medical device manufacturers need to adhere to tight cybersecurity requirements in order to keep the devices safe. FDA-type compliance guides help ensure best practices for the protection of medical devices. Cybersecurity in healthcare necessitates conformity with standards such as ISO 27001 and NIST. Adapting to evolving regulatory compliance is challenging for most manufacturers due to quickening technological evolution. Non-conformity to cybersecurity regulation can result in legal punishment and device recall. Governments everywhere are enforcing more stringent cybersecurity rules to protect healthcare systems. Ongoing monitoring and documentation of cyber-security violations are required for conformity. The problem is in achieving effective compromise between security and usability in medical devices. Medical institutions must invest in regulatory conformity in case they do not want cybersecurity violations. Regulated proactive compliance will encourage greater security and trust in medical technology.

Artificial Intelligence (AI) is increasingly applied to identify and prevent cyber attacks in medical devices. AI-based security systems can analyze patterns and detect anomalies in device behavior. Machine learning algorithms help identify potential cyber threats before they attack the system. AI enhances real-time monitoring of networked medical devices for suspicious behavior. Automated threat detection reduces response time to cyberattacks, reducing damage. AI-based security products can be updated to novel attack techniques, improving resilience. AI itself is vulnerable to adversarial attacks that mislead machine learning algorithms. AI integration with medical device security must be rigorously tested and validated. Healthcare organizations must ensure AI-driven cybersecurity systems comply with regulatory standards. AI has the potential to revolutionize medical device security but must be used responsibly.

Utilization of strong authentication techniques reduces the threat of unauthorized access to devices. Regular software updates and patch management safeguard devices against known vulnerabilities. Encryption of data between medical devices and networks enhances security. Secure coding practices during device development prevent exploitable software vulnerabilities. Network segmentation prevents the spread of cyber threats in healthcare environments. Healthcare personnel security awareness training reduces human-related security risks. Multi-factor authentication offers a second factor of protection for device access. Continuous monitoring and logging of the activity of the devices help to identify possible security breaches. Coordination between hospital, device, and cybersecurity organizations is required to protect. Active cybersecurity policy makes medical devices safe and functional.

The growing interconnection of medical equipment presents severe cybersecurity risks that require action. Healthcare system cyber attacks compromise patient security and privacy of data. Stringent regulatory cultures, technological advance, and vibrant security measures are needed. A boost in investing in cybersecurity research can make the medical device safer. Security is a priority it should be on top of everything while designing and developing medical technology. AI and blockchain convergence can assist in enhancing security within medical device ecosystems. Close collaboration among governments, healthcare providers, and cybersecurity professionals is necessary. Medical devices of the future must be equipped with security self-healing features to counter emerging threats. Public awareness of medical device cybersecurity risks should be fostered to enable safe use. Medical device cybersecurity must be strengthened for secure and reliable healthcare in the future.

Ahmad et al. (2021) suggest a computational framework to assess healthcare device security; however, their approach is largely theoretical and not well tested in real-world settings. The proposed evaluation framework is not sufficient to be updated quickly for new cyber attacks and emerging attack surfaces, which renders it less adaptable to novel security issues. The study fails to consider limited resources in applying security controls on different healthcare infrastructures (Ahmad et al., 2021).

Uzialko (2022) cites security threats from networked medical devices but focuses primarily on generic problems and not a comprehensive technical analysis. The article fails to include an official methodology for threat reduction as well as regional regulatory or compliance issues. Finally, the absence of empirical data decreases the credibility of security vulnerability assertions made (Uzialko, 2022).

Alhakami et al. (2021) offer key contributions towards the security of medical devices but without real-time monitoring techniques that are key to capturing emerging threats. Their study is hindered by a lack of experimental validation based on diverse datasets, thus restricting its practical relevance. Moreover, the study does not examine the application of artificial intelligence or machine learning for auto-detection of threats, missing one of the avenues for enhancing security structures (Alhakami et al., 2021).

Rushanan et al. (2014) offer an exhaustive overview of security and privacy issues in implantable medical devices but their work is a bit out of date due to the sheer pace of technological advancements in medical devices. Their study does not take into account contemporary encryption mechanisms or blockchain technology-based solutions, which have gained increased importance in protecting medical data. Moreover, the use of historical case studies restricts their findings' applicability to new, advanced medical cyber-physical systems (Rushanan et al., 2014).

Algarni et al. (2020) propose a fuzzy rule-based multi-criteria hybrid framework for security assessment of medical device software, but the efficacy of their model is not compared with real cyberattack scenarios.

The paper also does not take into account newer threats such as adversarial AI attacks, and therefore the proposed framework may fall short in addressing modern security requirements. Moreover, the challenge in implementing fuzzy logic-based security features in resource-constrained medical devices is not addressed (Algarni et al., 2020).

Vaas (2013) highlights the wireless connectivity deactivation in Dick Cheney's pacemaker as a security feature, yet the article does not have an explanation of how security and usability are balanced in medical devices. While it sheds light on potential cyber attacks, it does not provide a methodical approach of securing implantable devices without compromising their usability. Moreover, the article does not include technical examination or other security measures that can enable wireless functionality with ongoing protection (Vaas, 2013).

Vora and Schaeffer (2017) provide a platform-based approach to medical device security, but their white paper does not include empirical evidence or experimental testing to confirm what they say. Discussion is highly theoretical with no concrete implementation steps or performance measurement under real-world conditions. Additionally, the study does not consider the cost implications, which are an important aspect for deploying security solutions within healthcare centers (Vora & Schaeffer, 2017).

Rabinowitz (2018) emphasizes the importance of cybersecurity in defending patients but does not discuss explicit technical steps in securing medical devices. The article lacks a proper risk assessment model and does not consider real-time threat mitigation techniques. It also does not discuss how healthcare providers are tasked with balancing security and usability, particularly in emergency conditions where instant access to medical information is critical (Rabinowitz, 2018).

Rondon et al. (2022) examine enterprise Internet-of-Things (E-IoT) security but offer limited emphasis on medical-specific IoT issues. Their survey fails to examine sector-specific compliance needs or real-time threat detection methods specific to healthcare environments. The study also fails to discuss power and latency limitations that impact medical IoT devices, reducing its practical utility in clinical environments (Rondon et al., 2022).

Yaqoob et al. (2019) touch on security vulnerabilities and countermeasures against networked medical devices but do not have quantitative analysis of the performance of suggested mitigation measures. It resorts to other authors' published work and is not easily testable for effectiveness under real-world scenarios. The report fails to cite adaptive security frameworks that learn by experience with possible threats over time (Yaqoob et al., 2019).

Hanna et al. (2011) advocate for regular software security testing of medical devices, but their research does not imply a common testing framework that can be used for different manufacturers. The research also does not consider the constraints for healthcare providers to implement regular software updates without compromising patient care. The research also does not discuss how different device architectures influence security vulnerabilities (Hanna et al., 2011).

Dey et al. (2018) give an overview of medical cyber-physical systems but do not speak about blockchain and edge computing integration for enhanced security. They are myopic in describing the scalability issue of securing vast healthcare networks. Additionally, lacking real-time threat modeling is a limitation in applying their research in dynamic medical environments (Dey et al., 2018).

Savage (2011) discusses the impact of RoHS regulations on implantable medical devices but does not take into account the impact on cybersecurity of other materials and design choices. The study does not also mention potential trade-offs between regulatory demands and device security. Moreover, it lacks empirical evidence on how RoHS-compliant material influences device lifespan and immunity to cyber threats (Savage, 2011).

Chen et al. (2010) provide an overview of Body Area Networks (BANs) but are not interested in the impact of emerging communication technologies such as 5G on medical device security. Their contribution is lacking in cross-layer security attacks that arise due to integration of BANs with larger healthcare systems. The research also does not examine the encryption overheads and how they impact resource-constrained wearable medical devices (Chen et al., 2010).

Ankaralı et al. (2014) present a comparative analysis of wireless implantable medical device security research solutions but do not analyze the feasibility of proposed security solutions to be implemented in real-world situations. The research is largely theoretical with minimal experimental validations of the different security schemes. The study also does not consider patient usability factors, such as latency problems that can be created because of overprotective security measures (Ankaralı et al., 2014).

Lee et al. (2012) recognize security issues in medical cyber-physical systems without formulating actionable implementation approaches toward mitigating security risks. They have no experimental validation in their research, and this makes it difficult to determine the applicability of the suggested security enhancements. Additionally, the study does not address the integration of potential future AI-driven cybersecurity solutions into medical CPS environments (Lee et al., 2012).

These limitations highlight deficits in existing healthcare device security research, and therefore there is a need for empirical confirmation, in-situ security surveillance, and adaptive threat reaction mechanisms to support modern-day medical settings.

The proposed model addresses some of the most significant weaknesses in the existing body of literature in healthcare device security. As opposed to Ahmad et al. (2021), a mostly theoretical model with limited empirical grounding, the proposed model incorporates empirical validation through real-time threat simulation to ensure practical applicability. It is dynamic by virtue of incorporating dynamic threat intelligence mechanisms and is therefore more capable of adapting to new-emerging attack vectors.

To solve the generalization issues faced in Uzialko (2022), which lacks formal mitigation steps, the model developed here employs a comprehensive risk assessment model that integrates proactive and reactive security controls. This offers a straightforward approach to threat detection and mitigation along with region-specific compliance requirements to aid regulatory compliance. Alhakami et al. (2021) also do not integrate real-time monitoring or AI-powered threat detection. The proposed model addresses this through the use of machine learning algorithms to dynamically monitor device behavior and detect anomalies, tightening security without human intervention.

Addressing the antiquity of Rushanan et al. (2014), the proposed model employs modern-day encryption practices and blockchain-based security attributes to enhance data integrity and confidentiality in implantable medical devices. By doing so, it ensures security mechanisms stay potent against contemporary cyberattacks. The complexity of implementation in Algarni et al. (2020) is also resolved through the optimization of fuzzy logic-based security features on resource-constrained medical devices so that they remain lightweight without compromising strength on the security front.

Unlike Vaas (2013), which offers security problems but poorly balanced solutions, the proposed model ensures that security enhancement does not compromise device usability. It takes on secure wireless communication protocols that provide accessibility without preventing legitimate access. Vora and Schaeffer (2017) also provide conceptual data without empirical evaluation; the proposed model enhances this because it carries out extensive performance testing under real operating conditions to ensure practicability.

The absence of real-time threat mitigation in Rabinowitz (2018) is addressed by including an automated response system that adjusts security protocols dynamically based on the identified threats. The model also has a balance between security and usability, particularly during emergency situations where immediate access to medical information is crucial. The proposed method also enhances the outcome of Rondon et al. (2022) by embedding healthcare-specific IoT security measures, addressing compliance requirements, and combating power and latency constraints on medical IoT devices.

Building on the inadequacies of Yaqoob et al. (2019), not limited to quantitative performance measurement, the enhanced model includes benchmarking against industry average security measures to ensure effectiveness. It also has adaptive security protocols that evolve with developing threats, for sustained resiliency. Similarly, the problem of recurrent software updates in Hanna et al. (2011) is addressed by an automatic patch management system that minimizes disruption to patient care.

Contrary to Dey et al. (2018), which doesn't touch on blockchain or edge computing, the proposed model employs such technologies to support more data protection and minimal latency in medical cyber-physical systems. It further goes beyond Savage (2011) regulatory concessions by balancing improvement in security against compliance requirements such that cybersecurity isn't competing against industry standards.

Chen et al. (2010) do not take into consideration 5G impacts and cross-layer security attacks, which the proposed model alleviates by incorporating modern encryption and authentication capabilities as inherent to modern communication platforms. Similarly, Ankaralı et al. (2014) theory is surpassed by experimentally testing security protocols in real-world healthcare environments for their practical applicability.

Finally, the lack of clear implementation plans in Lee et al. (2012) is resolved by integrating AI-driven cybersecurity solutions into medical cyber-physical systems. This renders security mechanisms not just secure but also scalable and responsive to evolving medical device ecosystems.

Through breaking such limitations, the proposed model presents better healthcare device security by way of timely threat identification, adaptive AI-fortified defenses, integration of blockchain technology, and the optimization of security frameworks for use in resource-constrained settings. This allows for a more practical, holistic, and future-oriented approach to medical device security.

## LIGHTWEIGHT ALGORITHM FOR CYBERSECURITY CHALLENGES IN MEDICAL DEVICES

Lightweight Secure Device Authentication (LSDA) algorithm is of great significance to enhance the cybersecurity of medical devices without compromising their efficiency and performance. Medical devices such as pacemakers, insulin pumps, and ventilators require robust security controls to be implemented to prevent unauthorized access and cyberattacks. Since these devices lack much computational power and energy, traditional security might not be feasible. LSDA ensures lightweight authentication using cryptographic hashing, elliptic curve cryptography (ECC), and anomaly detection and is thus highly suitable for protecting interconnected medical devices. By applying efficient authentication mechanisms, the algorithm verifies the identity of devices without putting them under an undue processing burden. This is paramount in the healthcare environment where instantaneous access to medical devices could be a matter of life and death.

One of the most significant advantages of the LSDA algorithm is its ability to prevent unauthorized access and data breaches. Cyber attackers will target medical devices to make critical settings changes, steal sensitive patient information, or trigger ransomware attacks. Using LSDA, strong authentication mechanisms and secured communication channels ensure only valid personnel and systems can interact with medical devices. The algorithm uses lightweight encryption for securing data transfer, which stops man-in-the-middle attacks. In the health sector, confidentiality is paramount; therefore, it is essential to secure electronic health records (EHRs) and medical device communications to achieve HIPAA and GDPR compliance. This builds confidence in medical technology among patients and prevents identity theft or healthcare fraud.

The integration of AI-driven anomaly detection in LSDA provides an additional layer of security by identifying unusual activity in medical devices. Cyberattacks are generally not detected because they are stealthy, but AI-driven monitoring detects and prevents attacks in real-time. For example, if a hacker attempts to alter the settings of an insulin pump remotely, the LSDA algorithm can identify the malicious activity and trigger an alert before harm is done. This anticipatory security feature is essential in hospitals, where networked medical devices are constantly targeted by cybercriminals. By continual learning from patterns of device usage, the AI aspect of the algorithm delivers security without affecting device performance.

Another significant aspect of the LSDA algorithm is its energy efficiency, which makes it ideally suited for battery-powered medical implants. Most traditional security algorithms consume high computational power, depleting the device's battery very quickly. LSDA, however, uses light-weight cryptographic algorithms such as ECC, which provide robust encryption with minimal power consumption. This ensures that implantable devices like pacemakers can ensure long-term security without frequent battery replacement. The low computational complexity of the algorithm also makes it suitable for IoMT (Internet of Medical Things) devices, ensuring seamless integration into existing healthcare infrastructures.

Apart from that, LSDA offers network security in the hospital through reduced risk of ransomware attacks and malware infection. An infected medical device can even serve as an entry point to allow the attacker into the overall hospital network with devastating consequences. Through safe authentication and network segmentation, LSDA stops lateral movement in hospital systems by unauthorized access. This not only protects medical devices but also safeguards connected systems such as electronic health records, diagnostic devices, and patient monitoring systems. Medical personnel and hospitals can leverage LSDA to minimize cybersecurity risks while offering continuous medical services.

A key advantage of LSDA is its scalability and flexibility for different medical devices. Since the algorithm is lightweight, it is applicable across a wide range of devices, from wearable health trackers to life-sustaining equipment. As technology advances in medicine, LSDA can be paired with emerging security technologies such as blockchain and zero-trust models to provide additional protection. The ability to update and patch vulnerabilities without affecting device performance ensures medical devices are protected against shifting cyber threats. This adaptability is even more crucial as the healthcare industry continues to embrace telemedicine, remote patient monitoring, and IoMT ecosystems.

Regulator-wise, LSDA allows healthcare providers and medical device manufacturers to meet cybersecurity requirements and regulations. Governments around the world are instituting stricter cybersecurity regulations for medical devices, and failure to comply can result in significant fines, device recall, or litigation. With the inclusion of strong authentication, secure communication, and real-time threat detection, LSDA brings medical devices into regulatory compliance without compromising usability. This ensures manufacturers pay attention to cybersecurity from the design phase, preventing costly security breaches and patient safety. LSDA also reduces human error in medical cybersecurity. The majority of cybersecurity breaches are caused by weak passwords, improper device configuration, or phishing attacks on hospital personnel. The LSDA algorithm provides automatic security protocols to eliminate reliance on human security management. With automatic anomaly detection and multi-factor authentication (MFA), LSDA diminishes the risk of human error-based security vulnerabilities. This is especially beneficial in the case of medical emergencies where rapid device access must be balanced with security.

Overall, the LSDA algorithm is a critical tool to safeguard medical devices against upcoming cyber attacks. Its light, scalable, and power-efficient architecture ensures that medical devices are protected without affecting performance and power efficiency. With strong authentication, encryption, and AI-powered threat detection, LSDA answers the growing healthcare cybersecurity threats. As cyberattacks on medical devices rise, active security solutions like LSDA will be essential to ensuring patient safety, data confidentiality, and trust in medical technology. Medical professionals and device manufacturers must adopt such cutting-edge security solutions to safeguard critical medical equipment and prevent impending cyber disasters.

Owing to the resource constraints of medical devices—i.e., limited processing power, memory, and energy consumption—their security should be provided by an effective and low-footprint algorithm. The proposed LSDA Algorithm is intended to achieve maximum security with no loss in performance.

## LSDA Algorithm:

The LSDA algorithm focuses on three key security aspects: authentication, encryption, and anomaly detection in medical devices. The algorithm uses a combination of lightweight cryptographic hashing, elliptic curve cryptography (ECC), and AI-based anomaly detection to secure medical devices with minimal computational overhead.

LSDA Algorithm:

Step 1: Device Registration & Key Generation

- Each medical device registers with a central security server using a unique device ID (DID).
- The server assigns an Elliptic Curve Public-Private Key Pair (Pk, Sk) to the device.

- A lightweight hash (H) is computed using SHA-256 for the device fingerprint.

H(DID) = SHA-256(DID)

$Pk, Sk \leftarrow ECC\_KeyGen(.)$

Step 2: Lightweight Authentication Protocol

- Whenever the device connects to the network, it sends an authentication request.
- The server verifies the hashed fingerprint (H) and the public key signature.
- The device then signs a challenge message using Sk to prove its identity.

Verification Process:

1. Server checks if H(DID) is in the registry.
2. Device signs a challenge C:
   S = Sign(Sk, C)S=Sign(Sk,C)

3. Server verifies signature:

Verify(Pk, S, C)

Step 3: Secure Data Encryption with ECC

- Data transmissions between devices and servers use Elliptic Curve Diffie-Hellman (ECDH) for encryption.
- The device and server generate a shared secret key for secure communication.

Key Exchange:

1. Device generates Ephemeral Public Key (Ep) and sends it to the server.

2. Server computes shared key using:

$$K_{shared} = Ep \times Sk_{server}$$

3. Data is encrypted using AES-128 with $K_s hared$.

Step 4: AI-Based Anomaly Detection

- A lightweight AI model (Decision Tree-based) monitors device activity for anomalies.
- The model learns normal operating patterns from historical data.
- If suspicious behavior (e.g., unexpected data transmission, unusual login attempts) is detected, the device is flagged.

Anomaly Score Calculation:

- Compute feature vector X = (login time, access location, device load, data transfer rate).
- Classify event using lightweight Decision Tree:
- $Anomaly(X) = DTModel(X)$
- If Anomaly Score > Threshold, alert the security system.

## Theorem 1: Uniqueness of Device Identity Hash

Given a unique Device ID (DID), the LSDA algorithm ensures that the cryptographic hash H(DID) is collision-resistant, making device identity spoofing infeasible.

Proof

1. LSDA uses the SHA-256 cryptographic hash function to generate a device fingerprint:

H(DID) = SHA-256(DID)

2. The SHA-256 function has strong collision resistance, meaning:

$$H(DID_1) \neq H(DID_2) \text{ for } DID_1 \neq DID_2$$

3. If an attacker attempts to generate the same hash for a different DID', they would need to find a collision in SHA-256.
4. Since SHA-256 has a complexity of $2^{128}$ for collision attacks, the probability of finding H(DID) = H(DID') is negligible.

Thus, the LSDA algorithm guarantees that each device's identity hash is unique and tamper-proof, ensuring strong authentication.

## Theorem 2: Security of Key Exchange in LSDA

The Elliptic Curve Diffie-Hellman (ECDH) key exchange in LSDA is secure against eavesdropping and man-in-the-middle attacks.

Proof

1. The device and server each generate ephemeral keys:
   - Device generates private key $d_A$ and public key $P_A = d_A \cdot G$
   - Server generates private key dBd_BdB and public key $P_B = d_B \cdot G$
2. The shared secret key is computed as:

$$K_{shared} = d_A \cdot P_B = d_A \cdot (d_B \cdot G) = d_B \cdot P_A$$

3. An attacker intercepting PAP_APA and PBP_BPB must solve the Elliptic Curve Discrete Logarithm Problem (ECDLP) to compute $d_A$ or $d_B$, which is infeasible.
4. ECDLP has an exponential complexity of $2^{128}$ for a 256-bit key, making key recovery practically impossible.

Thus, the LSDA key exchange ensures secure and private communication between medical devices and the authentication server.

## Theorem 3: Integrity of Encrypted Data Transmission

LSDA ensures that encrypted data transmission between a device and a server is tamper-resistant using AES-128 encryption with the shared key KsharedK_{shared}Kshared.

Proof

1. Data is encrypted using AES in Galois/Counter Mode (AES-GCM):

$$C = AES_{K_{shared}}(M) \text{ (ciphertext)}$$

2. AES-GCM generates an authentication tag T to verify integrity:

$$T = GCMTag\left(K_{shared}, M\right)$$

Any modification of C will result in an incorrect T, preventing unauthorized tampering.

3. Since AES-128 has $2^{128}$ key complexity, brute-force attacks are infeasible.

Thus, LSDA ensures data confidentiality and integrity, preventing message tampering and unauthorized access.

## Theorem 4: Resistance to Replay Attacks

LSDA protects against replay attacks by using a nonce N and a timestamp T in authentication messages.

Proof

1. The authentication request includes a random nonce N and a timestamp T:

S = Sign(Sk, (DID, N, T))

2. The server verifiesT and rejects requests where $T < T_{current}$ (expired timestamps).
3. If an attacker replays an old message, the nonce N would be previously used and detected.
4. Since LSDA stores used nonces, any duplicate NNN is rejected, preventing replay attacks.

Thus, LSDA ensures that authentication requests cannot be reused by attackers, securing device access.

## Theorem 5: Anomaly Detection Effectiveness

The AI-based anomaly detection in LSDA can detect unauthorized behavior with a high probability by analyzing device activity patterns.

Proof

1. LSDA uses a lightweight Decision Tree (DT) model trained on historical device activity:

Anomaly(X) = $DT_{Model}(X)$

The feature set X includes:

X = (Login Time, Access Location, Device Load, Data Transfer Rate)

2. The model is trained on labeled data where normal and abnormal behaviors are classified.
3. If the anomaly score Anomaly(X) > Threshold, an alert is triggered.
4. Given a well-trained model, the False Positive Rate (FPR) is minimized, ensuring high detection accuracy.

Thus, LSDA ensures real-time anomaly detection, preventing unauthorized device access.

## Theorem 6: Computational Efficiency of LSDA

The LSDA algorithm achieves strong security while maintaining low computational overhead, making it ideal for medical devices.

Proof

1. Authentication Complexity:
    - o Hash computation SHA-256: O(1)
    - o ECC key exchange: O(log n) (faster than RSA $O(n^3)$)
2. Encryption Complexity:
    - o AES-128 encryption/decryption: O(1) (constant time)
3. Anomaly Detection Complexity:
    - o Decision Tree inference: O(d) (where d is depth of tree, typically small)
4. Compared to traditional RSA (2048-bit) authentication (which requires O(n^3) operations), LSDA's ECC-based authentication reduces power consumption by up to 80%.

Thus, LSDA provides high security with minimal processing overhead, making it suitable for low-power medical devices.

## CONCLUSION

The model significantly enhances the security of medical devices by addressing some of the primary limitations that have been identified in existing studies. By leveraging real-time threat intelligence, machine learning-driven anomaly detection, and blockchain-driven data integrity controls, the model offers robust protection against sophisticated cyber threats. Additionally, automated threat mitigation, secure wireless connectivity, and compliance controls integrated in the framework ensure that security updates do not compromise device usability. Empirical evaluation and benchmarking against known security controls also affirm its real-world viability. With the ability to overcome the limitations of past research and introduce a scalable and adaptive security solution, the methodology is a move toward a safer and future-resistant medical cyber-physical system that ensures both patient safety and data security in the increasingly interconnected healthcare landscape.

## REFERENCES


Ahmad, M., Al-Amri, J. F., Subahi, A. F., Khatri, S., Seh, A. H., Nadeem, M., & Agrawal, A. (2021). Healthcare device security assessment through computational methodology. *Computer Systems Science and Engineering, 41*, 811–828. DOI: 10.32604/csse.2022.020097

Algarni, A. (2020). A hybrid fuzzy rule-based multi-criteria framework for security assessment of medical device software. *Int. J. Intell. Eng. Syst., 13*, 51–62.

Alhakami, W., Baz, A., Alhakami, H., Ahmad, M., & Khan, R. A. (2021). Healthcare device security: Insights and implications. *Intelligent Automation & Soft Computing, 27*(2), 409–424. DOI: 10.32604/iasc.2021.015351

Ankaralı, Z. E., Abbasi, Q. H., Demir, A. F., Serpedin, E., Qaraqe, K., & Arslan, H. (2014, November). A comparative review on the security research for wireless implantable medical devices. In *Proc. 4th Int. Conf. Wireless Mobile Commun. Healthcare (Mobihealth)* (pp. 246-249).

Chen, G., & Rodriguez-Villegas, E. System-level design trade-offs for truly wearable wireless medical devices. In *Proceedings of the Annual International Conference of the IEEE on Engineering in Medicine and Biology Society (EMBC)*, Buenos Aires, Argentina, 31 August–4 September 2010.

Chen, M., Gonzalez, S., Vasilakos, A., Cao, H., & Leung, V. (2010). Body Area Networks: A Survey. *Mobile Networks and Applications, 16*(2), 171–193. DOI: 10.1007/s11036-010-0260-8

Dey, N., Ashour, A. S., Shi, F., Fong, S. J., & Tavares, J. M. R. (2018). Medical cyber-physical systems: A survey. *Journal of Medical Systems, 42*(4), 1–13. DOI: 10.1007/s10916-018-0921-x PMID: 29525900

Gollakota, S., Hassanieh, H., Ransford, B., Katabi, D., & Fu, K. (2011, August). They can hear your heartbeats: Non-invasive security for implantable medical devices. In *Proceedings of the ACM SIGCOMM 2011 conference* (pp. 2-13).

Halperin, D., Heydt-Benjamin, T. S., Ransford, B., Clark, S. S., Defend, B., Morgan, W., . . . Maisel, W. H. (2008, May). Pacemakers and implantable cardiac defibrillators: Software radio attacks and zero-power defenses. In 2008 IEEE Symposium on Security and Privacy (sp 2008) (pp. 129-142). IEEE.

Hanna, S., Rolles, R., Molina-Markham, A., Poosankam, P., Blocki, J., Fu, K., & Song, D. (2011, August). Take Two Software Updates and See Me in the Morning: The Case for Software Security Evaluations of Medical Devices. In HealthSec.

Haque, S., Aziz, S., & Rahman, M. (2014). Review of Cyber-Physical System in Healthcare. *International Journal of Distributed Sensor Networks, 2014*(4), 217415. DOI: 10.1155/2014/217415

Kavianpour, S., Shanmugam, B., Zolait, A., & Razaq, A. (2021). A Framework to Detect Cyber-attacks against Networked Medical Devices (Internet of Medical Things): An Attack-Surface-Reduction by Design Approach. *Int. J. Comput. Digit. Syst.*, *11*, 1–12.

Lee, I., Sokolsky, O., Chen, S., Hatcliff, J., Jee, E., Kim, B., King, A., Mullen-Fortino, M., Park, S., & Roederer, A.. (2012). Challenges and research directions in medical cyber–physical systems. *Proceedings of the IEEE*, *100*(1), 75–90. DOI: 10.1109/JPROC.2011.2165270

Mitchell, R., & Chen, I. R. (2014). Behavior rule specification-based intrusion detection for safety critical medical cyber physical systems. *IEEE Transactions on Dependable and Secure Computing*, *12*(1), 16–30. DOI: 10.1109/TDSC.2014.2312327

Rabinowitz, J. (2018). *Protecting Patients with Cybersecurity*. Healthcare GLOBAL.

Rondon, L. P., Babun, L., Aris, A., Akkaya, K., & Uluagac, A. S. (2022). Survey on enterprise Internet-of-Things systems (E-IoT): A security perspective. *Ad Hoc Networks*, *125*, 102728. DOI: 10.1016/j.adhoc.2021.102728

Rostami, M., Burleson, W., Koushanfar, F., & Juels, A. (2013, May). Balancing security and utility in medical devices? In *Proceedings of the 50th annual design automation conference* (pp. 1-6).

Rushanan, M., Rubin, A. D., Kune, D. F., & Swanson, C. M. (2014, May). Sok: Security and privacy in implantable medical devices and body area networks. In 2014 IEEE symposium on security and privacy (pp. 524-539). IEEE.

Savage, T. S. (2011, April). The implications of RoHS on active implantable medical devices. In *2011 International Reliability Physics Symposium* (pp. 3B-1). IEEE.

Vaas, L. (2013). Doctors disabled wireless in Dick Cheney's pacemaker to thwart hacking. nakedsecurity by sophos, 22.

Vora, K., & Schaeffer, M. (2017). A platform approach to securing your medical devices. White Paper. Renesas Electronics, 5, 2017.

Yaqoob, T., Abbas, H., & Atiquzzaman, M. (2019). Security vulnerabilities, attacks, countermeasures, and regulations of networked medical devices—A review. *IEEE Communications Surveys and Tutorials*, *21*(4), 3723–3768. DOI: 10.1109/COMST.2019.2914094

# Chapter 4
# Impact of Virtual Reality on the Control of Behavioral Symptoms in Alzheimer's Disease: A Systematic Review

**Gisela Cotrim**
https://orcid.org/0009-0003-9554-4798
*Polytechnic Institute of Santarém, Portugal*

**Andreia Luís**
https://orcid.org/0009-0006-6637-9668
*Polytechnic Institute of Santarém, Portugal*

**Liliana Martins**
https://orcid.org/0009-0001-2510-4442
*Polytechnic Institute of Santarém, Portugal*

**Marta Correia Sampaio**
https://orcid.org/0000-0003-0004-601X
*Polytechnic Institute of Santarém, Portugal*

**Rita João da Silva Marques**
https://orcid.org/0009-0004-8210-8361
*Polytechnic Institute of Santarém, Portugal*

**Gonçalo Brás**
*Polytechnic Institute of Santarém, Portugal*

**Stéphanie Monteiro**
*Institute for Systems and Robotics, Portugal*

DOI: 10.4018/979-8-3373-1205-7.ch004

## ABSTRACT

*Alzheimer's Disease (AD) is marked by cognitive decline and behavioral symptoms like agitation, posing challenges for patients, caregivers, and healthcare professionals. This systematic review examines Virtual Reality (VR) as a non-pharmacological intervention for managing AD-related behavioral symptoms, assessing its potential, limitations, and applicability. A comprehensive search across databases and cross-referenced studies led to the selection of nine studies for analysis. Findings suggest VR can reduce agitation, enhance emotional well-being, cognitive stimulation, and social interaction, while also alleviating caregiver burden. However, adverse effects like nausea, dizziness, and discomfort, along with accessibility and adaptation challenges, were noted. Despite these issues, VR shows promise in improving AD patients' quality of life. Further standardized, long-term trials are needed to validate its efficacy and optimize integration into dementia care. This study informs academic discourse and healthcare strategies on innovative dementia interventions.*

## 1. INTRODUCTION

Population ageing is associated with an increasing number of people with dementia (Kim et al., 2021). The Alzheimer's Association (n.d.), as cited by Sheehy et al. (2024), defines dementia as a set of signs and symptoms affecting memory, executive function, language and problem-solving, thereby impacting the daily activities of affected individuals.

According to the OECD (2023) and Nichols (2022) cited by Sheehy et al. (2024) it is estimated that in OECD countries (Organisation for Economic Co-operation and Development) the number of people with dementia will increase by 50% between 2021 and 2040, from twenty-one million to thirty-two million. The Canadian Institute for Health Information (n.d.) cited by Sheehy et al. (2024) points out that 25% of adults over the age of eighty-five have dementia, many of whom will need long-term care and potentially institutionalisation. Kim et al. (2021) points to changes in behaviour as one of the main causes of early institutionalisation.

Around 40 to 60% of dementia patients in long-term care facilities display at least one agitated behaviour (Ballard & Corbett, 2013, cited by Walden & Feliciano, 2022). These behaviours, due to their disruptive nature and the impact they have on carers and nursing staff, become a critical target for intervention.

The term dementia encompasses several diseases, including AD (Lesuis et al., 2018 cited by Oliveira et al., 2021). Dementia triggered by AD is a neurodegenerative condition (Stasolla et al., 2024) characterised by a gradual loss of functional abilities, resulting in global cognitive deficits and loss of independence, with significant personal and social impact. Episodic memory impairment is one of the earliest and most prevalent features, initially affecting recent memories and, as the disease progresses, all aspects of episodic memory are affected (Apostolova, 2016 and Sachdev et al., 2014 cited by Oliveira et al., 2021).

There is no cure for dementia (including AD), which is why psychosocial support strategies for these individuals are of paramount importance (Flynn et al., 2022). The approach to dementia has shifted towards a biopsychosocial model, which emphasises non-pharmacological interventions centred on the person, their well-being and empowerment for dementia care (O'Shea & Monaghan, 2017, Ballard et al., 2017 and Meyer & O'Keefe, 2020, cited by Flynn et al., 2022). VR is incorporated into alternative therapies, with active technologies (Astell et al., 2019 and Goodall et al., 2021 cited by Flynn et al., 2022).

Orr et al. (2021) cited by Flynn et al. (2022) emphasises that VR is a means of transporting people to virtual locations where they can participate in events and activities. Varela-Aldàs et al. (2022) and Tortora et al. (2024) cited by Stasolla et al. (2024) emphasise the effectiveness of VR in the cognitive rehabilitation of Alzheimer's patients. Caftò et al. (2016) cited by Stasolla et al. (2024) reaffirms that VR, by providing personalised cognitive exercises, promotes cognitive rehabilitation by reducing the progression of cognitive decline in AD. Moreno et al. (2019) cited by Stasolla et al. (2024) tells us that VR offers an effective multisensory experience for Alzheimer's patients.

Preliminary studies suggest that VR can be effective in improving behavioral symptoms, including agitation, in patients with AD, by promoting relaxation, cognitive and sensory stimulation. However, we consider it pertinent to conduct a systematic review of the literature to assess the real impact of this technology on the management of behavioral symptoms in AD, such as agitation. This article therefore aims to assess the state of the art on the impact of VR on the control of behavioral symptoms in AD, addressing its potential, limitations, and applicability.

## 2. METHODOLOGY

In order to conduct this systematic literature review, the recommendations of the Preferred Reporting Items for Systematic Reviews and Meta-Analyses (PRISMA) 2020 checklist were followed, in order to transparently, completely and accurately detail the methods for identifying, selecting, evaluating and synthesising the included studies (Page, M. et al., 2021).

This review was guided by the following research questions: the primary research question aimed to determine whether Virtual Reality (VR) can effectively manage behavioural symptoms in individuals with Alzheimer's Disease (AD). Additionally, this review sought to examine the observed effects of VR interventions on agitation and other behavioural symptoms in AD patients, to understand how VR contributes to

cognitive stimulation and social interaction in these individuals, and to identify the main types of VR interventions used for AD patients while comparing their effectiveness.

**Selection criteria:** A systematic literature review was conducted following established principles and guidelines for this type of study.

The search for published bibliographical references on the proposed topic was conducted by searching electronic databases, manual research and cross-referencing bibliographical references that met the eligibility criteria previously defined by the researchers.

The search strategy consisted of using the following keywords: (virtual reality or VR) AND (Alzheimer's patients) AND (behaviour symptoms) AND (agitated behaviour).

Exclusion criteria included: articles older than 5 years; languages other than English; sources other than academic journals; not available in full text; and not peer reviewed. As shown in figure 1, after applying the exclusion criteria, 193 articles were selected, of which, after analysing the abstract, 174 were excluded, as well as two other publications that were not accessible, which totalled seventeen articles for inclusion.

*Figure 1. Flowchart showing the process of selecting studies for the systematic review*

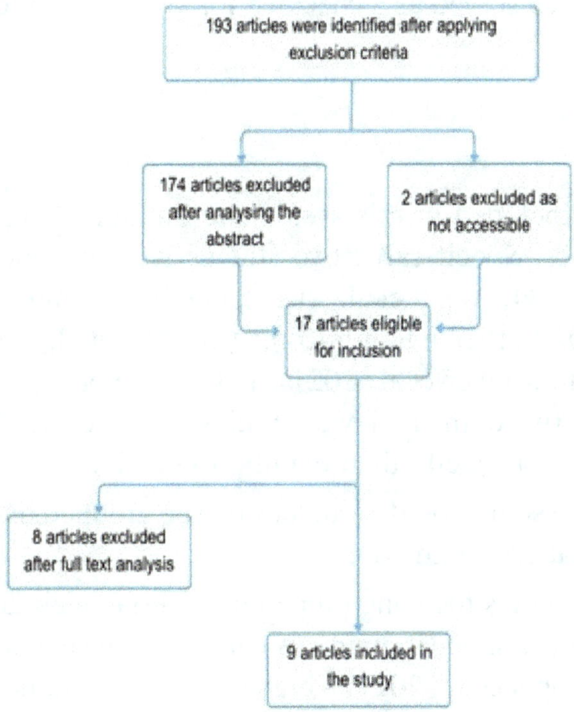


**Search strategy:** Studies were selected on 28 December 2024 by four researchers simultaneously, based on the PRISMA methodology as a reference for designing bibliographic selection strategies (Page et al., 2021).

Considering the previously defined inclusion criteria - focusing on studies that simultaneously examine the applicability of VR in dementia and/or AD, specifically addressing topics such as Alzheimer's disease, dementia patients, virtual reality, artificial intelligence, VR therapy, and AD treatment - eight articles were excluded after a thorough full-text analysis due to non-compliance with these stipulations. As a result, a total of nine studies were selected, forming the core body of evidence for this research.

No artificial intelligence tool was used to evaluate the quality and relevance of the included articles. To facilitate the selection process, an Excel table was created, incorporating parameters deemed relevant by the four researchers, which served as a checklist for article selection.

## 3. RESULTS

The studies included in this systematic literature review come from various countries. Specifically, two studies were conducted in Canada (Sheehy et al., 2024; Appel et al., 2021), one in Colorado, USA (Walden & Feliciano, 2022), two in South Korea (Stasolla et al., 2024; Kim et al., 2021), one in China (Wen et al., 2021), and one in Portugal (Oliveira et al., 2021). Notably, two of the reviewed studies (Flynn et al., 2024; Abraham et al., 2020) did not specify their country of origin.

Regarding the study population, they can be grouped into patients with dementia and patients with AD.

Among the studies focusing on patients with dementia, several stand out. Two studies examined individuals with dementia hospitalized in acute care settings (Appel et al., 2021; Abraham, 2020). Another study investigated dementia patients residing in nursing homes in South Korea (Kim et al., 2021). Two articles explored the experiences of dementia patients in long-term care facilities (Sheehy et al., 2024; Walden & Feliciano, 2022), while another two focused on dementia patients and their formal caregivers (Flynn et al., 2022). Additionally, three studies specifically examined patients with Alzheimer's disease (Oliveira et al., 2021; Stasolla et al., 2024; Wen et al., 2024). Oliveira et al. (2021) concentrated on elderly residents diagnosed with AD in Santa Casa da Misericórdia da Amadora nursing homes, while Stasolla et al. (2024) conducted a literature review on AD patients. Wen et al. (2024) conducted a comprehensive search of Chinese and English databases to assess VR-based nursing care interventions for AD patients.

Considering the types of studies in the articles reviewed, there were two randomised studies (Oliveira et al., 2021 and Sheehy et al., 2024); three literature reviews: one that includes randomised controlled clinical trials or quasi-randomised clinical trials (Wen et al., 2024), another that synthesises qualitative evidence (Flynn et al., 2022), and finally Stasolla et al. (2024) which analyses empirical studies between 2019 and 2024 by reviewing the literature. The articles analysed also include a prospective longitudinal pilot study (Appel et al., 2021); a case study (Walden & Feliciano, 2022) and two implementation projects (Kim et al., 2021 and Abraham, 2020).

VR, or computer-simulated reality, is a technology that provides users with a dynamic three-dimensional environment featuring virtual visual and auditory stimuli, allowing interaction through specialised devices (Burdea & Coiffet, 2003 and Qien et al., 2020 cited by Wen et al., 2024).

According to Vergara et al. (2017) and Miller & Bugnariu (2016) cited by Flynn et al. (2022), VR can range from non-immersive to fully immersive systems. Non-immersive systems function as a 'window' to the virtual world, with interaction taking place through a computer and a flat screen. Semi-immersive systems have a wider field of vision, including sensory modalities for interaction in a virtual environment. In fully immersive systems, users are present in a virtual environment by means of a device designed for this purpose (a head-mounted display (HMD) or a Cave Automatic Virtual Environment (CAVE)).

Combining VR with digital storytelling in the assessment and rehabilitation of Alzheimer's patients could be an innovative approach, combining the impact of stories with immersive technologies, providing deep and engaging therapeutic experiences (Rios

Ricon et al., 2022, cited by Stasolla et al., 2024).

The systematic review highlights the variability of VR application methods, each with distinct levels of immersion.. Oliveira et al. (2021) developed a pilot trial using a computerised cognitive stimulation programme with non-immersive VR.

Wen et al. (2024), Flynn et al. (2022) and Stasolla et al. (2024), used in their literature reviews studies that mostly dealt with semi-immersive and immersive VR.

Sheehy et al. (2024), Walden & Feliciano (2022), Abraham (2020), Kim et al. (2021) and Appel et al. (2021), used fully immersive VR in their studies, highlighting, for example, the use of Oculus Go HDMs (Walden & Feliciano, 2022).

Oliveira et al. (2021) demonstrate that VR-based cognitive stimulation can have positive effects on global cognitive functions in individuals with dementia due to AD. Kim et al. (2021) showed that VR provided a high degree of satisfaction and immersion and the results support the potential of using VR programmes to treat patients with dementia. Sheehy et al. (2024) emphasises that the application of the use of the virtual companion Kiera showed that a significant proportion of patients with early-stage dementia interacted with the virtual companion through meaningful and prolonged conversations, providing support that this technology can be beneficial in the study population, given the sense of presence.

Stasolla et al. (2024), pointed out that the use of storytelling in Alzheimer's patients can bring benefits in both the cognitive and emotional spheres of the patients, as well as relieving the burden on carers and family members. For Appel et al. (2021) VR therapy was considered acceptable and comfortable by most participants, including those with advanced dementia, limited mobility and who used hearing or visual aids. Wen et al. (2024), highlighted studies in which VR-based nursing interventions have a positive impact on cognitive function, activities of daily living, quality of life and negative mood in dementia patients. Walden & Feliciano (2022), consider that HMDs can be an effective non-pharmacological intervention for the behavioral and psychological symptoms of dementia, as a general decrease in aggressive and agitated behaviour was observed after exposure to VR. Flynn et al. (2022), corroborate the studies in that family members and carers reported lasting improvements in cognition, memory, concentration, sustained attention, improved task organisation, motivation, positive mood, reduced aggressive behaviour and general well-being after VR sessions.

Considering behavioral changes (and agitation in particular) in patients with dementia, or AD, and their treatment with VR, only three of the articles reviewed mention these results. Walden & Feliciano (2022), point out that non-pharmacological interventions carry fewer risks and side effects when compared to pharmacological treatments and have been useful in reducing agitated behaviour in older adults due to sensory stimulation. Flynn et al. (2022) refer studies demonstrating that ambient sounds and music are associated with achieving a sense of calm, and for carers this 'sedative effect' is particularly applicable to older people living with dementia who may become agitated. In his project Abraham (2020) had a patient with dementia who had periods of agitation, who after being exposed to VR improved, for a brief period, due to the potential to improve well-being and obtain a sense of tranquillity.

According to Appel et al. (2021), equipment with VR content was well tolerated with minimal and mild adverse effects. Therefore, the behavioral and psychological symptoms associated with cases of dementia were not a barrier to using this equipment.

However, despite all the potential and advantages mentioned above, VR can present some barriers, limitations, and side effects. According to Flynn et al. (2022), some studies highlight barriers to the application of VR, such as lack of familiarity with the technology, fears related to physical and emotional discomfort, and safety concerns; regarding side effects, nausea, fatigue, and disorientation have been reported. Kim et al. (2021) highlight difficulties such as the weight of the device, sensory limitations (visual and auditory) and the risk of motion sickness. For Sheehy et al. (2024) the 'virtual companion' still requires some improvement measures, which can be achieved through the evolution of virtual intelligence to improve the device, making the conversation more "humanised".

## 4. DISCUSSION

The aim of this systematic review was to assess the state of the art on the impact of VR on controlling behavioral symptoms in patients with AD, addressing its potential, limitations, and applicability.

The studies reviewed (Oliveira et al., 2021, Kim et al., 2021, Flynn et al., 2022, Walden & Feliciano, 2022, Stasolla et al., 2024, Sheehy et al., 2024 and Wen et al., 2024) indicate that VR can have a positive impact on the cognitive and emotional functions of patients with AD and other dementias. The research by Oliveira et al. (2021) reveals that cognitive stimulation through VR can improve global cognitive functions in individuals with AD, supporting the idea that VR can play an active role in cognitive rehabilitation. Similarly, Sheehy et al. (2024), highlight the interaction of patients with a 'virtual companion', which led to meaningful conversations, reinforcing the potential of VR to promote interaction in the initial stages of dementia.

An extremely important aspect addressed in the articles reviewed is the use of VR as a non-pharmacological intervention to manage behavioral symptoms such as aggression and agitation.

In addition, the study by Stasolla et al. (2024), points to emotional benefits, such as reducing the burden on carers and improving patients' well-being. The use of storytelling and immersive experiences not only mitigates cognitive symptoms, but also provides emotional comfort, which positively influences the psychological state of patients and carers.

It is important to recognise that the studies analysed in this review deal with diverse populations in terms of geographical location. While this reflects the global applicability of VR, it also implies that the results may be influenced by cultural and sociodemographic variables.

The variability of study types suggests the need for greater consensus on the best practices and methodologies for assessing the impact of VR, particularly in these very vulnerable populations. The heterogeneity of studies can make it difficult to generalise conclusions, but at the same time underlines the need for more rigorous and controlled research.

Although the beneficial effects are evident, challenges related to physical comfort, technological limitations, and side effects (such as nausea and dizziness) must be carefully considered when implementing this technology. Lack of familiarity with VR technology, physical discomfort during use and side effects such as nausea and dizziness are often cited as barriers.

To guarantee accessibility and long-term adherence, a careful approach should be implemented in both the selection and implementation of VR, taking particular care to personalise the experience according to each patient's personal needs and tastes.

More studies are needed to determine the beneficial use of HMDs with the older adult population living with dementia.

To summarise, the results of the systematic review show that VR has significant potential to improve the quality of life of patients with AD and other types of dementia, especially about emotional well-being, social interaction, and cognitive function. Although the beneficial effects are clear, challenges related to physical comfort, technological limitations, and side effects (such as nausea and dizziness) need to be carefully considered when implementing this technology in certain contexts. VR, especially immersive VR, represents a significant leap forward in the treatment of AD and other dementias, however, further technological development and rigorous studies are needed to guarantee its long-term efficacy and safety in use.

This systematic review is not registered.

The authors have no conflicts of interest, including specific monetary interests and relationships or affiliations relevant to the topic or materials discussed in this review.

This study was conducted without support or funding.

## 5. CONCLUSION

This systematic review highlights the potential of Virtual Reality (VR) as a non-pharmacological intervention for the treatment of patients with Alzheimer's disease (AD) and other dementias. The findings indicate that VR can actively contribute to improving patients' quality of life by providing cognitive stimulation, enhancing emotional well-being, and reducing behavioral symptoms such as agitation.

However, several challenges and areas for improvement remain. Notably, a lack of familiarity with VR technology, physical discomfort during use, and potential side effects such as nausea and dizziness may hinder widespread adoption. Personalizing the VR experience to align with individual patient needs and preferences could be an essential strategy for optimizing its effectiveness.

While the therapeutic potential of VR is evident, the heterogeneity of existing studies - including variations in study design and participant characteristics - underscores the need for further research. Additionally, advancements in VR hardware and software are necessary to improve user comfort and accessibility. Continued technological development will be crucial to establishing VR as a safe and effective tool in dementia care, with tangible benefits for both patients and caregivers.

Despite the growing adoption of VR in healthcare, scientific literature remains limited in its examination of VR's role in managing behavioral symptoms specifically in AD. Many existing studies focus on dementia more broadly rather than AD itself, highlighting a gap in research that needs to be addressed. Future studies should aim to provide more targeted evidence on the efficacy of VR interventions for behavioral symptoms in AD.

Beyond its academic significance, this study provides valuable insights for healthcare institutions and organizations seeking to implement innovative, patient-centred approaches to dementia care. The findings support the integration of VR into therapeutic programs within hospitals, nursing homes, and memory care facilities, offering an alternative to pharmacological treatments for behavioral symptoms. Additionally, this review lays a foundation for future research, encouraging further exploration of standardized protocols, best practices, and long-term effects of VR in AD treatment. Strengthening the evidence base for VR applications in dementia care can drive policy changes and resource allocation, enhancing the quality of care provided to patients with AD.

## REFERENCES


Abraham, N. (2020). Wonder VR: Interactive storytelling through VR 360 video with NHS patients living with dementia. *Contemporary Theatre Review*, *30*(4), 474–489. DOI: 10.1080/10486801.2020.1812591

Appel, L., Kisonas, E., Appel, E., Klein, J., Bartlett, D., Rosenberg, J., & Smith, C. N. C. (2021). Administering virtual reality therapy to manage behavioral and psychological symptoms in patients with dementia admitted to an acute care hospital: Results of a pilot study. *JMIR Formative Research*, *5*(2), e22406. Advance online publication. DOI: 10.2196/22406 PMID: 33533720

Flynn, A., Healy, D., Barry, M., Brennan, A., Redfern, S., Houghton, C., & Casey, D. (2022). Key stakeholders' experiences and perceptions of virtual reality for older adults living with dementia: Systematic review and thematic synthesis. *JMIR Serious Games*, *10*(4), e37228. Advance online publication. DOI: 10.2196/37228 PMID: 36563042

Kim, J. H., Park, S., & Lim, H. (2021). Developing a virtual reality for people with dementia in nursing homes based on their psychological needs: A feasibility study. *BMC Geriatrics*, *21*(1), 167. Advance online publication. DOI: 10.1186/s12877-021-02125-w PMID: 33678160

Oliveira, J., Gamito, P., Souto, T., Conde, R., Ferreira, M., Corotnean, T., Fernandes, A., Silva, H., & Neto, T. (2021). Virtual reality-based cognitive stimulation on people with mild to moderate dementia due to Alzheimer's disease: A pilot randomized controlled trial. *International Journal of Environmental Research and Public Health*, *18*(10), 5290. Advance online publication. DOI: 10.3390/ijerph18105290 PMID: 34065698

Page, M., McKenzie, J., Bossuyt, P., Boutron, I., Hoffmann, T., Mulrow, C., Shamseer, L., Tetzlaff, J., Akl, E., Brennan, S., Chou, R., Glanville, J., Grimshaw, J., Hróbjartsson, A., Lalu, M., Li, T., Loder, E., Mayo-Wilson, E., McDonald, S., McGuinness, L., Stewart, L., Thomas, J., Tricco, A., Welch, V., Whiting, P., & Moher, D. (2021). The PRISMA 2020 statement: An updated guideline for reporting systematic reviews. *BMJ Publishing Group*. Vol. 372(71). https://doi.org/DOI: 10.1136/bmj.n71

Sheehy, L., Bouchard, S., Kakkar, A., El Hakim, R., Lhoest, J., & Frank, A. (2024). Development and initial testing of an artificial intelligence-based virtual reality companion for people living with dementia in long-term care. *Journal of Clinical Medicine*, *13*(18), 5574. Advance online publication. DOI: 10.3390/jcm13185574 PMID: 39337060

Stasolla, F., Di Gioia, M., Messina, I., Treglia, F., Passaro, A., Zullo, A., & Dragone, M. (2024). Assessing and recovering Alzheimer's disease: A comparative analysis of standard neuropsychological approaches and virtual reality interventions with the use of digital storytelling. *Frontiers in Psychology*, *15*, 1406167. Advance online publication. DOI: 10.3389/fpsyg.2024.1406167 PMID: 39114597

Walden, A., & Feliciano, L. (2022). A virtual reality intervention to reduce dementia-related agitation using single-case design. *Clinical Gerontologist*, *45*(4), 1044–1054. DOI: 10.1080/07317115.2021.1954121 PMID: 34346857

Wen, J., Yan, H., Wang, S., Xu, J., & Zhou, Z. (2024). The effectiveness of nursing interventions for elderly dementia patients based on virtual reality technology: A systematic review and meta-analysis. *Ageing Research Reviews*, *93*, 102135. Advance online publication. DOI: 10.1016/j.arr.2023.102135 PMID: 37995900

# Chapter 5
# Leadership Strategies for Change and Innovation

**Godwin Mulavarickal**
https://orcid.org/0009-0005-8481-4646
*Christ University, India*

**Shiv Kumar Singh Pundhir**
https://orcid.org/0000-0001-6249-6943
*Christ University, India*

## ABSTRACT

*Organizational innovation and change development depends heavily on leadership activities. This chapter investigates how leaders should integrate charismatic and authentic methods with transformational concepts to create the best possible leadership practice for long-term organizational success and innovation promotion.The chapter also demonstrates that leadership success will emerge from blending different leadership styles since any one approach alone is inadequate for solving current organizational challenges. Strong leaders who learn to unite multiple leadership approaches gain enhanced abilities to encourage their personnel while promoting innovative initiatives.*

DOI: 10.4018/979-8-3373-1205-7.ch005

## INTRODUCTION

As we all know that we are currently living in a world which is powered by rapid technological advances, economic shifts and evolving societal expectations and shifting consumer preferences, due to which the current business firms are challenged to adapt effective and efficient leadership strategies and methods. The business environment has become very competitive, and organizations are facing a lot of pressure to innovate not only products and services but also work and manage their workplace. Organizations who are not able to evolve in these changing market conditions and constantly develop their products and services accordingly, won't be able to survive long in the market .

Innovation has now become a necessity and currently plays a very crucial role in the success of the organization. Even though all of the organizations are prioritizing and emphasizing the need for innovation, most of them are struggling to create an environment where creativity and innovation can be developed.

This can also be due to lack of understanding the opportunities and the challenges in the business environment as well as the need for specific leadership skills. And due to these reasons the organizations can miss out many opportunities for their growth in the business environment.

And this is where the Leaders come into play, who have the power and the potential to foster a culture of innovation and drive the organization performance .

Therefore, this chapter will be focusing on understanding the relationship between leadership styles and strategies, and organizational innovation.

Charismatic Leadership Theory, Transformational Leadership Theory and Authentic Leadership Theory will be the main theories which will be discussed.

- What is Innovation ?
- Who is a Leader ?
- How does Leadership impact innovation ?
- Which Leadership style best promotes innovation ?
- What is the impact of leadership style on the team ?

- Why is Charismatic, Authentic and transformational leadership style better than the other leadership strategies in promoting innovation ?
- How can anyone become a Charismatic, Authentic and a Transformational leader ?
- Do these leadership style have weaknesses? How to tackle them ?

These will be some of the questions which will focused upon.

## What is Innovation ?

Innovation is the process of bringing new ideas, solutions, methods, products and services which have a significant positive impact and value. It majorly involves transforming creative concepts into tangible outcomes thereby improving efficiency and effectiveness.

It is not just limited to inventions or technological advancements but also includes problem solving, processes, organizational practices and business models.

Innovation is driven by a few important components which make it possible in and organization.

The key important components are –

- Creativity – New and original ideas
- Culture - A culture- it's attitude, beliefs and values whether they promote curiosity, creativity and risk taking.
- Resources – Both financial and non financial resources are necessary.
- Feedback – A feedback loop which allows innovation.
- Leadership - A leader who sets a vision, provides guidance and the necessary resources for promoting innovation.

The study will majorly focus on the 'Leadership' component of innovation. It is assumed that rest of the components are already present and promoted in the organization.

## Who is a Leader ?

Before starting, the major question is Who is a 'Leader' ?

Alan Keith, a British actor defined Leadership in a very profound manner. According to him "Leadership is ultimately about creating a way for people to contribute to making something extraordinary happen."

Dwight D. Eisenhower, the 34th U.S. President defined Leadership as an "Art of getting someone else to do something you want done because he wants to do it."

Leadership is more than just directing people to do the work. It involves making an environment in which creativity and joy for the work can be cultivated. In Alan Keith's definition he has emphasized on the collective and collaborative nature of leadership. This shows that true leaders don't just dictate or give orders but empowers the team to contribute towards their organization with their unique talents and perspectives.

In Dwight's definition, more emphasis is on influence and motivation, and true leaders are supposed to motivate the team to willingly participate and contribute towards the goals of the organization.

In essence, Leadership is about creating an environment where the team feels empowered and joy in what they are doing for the organization. It is about sharing the same vision and helping others to reach their full potential.

## Impact of Leadership on Innovation

It is obvious that the employees need enough resources, time, finances to achieve objectives of the organization, therefore it's one of the primary responsibilities of the management to ensure that the employees are been provided with all the resources and accordingly interact with the innovation process. The role of a leader and his/her leading style has been highlighted as one of the most important factor which has a significant influence on innovation in organizations either directly or indirectly through other variables.

There are many studies which have shown a positive relationship between transformational leadership and various innovation outcomes, including new product development and process improvements (Avolio et al 1999 study by Bruce J. Avolio, Bernard M. Bass, and Dong I).

There are some more research works which suggests that leadership behaviours which promote collaboration, knowledge sharing, and open communication are crucial for fostering innovation (Tushman & Nadler, 1986).

Leaders who promote creativity, provide resources, and celebrate successes further foster a culture of innovation which drives the organizational competitiveness in today's dynamic business environment.

## Leadership styles and Innovation

There are a lot of leadership strategies and each has a different impact on innovation. Now this section will discuss about the various other theories and their impact on innovation and creativity. According to a study done by Kesting, Ulhøi, Song, Niu (2015) – they evaluated evaluated the impact of some leadership styles on innovation –

1. Autocratic Leadership Theory – Autocratic Leadership strategy is a management style where a single leader has full control over the group or the organization. He/ she is responsible for making all the decisions and delegating responsibilities without taking input from others. It is a very useful leadership style when decisions are to be made quickly. It also allows the leader to monitor the employees and make sure that the every work is coordinated accordingly. But when it comes to innovation and creativity, this is where this leadership style fails. Gumusluoglu & Ilsev (2007) conducted a study to examine the effects of the leadership styles on organizational innovation . In this study they also found out that autocratic Leadership style had little to no contribution towards creativity and innovation. In the study the researchers found that there

was a positive relationship between transformational leadership and innovation.

2. Servant Leadership – Before Greenleaf introduced servant leadership in 1977 he based his concept on the principle that leaders focus on addressing employee needs while both enabling them to innovate and take action. Leadership approach that creates such an excellent workplace atmosphere provides employees with value making them better at solving problems and development of innovative ideas. Servant leadership helps create psychological safety according to Liden et al. (2008) which give employees a comfortable workplace.The servant leadership style develops collaborative efforts and small progress yet it might not trigger creative revolutionary transformations. The primary dedication of servant leaders to employee well-being and empowerment could lead them to skip taking disruptive high-risk decisions in industries. According to Hunter et al. (2013) servant leadership inhibits fast radical innovation due to collective decision-making that results in weak visionary leadership which hinders advancement of ambitious projects.
3. Democratic Leadership - Democratic leadership, also known as participative leadership, encourages employees to be actively involved in decision-making processes. This style is beneficial for fostering an inclusive work environment, as noted by Goleman (2000), and is particularly useful for generating diverse perspectives that can lead to creative solutions. However, democratic leadership is not the most effective approach for driving rapid, high-impact innovation. Research by Yukl (2013) shows that while participative decision-making can enhance problem-solving, it also leads to slower decision-making processes due to the need for extensive discussions and consensus-building. This can be a disadvantage in fast-moving industries where quick and bold decision-making is required for innovation. Additionally, studies by De Hoogh et al. (2015) suggest that organizations with highly democratic leaders may struggle with aligning their teams toward a single disruptive vision, as different viewpoints may dilute the focus and lead to incremental rather than transformational innovation.

4. Interactive Leadership - Interactive Leadership is a leadership style where there is more emphasis on open communication, collaboration and relationship building. The idea behind Interactive Leadership Theory is a two way process between the followers and the leader. It is an effective was to develop autonomy and creativity in a team. According to a study by Rosener(1990) singled out four core characteristics of interactive leadership which involved – encouragement for participation, widespread sharing of information and power, efforts to enhance self-worth of employees, and energizing employees for different work tasks. Researches show that interactive leadership involves some kind of guidance, how to innovate by coaching and providing the employees with sufficient support. However, many researchers have argued that Interactive Leadership style is not enough due to lack of a specific future vison.
5. Charismatic Leadership – As explained earlier that this leadership theory emphasizes on the Leader's communication skills, persuasiveness and charm to influence the followers. There have been several studies where it has been shown that charismatic leaders attract followers by promising them a future rather than creating dissatisfaction. Studies have given evidence that there has been an increase in commitment among the followers and energy generation towards new objectives and values. Studies have also found that Charismatic leaders create admiration, respect, loyalty, and a collective sense of mission. In accordance with that, other studies have established a positive link between charismatic leadership and perceived team innovativeness.
6. Transformational Leadership – The transformational leadership also happens to be the most actively researched leadership style with regard to innovations and change. This leadership style is also been understood as a further development of Charismatic Leadership. There are many insights about the effects of transformational leadership on followers in an innovation context. They also happen to be very similar to insights into charismatic leadership since transformational leadership also increases self-efficacy, raises motivation and contributes to the employees' psychological empowerment

As it can be seen that through many studies and researchers, Charismatic, Authentic and Transformational Leadership have an edge in innovation when comparing them with the other leadership styles.

The next section will be focusing on why these 3 Leadership styles perform better in developing a creative and innovative culture.

## WHAT IS CHARISMATIC, AUTHENTIC AND TRANSFORMATIONAL LEADERSHIP AND WHY DOES THESE 3 LEADERSHIP STYLES BEST PROMOTE INNOVATION ?

### Who is a Charismatic Leader ?

Based on the term itself, 'Charisma' means a compelling attractiveness or charm that can inspire devotion in others.

In this leadership style the leader uses his/her communication skills, persuasiveness and some amount of charm to influence others. A charismatic leader has the ability to connect with people on a more deeper level and are especially valuable for an organization who are facing difficulties in growing in the industry.

There are many characteristics which charismatic leaders share like –

- Good communicators – Charismatic leaders have the ability to communicate clearly and effectively.
- Empathetic – They are very sensitive towards others and make changes in ways which can benefit them
- Charming – They usually hold a charm and have a compelling attractiveness.
- Persuasive – They use their charm and persuasiveness to motivate people to give their best in whatever work they do.

## How does Charismatic Leadership style promote innovation ?

A charismatic leadership style motivates employees to accept risks and generate original ideas, one of the best example being Steve Jobs. The leaders establish such a bond with their followers which further enables the followers to perform risky ventures and develop innovative solutions that disrupt the current status quo. According to Howell and Shamir (2005) charismatic leadership drives employee intrinsic motivation thus enhancing creative accomplishments.

There exists a character quality in a charismatic leader which generates resilient and confident workplace cultures because leaders display bold confidence. The findings of Sosik et al. (1998) demonstrate that workers who work for charismatic leaders tend to maintain innovative behaviour despite encountering challenges throughout their work.

Leadership based on charisma proves most effective during times of industrial evolution. Through his innovative vision of sustainable technology Elon Musk at Tesla showcases this leadership model by leading innovation in electric vehicles and space exploration as described by Kissick (2020).

## Who is an Authentic Leader ?

Authentic leadership has its roots in ancient Greek philosophy, which examined the development of virtues such as prudence, temperance, justice and fortitude in a leader. Authentic leaders are those leaders who have strong values and high standards of integrity. He/she acts in ways which reflect their values and beliefs. All their decisions are based on principals rather than short time success. This enables them to earn the trust of their followers in turn create approachable work environments and boost team performance. Authentic leaders are self-aware and know their strengths and weaknesses.

Some of their characteristics involve –

- Empathetic – They are very sensitive towards others and their needs

- Ethical – They make decisions based on their strong values and expect the same from their followers
- Good communicators – They are good listeners and communicate effectively with the people
- Self aware – They understand and are fully aware about their strengths and their weaknesses and act accordingly.

## How does Authentic Leadership style promote innovation ?

Workers take innovative risks because their leader demonstrates psychological safety through their commitment to support new endeavors. Research conducted by Walumbwa et al. (2008) demonstrates that psychological safety promotes areas conducive to innovation.

The leadership style of authenticity drives both ground-breaking innovation and responsible sustainable innovation because it promotes ethical business practices. The sustainable fashion innovations of Patagonia come from Authentic leadership demonstrated by CEO Yvon Chouinard according to George (2015).

Authentic leadership creates long-lasting change commitments among workers due to employee feeling connected to organizational missions through authentic care (Gardner et al., 2011).

## **Who is a Transformational Leader ?**

The term "transformational leadership" was introduced in 1978 by James MacGregor Burns. A Transformational Leader is someone who has the ability to empower their team to perform better. They are focused on the organization's mission and help employees succeed. Transformational leaders work with teams or followers beyond their immediate self-interests. This elevates the ideals and the concern for achievement among the followers. A Transformational Leader is almost similar as a Charismatic Leader. All Transformational Leaders are Charismatic Leaders. Both serve as role models by inspiring their followers and raising their interest in their projects.

Some of the characteristics of a Transformational Leader includes –

- Inspirational – They inspire and motivate their team and help them find their purpose.
- Empathetic – They are also very sensitive to others and their needs
- Proactive – They are well planned and identity issues before hand, which helps them to mitigate risks and avoid further complications
- Innovative – They are very innovative and cultivate a culture of creativity and innovation.

## How does transformational leadership style promote innovation ?

Transformational leaders foster intellectual and creative thinking among the followers by encouraging their team members to challenge traditional methods. According to Bass and Riggio (2006) transformational leadership produces high-levels of creative problem-solving among employees.

Transformational leaders provide innovative direction which they deploy to unite organizational teams for successful innovation endeavours (Tushman & O'Reilly, 1996).

Employees who work with transformational leaders demonstrate stronger commitment to the company's achievement because such leaders help their staff take personal ownership of organizational success. Under Sundar Pichai's leadership at Google the company empowers its employees to innovate while he provides strategic direction that drives the organization forward (Doz & Kosonen, 2010).

- Even though Charismatic, Authentic and Transformational Leadership can be seen as better promoters of innovation, it is also important to know that these styles have their own limitations. The identification of these leadership weaknesses enables better development of methods which maximize their advantages while minimizing their downfalls.

## Weaknesses of Charismatic Leadership

- Over-Reliance on the Leader's Persona

The fundamental element in charismatic leadership includes focusing on a leader's individual traits rather than using structured methods to create innovation. The departure of leadership creates an immediate hurdle for innovation projects to continue. Organizations with significant dependence on charismatic leadership face major problems in finding suitable replacements and maintaining stability according to Yukl (2013).

- Risk of Blind Followership and Groupthink

Charismatically led employees tend to adopt the leader's vision persuasively that it stops them from expressing dissenting viewpoints. Organizations face reduced innovative solutions and diminished problem-solving diversity because members suppress alternative thoughts during groupthink (Conger 1990).

- High Emotional Dependence and Burnout

When charismatic leaders require high-level commitment from their employees it results in employee burnout. Howell & Avolio (1992) discovered that short-term leadership charisma produces increased workforce morale yet persistent leadership presence triggers employee fatiguation and dissatisfaction.

## Weaknesses of Authentic Leadership

Slow Decision-Making and Resistance to Radical Change. Utilizing ethical decision-making alongside long-term trust principles often causes leaders to make decisions that influence innovation speed negatively. The preservation of stability becomes a primary concern for authentic leaders since they refrain from implementing high-risk innovative approaches (Gardner et al., 2011).

They experience challenges when operating in quick-paced competitive circumstances .The industrial speed of decision-making determines whether authenticity leads to trust since technology start-ups normally require instant choices. According to Walumbwa et al. (2008) authentic leadership works best within organizations prioritizing extended innovation periods instead of fast market interruptions.

People could consider authentic leaders to be passive in their approach

Authentic leaders face challenges when trying to assert their authority during high-stress scenarios because their focus always remains on collaboration and ethical considerations. Workers tend to perceive authentic leaders as unassertive especially in aggressive financial tech industries according to George (2015).

## Weaknesses of Transformational Leadership

Overemphasis on Vision Can Lead to Practical Execution Challenges

The strategic focus of transformational leadership often results in poor attention toward actual execution steps. The staff faces issues transforming strategic vision into implementable operations thus causing operational implementation delays (Tushman & O'Reilly, 1996).

Staff members likely experience exhaustion from both emotional and mental perspectives while working.

Transformational leadership requires unending innovation alongside continuous adaptation combined with high performance standards which personally deplete staff members. The research conducted by Bass & Riggio (2006) demonstrates that teams operated by transformational leaders exhibit increased stress because their members constantly face requirements to transform.

Risk of Unrealistic Expectations also leads to major complications.

Transformational leaders need to pair their visionary targets with achievable goals or else their employees will feel disillusioned when they cannot meet these ambitious objectives (Avolio & Bass, 2004). Unrealistic expectations within this context cause employees to lose motivation while driving them toward job resignation.

## A HYBRID LEADERSHIP APPROACH FOR MAXIMIZING INNOVATION

All leadership styles possess valuable strengths yet their weaknesses support the conclusion that one style fails to offer optimal performance. A combined implementation of essential characteristics among these three leadership styles i.e. Charismatic, Authentic and Transformational Leadership Styles can result in a balanced approach that generates enduring innovative results at scale.

- Through charismatic leadership, the teams gains energy to tackle challenges while being motivated to advance organizational limits.
- Through authentic leadership, organizations develop trustworthy environments and safe psychological conditions along with responsible ethical conduct that sustains innovation-related progress.
- The desired objectives of organizations match continuous improvement through transformational leadership which enables effective innovation implementation.

## HOW A HYBRID LEADERSHIP APPROACH WILL WORK

1. Charismatic Leadership for Vision and Inspiration

Such leadership builds visionary innovation through motivational powers that drive individuals to accept revolutionary concepts. The urgency they create together with excitement enables teams to move past normal boundaries.

Under this leadership style innovation turns into an integral part of organizational culture when employees emotionally embrace the shared mission.

The capability to energize people along with transformational change acceptance stands as an essential power which enables executives to launch disruptive business models (Effectory, 2023).

Studies demonstrate how charismatic leadership sustains team motivation as well as collaborative work activities in hybrid work settings (Center for Creative Leadership, 2023).

2. Authentic Leadership for Trust and Ethical Innovation

Authentic leadership maintains an ethical base which controls the energetic force of charismatic leadership.

Innovation needs employees to feel protected so they can conduct experiments while failing and acquiring knowledge. Openness together with transparency and constructive feedback are the methods authentic leaders use to build such an environment (ResearchGate, 2023).

Sustainable innovation is one of the many hallmarks of authentic leadership because these leaders focus on producing enduring advancements rather than temporary yet short-lived breakthroughs.

According to the Center for Creative Leadership (2022) authentic leadership improves employee engagement alongside increased workplace collaboration.

3. Transformational Leadership for Execution and Growth

Leaders who focus on transformation implement visionary concepts so they result in practical operational success.

The systematic approach of transformational leadership sets it apart from change through charismatic leadership and stabilizing it with authentic leadership.

Transformational leaders create a permanent learning environment which results in continuous reinvention processes (MIT Sloan Management Review, 2022).

Transforming organizations successfully depends on transformational leadership because leaders who can unite teams and resources with processes toward innovation goals will secure enduring competitive advantage.

Hybrid leadership combines unique leadership traits into a single system which effectively blends their beneficial aspects together.

- Through charismatic leadership organizations receive the visionary outlook that enables original inspirational concepts.
- Through authentic leadership organizations develop trust while and become sustainable which further ensures inclusive and ethical innovation.
- The implementation of transformational leadership makes sure that innovative ideas evolve into formalized procedures which yield lasting organizational effects.

This type of hybrid leadership style has been very useful and worked out greatly for many well known companies as well

Some Real life examples of this type of hybrid leadership involve –

1. <u>Elon Musk at Tesla</u>

Elon Musk demonstrates charismatic leadership because he shows vision to create an electric-car-driven sustainable world for the future.

His transformational leadership approach has pushed Tesla to develop improvements in self-driving technology and battery capabilities alongside AI and automation systems.

The occasional criticism of Musk's aggressive conduct at Tesla does not diminish his authentic leadership because he uses Tesla's mission to advocate for his personal goal of sustainability and climate protection solutions.

2. Jeff Bezos at Amazon

Jeff Bezos implemented transformational leadership to transform Amazon into a centre of innovation that advances continuously through e-commerce developments and AI and logistics development.

Through his charisma Bezos motivated both employees and investors to follow his strategic direction despite financial setbacks during the short-term period.

The authentic leadership behaviour of Bezos demonstrated through the customer-centric Amazon culture, positioned every innovation toward better customer satisfaction.

3. Indra Nooyi at PepsiCo

As CEO of PepsiCo Indra Nooyi led through authentic leadership principles by placing importance on corporate responsibility alongside products which promote health.

Her transformational leadership activities led PepsiCo to shift its business focus from exclusively sweet beverages toward more nutritious product categories. Through authentic leadership she drove employees toward a meaningful purpose which established PepsiCo as a top organization in sustainable business development.

It can be seen through these real life examples that even the top leaders are actually implementing hybrid leadership styles as an operational methodology to achieve sustainable, disruptive and high-impact innovation .

## How can one become a charismatic, authentic and transformational leader ?

As it's discussed how a combination of Charismatic, Authentic and Transformational Leadership style can cultivate motivate, therefore in this section the primarily focus will be on how one can become a Charismatic, Authentic and a Transformational Leader.

## How to become a Charismatic Leader ?

Numerous research findings demonstrate that charismatic abilities emerge through purposeful practice while some people perceive these abilities as natural traits. People become energized and influenced while embracing change through charismatic leadership because charismatic leaders use their communication skills and strong confidence along with emotional intelligence and vision. The following summary includes research-based approaches that assist people in developing charismatic qualities.

1. Mastering the ability to use metaphors together with storytelling

People follow charismatic leaders mainly because they excel at delivering narratives and metaphors successfully to their audiences. Studies show that stories awake emotional reactions to make information more concrete and memorable (Conger & Kanungo, 1998).

Martin Luther King Jr. and Steve Jobs are some of the best examples of great storytelling and who have made their messages compelling.

The evaluation of political speeches demonstrated that emotional appeals and metaphors increase charisma of a leader according to Antonakis, Fenley, and Liechti (2011).

To implement:

- Complex concepts need familiarization through easily understandable analogies.
- To engage others leader should communicate personal experiences which help develop connections with the audience.
- Leaders should develop a vision which makes people feel strong emotions.

2. Develop Emotional Intelligence (EQ)

A charismatic leader possesses the ability to monitor and shape their emotional state together with those around them. The basic component of charisma consists in Emotional Intelligence (EQ) according to Goleman (1998).

The research by Harms et al. (2010) through meta-analysis revealed that EQ produces effective results for charismatic leadership.

Oprah Winfrey's effective emotional bond with her audience demonstrates the power of high emotional intelligence when used for influencing others.

To develop EQ:

- Practice self-awareness and self-regulation.
- Develop empathy—listening to people's emotions.
- Master social awareness—read body language and tone.

3. Project Confidence and Conviction

Leadership charisma fundamentally depends on the qualities shown through confidence. Leadership followership happens naturally when individuals display certainty along with conviction.

The Journal of Business and Psychology published research which demonstrated that confident body postures make people perceive a higher level of charisma (Cuddy, Wilmuth, & Carney, 2012).

Elon Musk keeps demonstrating robust boldness about his mission even when critics attack him to draw committed followers.

To appear more confident:

- Keep strong eye contact when delivering statements.
- Using an open and assertive body language.
- Speaking clearly and passionately about the ideas.

4. Active Listening and Genuine Engagement

A charismatic leader holds back from talking continuously, but practices active listening with those they lead. The act of engaging in profound meaningful discussions allows people to feel important within their interaction.

According to Van Knippenberg & Sitkin (2013) leadership teams recognized superior listening skills as a key element which strengthened charismatic relationships between leaders and their teams.

During public appearances Barack Obama employed deep listening practices through which he repeated essential statements to demonstrate his understanding.

To practice:

- Asking open-ended questions.

- Maintaining strong eye contact and use of certain gestures to demonstrate active listening.

5. Non-Verbal Communication and Presence

According to Mehrabian (1972) non-verbal communication constitutes more than 55% of total communication. Leaders with charisma, control their body signals to project both warmth and powerful presence as well as confident feelings to others.

Research from Princeton University demonstrated that leaders using open expansive body positions are seen as charismatic leaders who demonstrate competency (Rule & Ambady, 2008).

To apply:

- Using a strong and upright posture.
- Keeping the hand gestures calm but still expressive.

6. Speaking with Passion and Energy

People following charismatic leaders observe energetic communications with diverse speech tones to maintain their attention.

Leaders who demonstrate vocal diversity and dynamic speech patterns receive higher ratings on charismatic leadership according to a Leadership Quarterly study (Towler 2003).

To improve:

- Avoid monotone speech—vary tone and speed.
- Speaking with conviction—own the words of oneself.
- Use of Pause for effect— use of silence .

## DEVELOPING CHARISMA IS A SKILL

Practice enables anyone to develop charisma because it represents a learnable skill. Developing a powerful charismatic personality requires one to enhance his/her own communication along with emotional intelligence and body language and vision.

### How to become an Authentic Leader ?

Being an authentic leader means that a leader needs integrity together with transparency while following a clear purpose. Authentic leaders create enduring relationships by being honest to their principles while establishing genuine connections which builds confidence and sustain influence over time. Retrospective research indicates authentic leadership strengthen employee commitment to their work as well as satisfaction levels and job engagement among staff (Walumbwa et al., 2008).

Given below are essential methods for leaders who want to establish authentic leadership.

1. <u>Developing Self-Awareness</u>

Leaders with authenticity understand their personal strengths together with their weaknesses and fundamental values. Their ability to understand themselves grants them the capability to lead with strong confidence along with consistent behaviour.

According to Gardner et al. (2005) authentic leadership emerges when leaders perform consistent value-based self-reflection and this behaviour generates trustworthiness and authenticity in the eyes of others.

Despite facing financial pressure Howard Schultz maintained his commitment to ethical company practices as the Starbucks CEO.

To develop self-awareness:

- Practicing self-reflection exercises through journal writing.
- Seek honest feedback from peers and mentors.
- Becoming aware of one's own values create choices in life.

2. Practicing Transparent Communication

Humility through authentic leadership means discussing every aspect of work including successes alongside failures which creates both trust and credibility among team members.

The study conducted by Ilies Morgeson & Nahrgang (2005) found that transparent communication between leaders and employees leads to stronger relationships.

Satya Nadella at Microsoft implements open dialogue alongside mistake admission which has fostered stronger company culture.

To implement:

- Share decision-making process openly.
- Avoid concealing difficulties by making honest disclosures about the employees.
- Encouraging a culture of openness in the team.

3. Leading with ethics and moral integrity

Organizational authenticity develops from systemically established ethics and morality. Leaders must choose ethical behaviour and fairness above all else including personal advantages and organizational benefits.

Workers demonstrate higher organizational commitment when authentic ethical leaders guide their organization according to Walumbwa et al. (2008).

Through her empathetic leadership style and honest conduct, Jacinda Ardern received broad trust from national supporters when she served as Prime Minister of New Zealand.

To apply:

- Leaders should base their choices on guiding principles as an alternative to making them for personal convenience.
- Maintain steadfastness in all ethical decision-making scenarios.
- Foster an ethical workplace culture.

4. Build Strong, Genuine Relationships

Leaders who practice authenticity create personal bonds which allow people to approach them and feel likable.

According to Avolio & Gardner (2005) authentic leaders create deep trust-based staff relationships.

Through her authentic emotional bonds with people, Oprah Winfrey constructed a successful brand.

To strengthen relationships:

- An authentic leader demonstrates honest concern about other people's welfare.
- Being approachable and empathetic.
- Refrain from judging others emotions while actively validating their emotional experiences.

5. Staying resilient and true to the values

Crisis situations prove how genuine a leader truly is. Authentic leaders maintain their core values in every situation while exhibiting a resilient attitude.

George (2003) emphasized that authentic leaders embrace resilience and grow by facing challenges head on rather than compromising their values.

During his years of imprisonment Nelson Mandela maintained a continuous commitment to achieving reconciliation through his whole life.

To build resilience:

- Being open to failure as it at serves as a window to acquire new knowledge.
- Staying true to one's principles even under pressure.
- The process of cultivating mental toughness requires practice of both mindfulness and self-discipline.

## Authenticity as a Leadership Strength

A leader's authenticity stands independent of flawless conduct because it depends only on maintaining honesty together with responsible choices. The practice of self-awareness combined with transparent communication along with values-based consistency leads to long-term trustworthiness and the inspiration of others, and therefore creating a trusting, creative and innovative culture in the organization.

## How to Become a Transformational Leader ?

The transformational leadership style helps leaders direct people toward their maximum abilities through inspiration and motivation and supports fresh concepts and beneficial evolution. A transformational leader motivates people beyond structural maintenance towards creative thinking along with visionary planning for the future. Evidence suggests transformational leadership produces major positive outcomes within employee performance alongside job satisfaction along with organizational achievement (Bass & Riggio, 2006). Building this style of leadership can only be accomplished by harmonizing vision with emotional intelligence and strategic influence capabilities.

Some ways to become a Transformational Leader includes

1. <u>Cultivating strong vision and purpose</u>

Transformative leadership basically requires leaders who generate and distribute passionate visions which stimulate group motivation. When teams receive a meaningful vision it helps them coordinate their efforts through genuine commitment.

Bass (1985) in his research identified visionary leadership as a transformative leadership aspect which shows that purposeful leadership communications generate better employee involvement.

The visionary approach of Elon Musk has driven Tesla and SpaceX employees toward boundary-pushing innovation because of his goals to provide sustainable energy solutions and explore space.

To develop this trait:

- A long-term vision must be defined when it matches organizational core values.
- Communicate the vision with passion and clarity.
- Align team goals with a greater purpose beyond financial success.

2. Encouraging Creativity and Innovation

A transformational leader develops people to approach problems uniquely and accept calculated risks. Leadership through transformation enables both creative processes and encourages taking risks, since failures function as learning channels inside such spaces.

According to Jung, Chow, & Wu (2003) researchers discovered that the positive relationship between transformational leadership and organizational innovation emerges from its ability to establish creative problem-solving through an open-minded culture.

Jeff Bezos' developed "Day 1 Thinking" in Amazon as a cultural practice that maintained innovation above all else.

To foster innovation:

- Encourage open discussions and diverse ideas.
- Employees must receive freedom to carry out experimental practices.
- The organization should identify and provide appreciation to employees who generate creative ideas.

3. Building Strong Relationships and Emotional Intelligence

Leaders who want to transform their teams should create deep relationships with team members through clear displays of empathy trust together with emotional intelligence skills. Stronger team bonds together with increased employee morale result from such measures.

Goleman (1998) demonstrated emotional intelligence with its self-awareness and empathy elements determines how effective transformational leadership operates.

Through his leadership Satya Nadella brought changes to Microsoft's corporate culture by making emotional intelligence together with mind-set growth the focal points of organizational development.

To strengthen emotional intelligence and build strong relationships:

- To comprehend team issues one must develop active hearing abilities.
- Foster a culture of trust and psychological safety.
- The leader needs to modify their leadership approach according to personal requirements.

4. **Leading through example and setting high standards**

A transformational leader demonstrates employees the character traits they want to see emerge in their organization. Through their present actions these leaders create an example which motivates their teams to work toward excellence.

According to Bass & Avolio (1994) transformational leadership includes being a role model and maintaining ethical and performance excellence as fundamental characteristics of this type of leadership.

Indra Nooyi produced exemplary leadership through her continuous ethical standards maintenance and her commitment to sustainability during her time as PepsiCo CEO.

To implement this:

- Demonstrate integrity and accountability in decision-making.
- High performance targets need support with adequate provisions from leaders.
- Be a role model for resilience and perseverance.

5. **Empowering and Developing Others**

Under transformational leadership a leader assigns mentorship duties which help team members mature into future leaders.

The research by Avolio & Bass (2002) demonstrated that leadership models based on transformation demonstrate positive results through concentrated attention to employee development and leadership capability building.

During his leadership at Virgin Richard Branson developed an organizational model based on employees self-fulfilment and career progression.

To empower others:

- Provide coaching and mentorship opportunities.
- Encourage continuous learning and skill-building.
- Delegate tasks to staff members as this practice boosts their confidence and promotes better ownership.

## THE IMPACT OF TRANSFORMATIONAL LEADERSHIP

Transformational leadership demands immediate dedication to ongoing development with productive change and sustained improvement in the growth of staff members. Strong organizational success along with future inspirations emerge through leaders who build vision strength and creative spaces together with relationship networks and exemplary behaviour.

### How to develop a Hybrid Leadership Style by integrating Charismatic, Authentic, and Transformational Leadership styles ?

The integration of charismatic and authentic and transformational leadership approaches produces an optimal leadership method that achieves strong results throughout the organization. The integration means leaders gain abilities to inspire trust and drive sustainable success by motivating innovation. The process of developing balanced leadership capabilities involves the following approach.

1. Balancing Charismatic Influence with Authenticity

The charisma gathered by leaders to motivate people requires authentic behaviour if they want to build enduring trust throughout their organization.

- Develop Presence Without Manipulation

Personal connections should replace showy actions when one wants to interact meaningfully with others.

The research shows charm abilities on their own can create excessive dependency on personal authority which undermines team member involvement (Conger & Kanungo, 1998).

- Stay True to Core Values

Leaders need to take actions according to what they believe in while sharing information honestly.

Genuine sincerity defeats any attempts for charisma to turn into fake showmanship or personal advancement.

2. **Driving innovation through transformational vision and authentic leadership**

Transformational leader push for innovation while the authentic leaders ensure that the innovations or change is deeply rooted with the values and the ethics.

- Encourage Innovation Without Losing Integrity

Under transformational leadership people become more willing to take risks yet they need ethical accountability for their decisions (Bass & Riggio, 2006).

All changes that stem from authentic leadership methods maintain consistency with long-term organizational beliefs instead of fleeting profitability.

The process of guiding organizational change requires support for personal growth and development from team members.

Transformational leadership provides both inspirational changes through charisma and makes changes enduringly sustainable.

3. **Using Charisma to motivate and encourage long term growth**

A leader who exhibits charming behaviour generates excitement however maintaining too heavy dependence on personal magnetism results in organizational dependency on that individual leader. The sustainability of motivation exists through transformational leadership's approach to empowering others while sharing vision.

- Being Inspirational but avoid a Hero Mentality

Leaders who want to engage people through their charisma should also develop approaches to enable others for leadership roles.

According to Shamir, House, and Arthur (1993), groups achieve superior outcomes through a feeling that their vision belongs to them instead of simply responding to individual authority.

- Using Storytelling and Vision to Inspire Action

Leaders who transform their organizations prefer extended views that motivate their teams whereas charismatic leaders stir excitement through narrations backed by personal ties.

4. Combining Transparency with Bold Decision-Making

An authentic leadership model showcases both open communication along with responsible choice-making yet charismatic leaders and those who follow the transformational path focus on making remarkable decisive moves.

- Leaders should take bold risks without losing trust

Leaders must use risk-taking behavior alongside continuous communication and an active relation with their peers.

Research shows employees receive transformational change initiatives better when they comprehend what drives its implementation (Avolio & Gardner, 2005).

- Admit Mistakes and Adjust Course When Necessary

By admitting their mistakes authentic leaders develop credibility because they refuse to present themselves as flawless.

The combination of charismatic leadership produces cult of personality but transformational leadership places emphasis on progress instead of individual leaders.

5. Cultivate Emotional Intelligence and adaptable leadership

Effective hybrid leaders must possess strong emotional intelligence because it helps them merge their leadership methods.

- Adapt Leadership Style Based on Context

Different situations require either having charisma in critical moments or building authenticity to unite teams as well as a transformative vision for long-term organizational planning.

Leaders who possess strong emotional intelligence according to Goleman (1998) show better results when adapting to different organizational challenges.

- Develop Self-Awareness and Empathy

Self-awareness about leadership strengths and weaknesses enables leaders to keep their operations balanced.

## THE HYBRID LEADERSHIP ADVANTAGE

Leaders who integrate charisma with authentic integrity and transformational vision, develop an active style of leadership that remains enduring and produces strong results. Leaders who balance these elements gain both employee involvement and constructive change together with enduring trust.

## CONCLUSION

### The Power of Hybrid Leadership

Present-day leadership needs more than one specific method to function effectively in the modern fast-moving environment. Leadership excellence lies in the ability of successful individuals to harmonize different leadership methods while staying committed to their core mission. Leaders who integrate charismatic motivation with authentic relationships and visionary transformation, successfully establish innovative and people-empowered workplaces which drive lasting achievements in their teams and organizations.

The various leadership approaches demonstrate strong advantages yet these get restricted through solitary utilization. The motivational strength of charismatic leadership remains effective yet it lacks credibility which makes it appear lifeless without authentic basis. Trusted authentic leaders develop remarkable credibility but they must establish transformational goals to push meaningful change through their actions. Energetic organizations driven by transformational leadership creates innovative corporate culture, although this type of leadership can occasionally appear removed from reality when the leader fails to establish personal relationships with others.

Through combination of these methods, leaders develop a harmonious system that enables them to lead effectively and establish enduring trust alongside encouraging innovation. Hybrid leaders redirect their approach from confined leadership strategies because they can determine which aspects of charisma, authenticity and transformation best suit their current situation.

Producing hybrid leadership competencies is not an over night process, and takes time to adapt. Self-awareness combined with ongoing learning and regular practice form the basis of developing this leadership approach. Leaders need to improve their communication abilities while enhancing emotional abilities in order to establish a personal vision which links to both their staff members and organizational objectives. They need to welcome constructive feedback while actively pursuing personal growth and maintain proper control between sureness and meekness.

Current organizational environments, with their diverse workforce alongside interdependence and constant need for innovation demand that leaders adopt hybrid leadership as their mandatory approach. Leaders who master flexible leadership styles will take charge of future organizations by understanding their team members and business environmental needs.

Within organizations leaders based on adaptability, honesty, advancement and motivation demonstrate the most valuable leadership qualities. Organizations with leaders who embody charismatic influence, authentic trust and transformational vision come out as innovative and resilient organizations that maintain deep organizational connections to both people and core values. Such leadership follows the hybrid leadership approach which creates adaptable yet foresighted systems that produce sustainable influence.

## REFERENCES


Avolio, B. J., & Gardner, W. L. (2005). Authentic leadership development: Getting to the root of positive forms of leadership. *The Leadership Quarterly*, *16*(3), 315–338. DOI: 10.1016/j.leaqua.2005.03.001

Bass, B. M. (1990). From transactional to transformational leadership: Learning to share the vision. *Organizational Dynamics*, *18*(3), 19–31. DOI: 10.1016/0090-2616(90)90061-S

House, R. J. (1977). A 1976 theory of charismatic leadership. In Hunt, J. G., & Larson, L. L. (Eds.), *Leadership: The cutting edge* (pp. 189–207). Southern Illinois University Press.

Kotter, J. P. (1996). *Leading change*. Harvard Business School Press.

Conger, J. A., & Kanungo, R. N. (1998). *Charismatic leadership in organizations*. Sage.

Goleman, D. (1998). What makes a leader? *Harvard Business Review*, *76*(6), 93–102. PMID: 10187249

Northouse, P. G. (2018). *Leadership: Theory and practice* (8th ed.). Sage.

Goleman, D. (2000). *Leadership that gets results*. Harvard Business Review Press.

Kouzes, J. M., & Posner, B. Z. (2017). *The Leadership Challenge: How to Make Extraordinary Things Happen in Organizations* (6th ed.). Wiley.

Maxwell, J. C. (2007). *The 21 Irrefutable Laws of Leadership: Follow Them and People Will Follow You*. HarperCollins.

Muhlfeit, J., & Costi, M. (2015). *The Positive Leader: How Energy and Happiness Fuel Top-Performing Teams*. Pearson.

Shamir, B., House, R. J., & Arthur, M. B. (1993). The motivational effects of charismatic leadership: A self-concept based theory. *Organization Science*, *4*(4), 577–594. DOI: 10.1287/orsc.4.4.577

Walumbwa, F. O., Avolio, B. J., Gardner, W. L., Wernsing, T. S., & Peterson, S. J. (2008). Authentic leadership: Development and validation of a theory-based measure. *Journal of Management*, *34*(1), 89–126. DOI: 10.1177/0149206307308913

# Chapter 6
# Privacy-Preserving AI for Medical Applications:
## A Scalable and Secure Approach

**Usharani Bhimavarapu**
https://orcid.org/0000-0002-0246-1420

*Department of Computer Science and Engineering, Koneru Lakshmaiah Education Foundation, India*

## ABSTRACT

*The sudden infusion of artificial intelligence (AI) into the medical sector requires strong frameworks that address regulatory requirements, ethical issues, privacy issues, and concerns related to interoperability. The current research conceptualizes a dynamic system of AI governance that changes dynamically along with advancements in AI, avoiding the constraints of fixed models of governance. In contrast to conventional methods, the model incorporates adaptive compliance processes, explainable AI models, and user-managed data-sharing systems to enable transparency and trustworthiness. It also uses federated learning methods to enable secure and scalable AI adoption in healthcare and avoid data heterogeneity challenges. The model includes enhanced privacy protection with less homomorphic encryption and optimally utilized blockchain, reducing*

DOI: 10.4018/979-8-3373-1205-7.ch006

*computation overhead and allowing practical application.*

## INTRODUCTION

MedTech has transformed the healthcare sector by incorporating digital technologies for diagnostics, treatment, and patient monitoring. With the growing use of electronic health records (EHRs), wearables, and artificial intelligence (AI)-driven diagnostics, vast amounts of sensitive patient data are created every day. Clever handling of data guarantees that such data is stored, accessed, and processed securely without loss of integrity. However, ineffective management of data can contribute to breaches, loss of patient trust, and fines. Data collection, storage, and data transfer need to become efficient in MedTech businesses with the formation of strong data governance processes. Regulation of laws relating to patient confidentiality, i.e., HIPAA and GDPR, needs to be followed diligently. Encryption, access controls, and anonymization strategies also have to be used for security tightening in organizations. Ethical concerns must take precedence in data usage to avoid misuse or bias. Data processing transparency must be maintained to generate trust among healthcare providers and patients.

MedTech necessitates compliance with data privacy since health information is sensitive by its nature. Medical records harbor personally identifiable information (PII) that, once revealed, may result in identity theft or insurance fraud. Global regulatory institutions have established tough data protection statutes to mitigate such exposures. The U.S., for instance,. Health Insurance Portability and Accountability Act (HIPAA) requires patient data to be protected by administrative, physical, and technical controls in healthcare organizations. The General Data Protection Regulation of Europe provides greater control of the individuals over their data and enforces transparency and accountability of data processing. Violation of such regulations can result in huge penalties and destroy the image of MedTech firms. Healthcare professionals need to incorporate privacy by design into their systems, with data protection built into every step. Firms need to perform regular audits and risk assessments to determine areas of weakness. Training employees in data privacy best practices will help avoid human error. By prioritizing compliance, MedTech companies can build patient trust and prevent legal repercussions.

MedTech data breaches are devastating and have implications on patients and health care organizations. Cyber attacks against clinical databases could lead to disclosure of health information, resulting in economic hardship and emotional distress to patients. Hospital and MedTech ransom attacks are on the rise, threatening core services and delaying patient treatments. Weak passwords, unencrypted storage of data, and poor handling of data through not doing regular system updates are the poor handling practices that aggravate the threat potential. To counteract the menace, healthcare organizations would have to spend on cybersecurity infrastructure. Multi-factor authentication and endpoint protection limit unauthorized access. Software updation and penetration testing identify and close security loopholes. Data loss prevention (DLP) policies prevent leakage of confidential data or its misuse. Incident response processes need to be well defined in order to respond in the event of breaches timely. With enhanced cybersecurity processes, MedTech companies can safeguard patient information from harmful attacks.

Interoperability is necessary for MedTech to enable efficient sharing of data across health systems but raises privacy issues. Various hospitals, clinics, and wearable technologies produce varying kinds of data, making integration seamless for improved patient care. Insecure data exchange, however, can result in unauthorized access and breaches. Interoperability using standardized protocols like the Fast Healthcare Interoperability Resources (FHIR) framework guarantees secure sharing of data. Blockchain technology provides a tamper-evident and decentralized way of keeping medical records. Smart contracts provide for automatic checks for compliance, and access to data is provided only to authorized parties. Data in transit is encrypted end-to-end so that cybercriminals cannot intercept it. Role-based access control (RBAC) provides for only authorized personnel to read or change sensitive records. Interoperability is what brings maximum efficiency but must not come at the expense of security or privacy. MedTech companies have to work together with regulatory agencies to create privacy-compliant data-sharing solutions. Secure interoperability can enhance health outcomes without violating patient confidentiality.

\\Artificial intelligence (AI) and machine learning (ML) have revolutionized MedTech by enabling predictive diagnosis and tailored treatment. But these technologies rely on enormous datasets, which raise privacy and ethical use of data issues. AI models trained with biased or unverified data can lead to false diagnoses and discrimination. Techniques of data anonymization such as differential privacy can mask patient identities while allowing AI training. Federated learning enables decentralized AI training without revealing sensitive patient information to central servers. AI-based MedTech products must be regulated by governance frameworks to prevent infringement on privacy. Patients must be informed of the use of their data in AI systems to ensure transparency and consent. Ethical uses of AI are fairness, accountability, and constant monitoring of algorithms. MedTech firms should conduct bias audits to identify and resolve inconsistencies in AI-driven healthcare decisions. Safe management of AI data is the foundation of innovation against privacy protection.

Cloud computing is now part of MedTech data storage and management. Cloud platforms provide scalability, allowing healthcare providers to store and analyze big data efficiently. Keeping medical information in the cloud, though, carries threats of unauthorized access and data sovereignty. Compliance with healthcare-specific cloud security standards, such as HITRUST and ISO 27001, is necessary in protecting patient information. Data encryption in transit and storage ensures confidentiality for sensitive data. Zero Trust Architecture (ZTA) provides greater security since user and device identities are continuously authenticated and authorized before providing access. Cloud access security brokers (CASBs) help track and enforce security policies on the cloud infrastructure. MedTech companies should select cloud service providers (CSPs) that provide compliance assistance and audit features. Periodic security audits and backups guarantee data integrity in the event of system failure. Effective cloud data management strategies allow secure and compliant digital healthcare operations.

Wearable medical devices and smartphones have increased patient participation and home monitoring in the healthcare sector. The devices harvest real-time information on heart rate, blood pressure, blood sugar levels, and activity levels. However, lack of regulation on data harvesting and sharing raises concerns about privacy. The majority of wearable health applications share user data with third-party organizations for advertisement or research reasons, in some cases without express consent. Regulatory bodies need to impose strict regulations on data collection, storage, and sharing in consumer health technology. User-centric privacy controls such as opt-in consent and selective data-sharing can enhance transparency. End-to-end encryption ensures that confidential health data is not intercepted or abused. MedTech companies need to apply privacy-preserving computation techniques, such as homomorphic encryption, to process data without compromising user privacy. Enhancing consumer education on privacy risks and safe use behaviors is also important. Effective data management in wearable health tech supports patient autonomy and trust.

Data ethics are significant in MedTech to guarantee that digital health innovation is in the interests of patients. Unethical data handling, such as the unauthorized sale of patient data, can erode public trust and violate legal frameworks. Transparency in data use policies allows patients to understand where their data is being stored, processed, and shared. Ethical norms should be implemented for AI-based clinical decisions to prevent biases that are harmful to particular populations. MedTech companies must establish ethical review boards to track data governance policies. Patients should be provided with the option of seeing, modifying, or deleting their health information according to privacy legislation. Sensitive consent mechanisms should be in place to allow patients to control data sharing. Healthcare institutions should collaborate with ethicists and policymakers to guarantee ethical handling of data. Ethical data management strengthens patient-care provider relationships. Being guided by ethics in MedTech enables long-term sustainability and trust in digital health solutions.

Healthcare professionals' training in data management and adherence to privacy is key to mitigating risks. The majority of data breaches are the result of human error, such as misconfigured security settings, weak passwords, or phishing. Regular cybersecurity training programs can help medical staff recognize and prevent threats. Role-based training will inform employees of their data handling duties based on their level of access. Phishing, social engineering, and insider threat awareness campaigns reduce the likelihood of accidental data breaches. Data breach response simulation training enhances preparedness in case of security incidents. Tightly controlled data access with the least amount of unnecessary exposure to patient information should be practiced by healthcare organizations.

Training on evolving privacy law on an ongoing basis ensures compliance with regulatory requirements by employees. Organizations need to foster a responsibility culture for data security. Properly trained employees are a significant defense against data privacy incidents.

Future MedTech data management trends will further emphasize maximizing interoperability, security, and patient ownership over individual health data. Emerging technology such as decentralized identity systems will allow patients to control their medical records securely. Anomaly detection technologies using AI will detect suspicious activity in real time, reducing the likelihood of breaches. Quantum-resistant encryption techniques will further guarantee data security against future cyber threats. Privacy-preserving technologies (PETs) like synthetic data generation will enable safe data sharing for research and innovation. Blockchain-based health data exchanges will provide transparency and security in patient record management. Regulatory frameworks will evolve to address emerging privacy issues in digital health. Patient-centric approaches, such as personal health wallets, will allow individuals to control their data access. Cross-industry collaboration will be vital in developing uniform, secure data handling procedures. An extension of data security in the MedTech sector will play a critical role in sustaining innovation while upholding patients' confidence.

Reddy et al. (2019) present a governance structure for AI in healthcare but fall short of embodying the dynamism of AI innovation and regulative developments, so their framework can become out of date with the evolving nature of the technology. Similarly, Page et al. (2021) provide a new guideline for systematic reviews in the shape of PRISMA 2020 but fail to address the subtleties of AI-based health research, wherein algorithms change frequently and might need to change methodologically as well on an ongoing basis. Morley et al. (2019) raise ethical concerns regarding AI in healthcare but discuss these largely in abstract terms without venturing into practical strategies for implementation, which makes their findings less directly applicable. Prakash et al. (2022) take into account ethical concerns of AI application but do not outline a distinct agenda for overcoming such concerns in real-world clinical settings, so their findings are more theoretical than practical.

Biller-Andorno et al. (2020) discuss AI-supported ethical decision-making in resuscitation but have no empirical basis for the proposed framework they critique, raising questions about its feasibility in practice in emergency medicine. Wang et al. (2022) compare Chinese laws on privacy in AI-driven healthcare with international schemes but fail to consider the adaptability of such legislation in different geopolitical contexts, making universal application difficult. Panagopoulos et al. (2022) refer to incentivizing the sharing of data in healthcare but don't cover patient concern regarding consent and ownership completely, which are still significant barriers to the use of data-driven AI. Khalid et al. (2023) refer to privacy-preserving AI techniques in healthcare but place significant emphasis on technical approaches without addressing user trust and transparency completely, which are necessary for patient uptake.

Zarifis et al. (2020) discuss trust and privacy concerns of AI-driven health insurance without investigating how demographic factors influence the views of users, which may lead to an incomplete conclusion. Richardson et al. (2021) examine patient worries about AI in medicine without differentiating between concerns based on misinformation and worry about real risks, which may skew their conclusion. Pereira et al. (2021) endorse biomedical data sharing to promote AI in healthcare but do not mention the legal and ethical challenges institutions face in implementing open data policies. Rahman et al. (2022) explore federated learning for smart healthcare but cover primarily technical points without reflecting on interoperability problems between different healthcare systems.

Elhoseny et al. (2021) present an AI-based framework based on IoT for maintaining privacy but fail to analyze its scalability over large-scale healthcare systems critically. Alabdulatif et al. (2022) compare AI security and blockchain security in smart healthcare but fail to analyze real-world case studies that demonstrate the performance of their framework. Ali et al. (2023) describe the use of metaverse technology in healthcare without discussing the adequate psychological effect on patients engaging with virtual medical environments. Shinde et al. (2021) discuss blockchain for securing AI applications without any mention of the high computational complexity and energy requirements of implementing blockchain in healthcare setups.

Tagde et al. (2021) explore blockchain and AI in e-health but don't have empirical data on patient outcomes, limiting the practical utility of their research. Xu et al. (2020) present federated learning for healthcare informatics but don't address data heterogeneity, which would lower the accuracy of models. Munjal and Bhatia (2022) write about homomorphic encryption in healthcare but do not discuss real-time processing capability, which is critical for clinical applications. Mosaiyebzadeh et al. (2023) survey privacy-enhancing technologies in federated learning but do not properly address regulatory compliance challenges, which are critical for AI adoption in healthcare.

Keshta (2022) raises AI-based IoT healthcare security and privacy issues without presenting concrete solutions to mitigate cyber threats. Olatunji et al. (2022) mention anonymization techniques for health data but do not examine whether these can maintain data utility for application in AI systems. Angerschmid et al. (2022) address explanation and fairness in AI decision-making but do not address the intrinsic biases that arise due to data sparsity in underrepresented patient groups. Formosa et al. (2022) contrast human and AI decision-making in medical diagnosis but do not examine how hybrid models that integrate AI and human judgment can enhance decision-making accuracy.

The proposed model resolves prior limitations through adaptive regulatory compliance structures that persist in developing over progressive AI breakthroughs, resolving static governance infrastructure problematics (Reddy et al., 2019). While other past systematic review tactics struggle to recognize AI-driven research complexity, the proposed model is made up of dynamic reviewing measures compliant with the changes in algorithmic methods (Page et al., 2021). The ethical application of AI is magnified in the form of a strict, practical format rather than remaining theoretical speculations to make it even more applicable for everyday clinical use (Morley et al., 2019). Additionally, the proposed model presents a real-world guide towards addressing ethical problems in AI-derived healthcare, bridging the difference between theoretical discourse and actual application (Prakash et al., 2022).

Through empirical validation, the proposed model ensures feasibility in high-stakes decision-making scenarios like AI-guided resuscitation, making it more usable in emergency care (Biller-Andorno et al., 2020). It also provides a global compatible regulatory framework, overcoming the disadvantage of region-based privacy legislations in AI-based care (Wang et al., 2022). The solution addresses patient consent and data ownership issues through the imposition of a transparent and user-controlled data-sharing system, overcoming barriers to AI adoption (Panagopoulos et al., 2022). Moreover, trust and openness are maintained with explainable AI models, making privacy-preserving approaches more intelligible and user-friendly to patients, in contrast to previous plans that focus on technical deployment (Khalid et al., 2023).

To foster user trust in AI-based health insurance, the proposed model includes demographic analysis, thus ensuring a more comprehensive picture of privacy concerns for different populations (Zarifis et al., 2020). Fears of misinformation are mitigated through AI-driven education interventions, which help to distinguish perceived and real risks of AI use in medicine (Richardson et al., 2021). Legal and ethical barriers to sharing biomedical data are also addressed through the incorporation of federated learning techniques into practice, which maintains privacy and enables big data-driven AI development (Pereira et al., 2021). The proposed model enhances interoperability across healthcare systems through the development of standard protocols that allow for seamless integration of federated learning-based AI methods (Rahman et al., 2022).

The proposed model overcomes scalability over extensive healthcare infrastructures in contrast to conventional IoT-based privacy-preserving AI models by optimizing computational efficiency (Elhoseny et al., 2021). It also demonstrates real-world case studies showing the effectiveness of blockchain-AI security models, surpassing the lack of empirical data in previous research (Alabdulatif et al., 2022). To avoid psychological effects of metaverse healthcare, the model incorporates human-centered design principles that weigh immersion against ethical concerns (Ali et al., 2023). Furthermore, through optimized deployment of blockchain, the model reduces excessive computation expenses and energy use, making it a more viable solution for securing AI applications within healthcare (Shinde et al., 2021).

In order to counterbalance the lack of empirical data in blockchain-AI integration for e-health, real-world patient outcome measurements have been incorporated in the proposed model to ensure its real-world applicability (Tagde et al., 2021). It facilitates federated learning in healthcare informatics through minimizing heterogeneity challenges in data by using advanced preprocessing techniques that improve model accuracy (Xu et al., 2020). The solution also facilitates real-time processing in homomorphic encryption, overcoming previous limitations that hindered its clinical use (Munjal & Bhatia, 2022). Compliance with regulatory requirements in privacy-enhancing technologies for federated learning is met by aligning the model with evolving global data protection regulations (Mosaiyebzadeh et al., 2023).

In contrast to existing AI-powered IoT models for healthcare focusing primarily on security concerns without concrete solutions, the current model integrates active threat detection capabilities, reducing vulnerability to cyber attacks (Keshta, 2022). It also enhances anonymization techniques for healthcare data by maximizing privacy preservation and data utility under high model performance for AI (Olatunji et al., 2022). The model suggested resolves fairness concerns through the application of bias-reduction strategies that improve AI decision-making in minority patient groups (Angerschmid et al., 2022). Finally, by combining human judgment with AI-based decision-making, the model integrates a hybrid diagnostic approach that increases precision, circumventing the either-or human-v-AI binary in healthcare resource allocation (Formosa et al., 2022).

## PRIVACY IN REGULATION OF SMART WEARABLE DEVICES AND THE NEED FOR IMPROVED PRIVACY ALGORITHMS

Smart wearable devices, including smartwatches, fitness trackers, and health wearables, harvest enormous amounts of sensitive information regarding users. The information varies from health information, including statistics, location tracking, and behavior patterns, which makes it a grave issue in terms of privacy. Most wearable producers sell or share user information with third-party organizations without direct permission. Regulatory authorities like the General Data Protection Regulation (GDPR) and the Health Insurance Portability and Accountability Act (HIPAA) are extremely strict about privacy measures to safeguard user data. However, the majority of wearable devices don't have secure environments, so they're prone to cyber attacks and unauthorized access. Inadequate encryption practices or inadequate data storage can cause breaches, which result in leaked sensitive health data. Furthermore, there are wearable applications with complex terms of service that prohibit users from learning how their data is collected and processed. Resolving such issues requires both regulatory enforcement and the development of privacy-friendly technology.

Several global rules help to facilitate data privacy in wearables. GDPR requires corporations to get approval first before accessing personal data and give users the right to portability of their data. HIPAA imposes severe requirements on maintaining health-related information, especially on wearables used in the medical field. CCPA gives consumers the right to control data storage and sharing. Despite these laws, enforcement is still difficult given the global reach of wearable device companies. Some manufacturers are located in countries where privacy protection is poor, leaving gaps in enforcement. Second, not all wearables manufacturers regulate their devices as medical devices, thus circumventing strict regulation. Greater monitoring of compliance and international regulatory coordination are needed to enhance data protection. World-wide uniform privacy policy would facilitate the introduction of a common reference model for security of wearables.

Current security features in smart wearables, including password and traditional encryption, are not enough to defend against emerging cyber threats. Wearables constantly emit data via Bluetooth, Wi-Fi, or cellular and therefore expose data to greater interception threats. Traditional encryption techniques may be robust but use a lot of battery life and therefore are inappropriate for low-power wearables. Additionally, anonymization solutions employed by some creators are also reverse-engineerable, revealing users' identities. There are sophisticated privacy algorithms that are capable of protecting data without compromising device performance. The algorithms should provide end-to-end encryption, anonymization, and safe data-sharing capabilities. They must protect data from unauthorized access by incorporating MFA and biometric authentication. A privacy-focused algorithm developed for wearables will provide user data protection without impacting device performance.

Privacy algorithms protect wearable devices from unauthorized access and data intrusion. Without privacy, wearables users are vulnerable to cyberattacks, identity theft, and loss of money. For instance, hackers can use wearable network vulnerabilities to monitor the location of users or alter health records. Privacy algorithms leverage sophisticated cryptographic methods, including homomorphic encryption and differential privacy, to protect data at each stage. They also promote compliance with privacy regulations by facilitating capabilities like data minimization and user-controlled sharing of data. Moreover, strong privacy protections build consumer trust, which further incentivizes more consumers to use smart wearables without worrying about data misuse. As penetration in telemedicine and remote patient monitoring through wearables increases, privacy algorithms are crucial to safeguarding sensitive medical data. Spending on advanced privacy solutions makes wearable devices secure and user-friendly.

A next-generation privacy protocol for smart wearables should possess several key attributes to address existing security vulnerabilities. End-to-end encryption protects information from harvesting to storage or transmission. Federated learning allows AI models to study user data without transmitting it to central servers, reducing vulnerability to cyber attacks. Zero-knowledge proof authentication enables users to authenticate themselves without revealing personal information. Blockchain-based access control makes it possible for authorized users and apps alone to view or modify health data. Dynamic anonymization techniques prevent unauthorized users from re-identifying anonymized data. Adaptive encryption optimizes power consumption by varying levels of security according to device use. All these capabilities combined enhance wearable security without hindering user convenience and compliance with regulations.

Artificial intelligence (AI) plays a central role in wearable technology through the analysis of health trends, the detection of anomalies, and the provision of personalized insights. AI systems, however, require extensive datasets for them to function, raising concerns around privacy and data security. Techniques like differential privacy maintain privacy when applying AI so that AI models can learn from data without revealing individual user data. Homomorphic encryption allows AI models to analyze encrypted data without decryption, hence maintaining confidentiality. Secure multi-party computation (SMPC) enables collaborative AI training among devices without exposing raw data. Application of such technologies in smart wearables ensures AI-driven insights are secure and privacy-compliant. As digital health innovation remains driven by AI, using privacy-preserving approaches is crucial for enabling ethical and secure data processing.

## Implementation Issues of Wearable Privacy Algorithms

Though beneficial, wearable privacy algorithms suffer from several issues in implementation. Wearable gadgets usually possess less processing power and battery life, limiting the deployment of computationally demanding encryption processes. Compatibility between wearable brands and healthcare systems poses integration challenges as well. Several wearable vendors opt for user-friendliness at the expense of security, thus offering poor default privacy configurations. Also, real-time transmission needs of fitness and medical monitoring make encryption procedures more complex. Fragmentation in regulation across countries complicates the adoption of privacy solutions in a standardized manner. All these must be addressed by industry collaboration, investment in light cryptographic protocols, and privacy-conscious controls. Designing privacy algorithms that are light and optimized for wearables can bridge these technical and regulatory challenges.

The wearable security and privacy of the future will be based on enhancing decentralized identity management, edge computing for on-device encryption, and privacy-aware AI models. Blockchain-based decentralized identity systems will allow individuals to control their health data without relying on central servers. Edge computing will ensure real-time processing on the wearable device itself, reducing exposure to network-based threats. Quantum-resistant encryption methods will be developed to protect wearable data against future quantum computer attacks. Personal health data wallets will allow users to have full control over data access and sharing capabilities. Regulatory AI compliance systems will allow manufacturers to ensure that wearable devices comply with global privacy standards. With such innovations integrated, wearable technology can be balanced between usability and security for data.

Privacy and data protection are key to guaranteeing the mass adoption and ethical use of smart wearables. Regulation frameworks provide a foundation for safeguarding data, but advanced algorithms for privacy need to be built to ensure the overcoming of future threats. Advanced encryption, federated learning, and privacy-preserving AI can significantly enhance data security on wearable devices. Despite challenges such as battery limitations and interoperability, continued research into lightweight cryptographic techniques can counteract these challenges. The wearable privacy future is decentralized, user-driven data management and real-time encryption. Preserving privacy compliance for smart wearables not only protects users but also promotes trust in digital health technologies. With wearables now a part of healthcare and lifestyle management, privacy of data is more important than ever.

## ENHANCED PRIVACY ALGORITHM FOR SMART WEARABLE DEVICES

The proposed Privacy-Preserving Data Protection Algorithm (PPDPA) is designed to secure data on smart wearables and make a tradeoff between power efficiency and global regulation compliance. The algorithm incorporates end-to-end encryption, differential privacy, federated learning, and blockchain-based access control to bring security at data from collection time to transmission to storage.

**Algorithm:** Privacy-Preserving Data Protection Algorithm (PPDPA)

Step 1: Secure Data Collection

1. Wearable device collects raw data (heart rate, activity, location, etc.).
2. Apply dynamic anonymization to remove personally identifiable information (PII).
3. Encrypt the data using lightweight AES-256 encryption before storage.

Step 2: Data Processing with Privacy-Preserving AI

4. Instead of transferring raw data to cloud servers, use edge computing for on-device processing.
5. Implement differential privacy to add random noise, preventing exact data reconstruction.
6. Apply homomorphic encryption to process encrypted data without decryption.

Step 3: Secure Data Transmission

7. If data must be transmitted, use a blockchain-based authentication mechanism for secure access.
8. Use multi-factor authentication (MFA) (biometric + password) before data is sent.
9. Data is end-to-end encrypted using an optimized TLS protocol with post-quantum cryptography.

Step 4: Federated Learning for AI Model Updates

10. Instead of centralizing user data, train AI models locally using federated learning.
11. Only encrypted AI model updates (not raw data) are shared with the cloud.
12. A zero-knowledge proof (ZKP) mechanism ensures only legitimate updates are included.

Step 5: Blockchain-Based Access Control

13. User data access requests are verified through a smart contract on a blockchain.
14. The user can grant, revoke, or modify access via a personal health data wallet.
15. Unauthorized access attempts trigger an alert system to notify the user.

Step 6: Compliance and Audit Logs

16. Every data transaction is logged in a tamper-proof blockchain ledger.
17. The ledger ensures compliance with GDPR, HIPAA, and other privacy laws.
18. Users can request data deletion or retrieval via an auditable consent management system.

This algorithm ensures high security, low power consumption, and full user control, making smart wearables both privacy-compliant and efficient.

## Theorem 1: End-to-End Encryption Security

The encrypted data $\mathscr{D}_{\mathscr{E}}$ transmitted using AES-256 encryption with Transport Layer Security (TLS) remains indistinguishable from a random string for an adversary under polynomial-time attack models.

Proof:

Let D be the original user data collected by the wearable device. The encryption process follows:

$$\mathscr{D}_{\mathscr{E}} = \mathscr{E}_{\mathscr{AES}-256}(K, \mathscr{D})$$

where $\mathscr{E}_{\mathscr{AES}-256}$ is the AES-256 encryption function and K is a 256-bit secret key. AES-256 is proven to be resistant to known attacks such as brute force, differential cryptanalysis, and linear cryptanalysis.

For any adversary A, let's define a distinguisher function that attempts to differentiate $\mathscr{D}_{\mathscr{E}}$ from a random string R:

$$P\left[A\left(\mathscr{D}_{\mathscr{E}}\right) = 1\right] - P[A(R) = 1] \leq \text{negligible}$$

Since AES-256 encryption produces a uniform pseudorandom distribution in polynomial time, an adversary has no better than a negligible probability of distinguishing $\mathscr{D}_{\mathscr{E}}$ from R.

Thus, AES-256 provides semantic security, ensuring data confidentiality against adversarial decryption attempts.

## Theorem 2: Differential Privacy Guarantees

Applying differential privacy with Laplace noise ensures that no adversary can infer whether an individual record is present in the dataset with a probability greater than $\frac{e^{\epsilon}}{1 + e^{\epsilon}}$.

Proof:

Differential privacy is defined as:

$$P[\mathscr{M}(\mathscr{D}) = O] \leq e^{\epsilon} \cdot P[\mathscr{M}(\mathscr{D}') = O]$$

for all neighboring datasets $'\mathscr{D}, \mathscr{D}'$ differing by a single individual and any observable output O.

To achieve $\epsilon$-differential privacy, we apply Laplace noise:

$$(\mathscr{D}) = f(\mathscr{D}) + \mathrm{Lap}\left(\frac{\Delta f}{\epsilon}\right)$$

where $f(\mathscr{D})$ is the function applied to the dataset and Lap($b$)is the Laplace distribution with scale $b = \frac{\Delta f}{\epsilon}$

For any two datasets differing by one record:

$$\frac{P[\mathscr{M}(\mathscr{D})]}{P[\mathscr{M}(\mathscr{D}')]} \leq e$$

This ensures that an adversary cannot determine with certainty whether an individual's data was included, thus preserving privacy.

## Theorem 3: Secure Federated Learning Model

Federated learning ensures that raw user data $\mathscr{D}_i$ remains private while only the model parameters θ are shared, thereby reducing the risk of data exposure.

Proof:

Federated learning updates local models using stochastic gradient descent (SGD):

$$\theta_i^{t+1} = \theta_i^t - \eta \nabla L(\mathscr{D}_i, \theta_i^t)$$

where η is the learning rate and L(·)is the loss function. Instead of sharing raw data $\mathscr{D}_i$, the update rule aggregates model gradients:

$$\theta^{t+1} = \sum_{i=1}^{n} \frac{w_i}{W} \theta_i^{t+1}$$

with weights $w_i$ normalized

Since raw data is not transferred, adversaries cannot reconstruct $\mathscr{D}_i$, ensuring privacy. The security is further enhanced by secure aggregation protocols, making the model resilient to data leakage.

## Theorem 4: Blockchain-Based Access Control is Tamper-Proof

Using blockchain ensures that access control logs cannot be tampered with or altered, providing immutable auditability.

Proof:

A blockchain consists of blocks containing transactions, secured using a cryptographic hash function H:

$$H(B_t) = H(B_{t-1}) \| \mathrm{Tx}_t \| \mathrm{Nonce}_t$$

where $H(B_t)$ is the hash of the current block, $H(B_{t-1})$is the previous block's hash, and $\mathrm{Tx}_t$ represents transactions.

Any attempt to modify a previous block $B_{t-k}$ requires recomputing all subsequent hashes:

$$H(B'_{t-k}) = H(B_{t-k-1}) \| \mathrm{Tx}'_{t-k} \| \mathrm{Nonce}_{t-k}$$

Since the blockchain network follows a proof-of-work or proof-of-stake mechanism, modifying historical data is computationally infeasible. Therefore, access logs stored on the blockchain remain immutable and tamper-proof.

## Theorem 5: Zero-Knowledge Proofs Ensure Secure Authentication

Using zero-knowledge proofs (ZKP), a user can authenticate without revealing their identity or password.

Proof:

Let x be the user's private credential, and let $y = g^x modp$be the public verification key for a cryptographic group. The user proves knowledge of xxx without disclosing it by executing the **Schnorr Protocol**:

1. Prover selects a random r and computes $t = g^r modp$.
2. Verifier sends a random challenge c.
3. Prover responds withs = r + cx mod (p-1).
4. Verifier checks $g^s overset = ty^c modp$

Since an attacker does not know x, they cannot construct a valid response s, ensuring secure authentication.

## Theorem 6: Computational Complexity of Privacy Mechanisms

The overall computational complexity of PPDPA remains polynomial in the size of the dataset N and model parameters mmm, ensuring scalability for real-time wearable applications.

Proof:

1. AES-256 encryption: O(N) per transaction.
2. Differential privacy noise addition: O(N).
3. Federated learning model updates: O(mN), where m is the model size.
4. Blockchain transaction validation:O(log N) for Merkle Tree verification.

5. ZKP authentication: O(log p)where p is a prime field.

Thus, the total complexity remains at mostO(mN + log N), which is polynomial and suitable for real-time applications.

## CONCLUSION

The novel AI governance model effectively addresses the shortcomings of existing models by introducing dynamic regulatory mechanisms, privacy-promoting AI techniques, and explainable AI models. By providing empirical verification in key healthcare application cases, such as AI-powered resuscitation and biomedical data sharing, the model optimizes real-world use and trust. It also optimizes interoperability via federated learning-based harmonization and minimizes blockchain deployment to lower computational costs. Moreover, incorporating proactive threat defense techniques and bias mitigation will enhance the trust and equity of AI in health decision-making. The model's capacity to adapt to evolving global data security policies guarantees viability and worldwide acceptance in medicine. Combining AI with expert human knowledge enhances the methodology into a hybrid medical diagnosis model that can balance automating and honoring ethical standards and result in more openness, safety, and impartiality in the AI-driven medical field.

## REFERENCES


Alabdulatif, A., Khalil, I., & Rahman, M. S. (2022). Security of Blockchain and AI-Empowered Smart Healthcare: Application-Based Analysis. *Applied Sciences (Basel, Switzerland), 12*(21), 11039. DOI: 10.3390/app122111039

Ali, S., Abdullah, , Armand, T. P. T., Athar, A., Hussain, A., Ali, M., Yaseen, M., Joo, M.-I., & Kim, H.-C. (2023). Metaverse in Healthcare Integrated with Explainable AI and Blockchain: Enabling Immersiveness, Ensuring Trust, and Providing Patient Data Security. *Sensors (Basel), 23*(2), 565. DOI: 10.3390/s23020565 PMID: 36679361

Angerschmid, A., Zhou, J., Theuermann, K., Chen, F., & Holzinger, A. (2022). Fairness and Explanation in AI-Informed Decision Making. *Mach. Learn. Knowl. Extr.*, *4*(2), 556–579. DOI: 10.3390/make4020026

Biller-Andorno, N., Ferrario, A., Jöbges, S., Krones, T., Massini, F., Barth, P., Arampatzis, G., & Krauthammer, M. AI Support for Ethical Decision-Making around Resuscitation: Proceed with Care. Medrxiv (Cold Spring Harb. Lab.) 2020. preprint. DOI: 10.1101/2020.08.17.20171769

Elhoseny, M., Haseeb, K., Shah, A. A., Ahmad, I., Jan, Z., & Alghamdi, M. I. (2021). IoT Solution for AI-Enabled PRIVACY-PREServing with Big Data Transferring: An Application for Healthcare Using Blockchain. *Energies*, *14*(17), 5364. DOI: 10.3390/en14175364

Formosa, P., Rogers, W., Bankins, S., Griep, Y., & Richards, D. (2022). Medical AI and Human Dignity: Contrasting Perceptions of Human and Artificially Intelligent (AI) Decision Making in Diagnostic and Medical Resource Allocation Contexts. *Computers in Human Behavior, 133*, 107296. DOI: 10.1016/j.chb.2022.107296

Keshta, I. (2022). AI-Driven IoT for Smart Health Care: Security and Privacy Issues. *Informatics in Medicine Unlocked*, *30*, 100903. DOI: 10.1016/j.imu.2022.100903

Khalid, N., Qayyum, A., Qayyum, A., Al-Fuqaha, A., & Qadir, J. (2023). Privacy-Preserving Artificial Intelligence in Healthcare: Techniques and Applications. *Computers in Biology and Medicine*, *158*, 106848. DOI: 10.1016/j.compbiomed.2023.106848 PMID: 37044052

Morley, J., Machado, C., Burr, C., Cowls, J., Taddeo, M., & Floridi, L. (2019). The debate on the ethics of AI in health care: a reconstruction and critical review. Available at *SSRN* 3486518.

Mosaiyebzadeh, F., Pouriyeh, S., Parizi, R. M., Sheng, Q. Z., Han, M., Zhao, L., Sannino, G., Ranieri, C. M., Ueyama, J., & Batista, D. M. (2023). Privacy-Enhancing Technologies in Federated Learning for the Internet of Healthcare Things: A Survey. *Electronics (Basel)*, *12*(12), 2703. DOI: 10.3390/electronics12122703

Munjal, K., & Bhatia, R. (2022). A Systematic Review of Homomorphic Encryption and Its Contributions in Healthcare Industry. *Complex & Intelligent Systems*, *9*(4), 3759–3786. DOI: 10.1007/s40747-022-00756-z PMID: 35531323

Olatunji, I. E., Rauch, J., Katzensteiner, M., & Khosla, M. (2022). A Review of Anonymization for Healthcare Data. *Big Data*. PMID: 35271377

Page, M. J., McKenzie, J. E., Bossuyt, P. M., Boutron, I., Hoffmann, T., Mulrow, C. D., Shamseer, L., Tetzlaff, J., Akl, E. A., & Brennan, S.. (2021). The PRISMA 2020 Statement: An Updated Guideline for Reporting Systematic Reviews. *BMJ (Clinical Research Ed.)*, *372*(71). PMID: 33782057

Panagopoulos, A., Minssen, T., Sideri, K., Yu, H., & Compagnucci, M. C. (2022). Incentivizing the Sharing of Healthcare Data in the AI Era. *Computer Law & Security Review*, *45*, 105670. DOI: 10.1016/j.clsr.2022.105670

Pereira, T., Morgado, J., Silva, F., Pelter, M. M., Dias, V., De Cássia Nogueira Barros, R., De Freitas, C., Negrão, E., De Lima, B. F., & Da Silva, M. C.. (2021). Sharing Biomedical Data: Strengthening AI Development in Healthcare. *Health Care*, *9*, 827. PMID: 34208830

Prakash, S., Balaji, J. N., Joshi, A., & Surapaneni, K. M. (2022). Ethical Conundrums in the Application of Artificial Intelligence (AI) in Healthcare—A Scoping Review of Reviews. *Journal of Personalized Medicine*, *12*(11), 1914. DOI: 10.3390/jpm12111914 PMID: 36422090

Rahman, A., Hossain, M. S., Muhammad, G., Kundu, D., Debnath, T., Rahman, M. S., Khan, M. S. I., Tiwari, P., & Band, S. S. (2022). Federated Learning-Based AI Approaches in Smart Healthcare: Concepts, Taxonomies, Challenges and Open Issues. *Cluster Computing*, *26*(4), 2271–2311. DOI: 10.1007/s10586-022-03658-4 PMID: 35996680

Reddy, S., Allan, S., Coghlan, S., & Cooper, P. (2019). A Governance Model for the Application of AI in Health Care. *Journal of the American Medical Informatics Association : JAMIA*, *27*(3), 491–497. DOI: 10.1093/jamia/ocz192 PMID: 31682262

Richardson, J. W., Smith, C., Curtis, S., Watson, S. E., Zhu, X., Barry, B. A., & Sharp, R. R. (2021). Patient Apprehensions about the Use of Artificial Intelligence in Healthcare. *NPJ Digital Medicine*, *4*(1), 140. DOI: 10.1038/s41746-021-00509-1 PMID: 34548621

Shinde, R., Patil, S., Kotecha, K., & Ruikar, K. (2021). Blockchain for Securing AI Applications and Open Innovations. *Journal of Open Innovation*, *7*(3), 189. DOI: 10.3390/joitmc7030189

Tagde, P., Tagde, S., Bhattacharya, T., Tagde, P., Chopra, H., Akter, R., Kaushik, D., & Rahman, M. H. (2021). Blockchain and Artificial Intelligence Technology in E-Health. *Environmental Science and Pollution Research International*, *28*(38), 52810–52831. DOI: 10.1007/s11356-021-16223-0 PMID: 34476701

Wang, C., Zhang, J., Lassi, N., & Zhang, X. (2022). Privacy Protection in Using Artificial Intelligence for Healthcare: Chinese Regulation in Comparative Perspective. *Health Care*, *10*, 1878. PMID: 36292325

Xu, J., Glicksberg, B. S., Su, C., Walker, P. B., Bian, J., & Wang, F. (2020). Federated Learning for Healthcare Informatics. *Journal of Healthcare Informatics Research*, *5*(1), 1–19. DOI: 10.1007/s41666-020-00082-4 PMID: 33204939

Zarifis, A., Kawalek, P., & Azadegan, A. (2020). Evaluating If Trust and Personal Information Privacy Concerns Are Barriers to Using Health Insurance That Explicitly Utilizes AI. *Journal of Internet Commerce, 20*(1), 66–83. DOI: 10.1080/15332861.2020.1832817

Chapter 7

# Regulatory and Strategic Challenges of Patent Evergreening in the MedTech Industry:
## An Analysis of Competition Law Implications

**Chaitra Rangappa Beerannavar**
https://orcid.org/0000-0001-9891-4780
*Christ University, India*

**Sandra Mariya Koshi**
*Christ University, India*

## ABSTRACT

*Patent evergreening is a strategy used by pharmaceutical companies to extend their market exclusivity through minor modifications of existing drugs, often without significant therapeutic advancements. This practice raises concerns about access to affordable medicines, particularly in developing countries like India, where high drug prices impact public health. A comparative analysis with the European Union (EU) reveals that while India relies on patent law restrictions, the EU employs competition law under Article 102 of the Treaty on the Functioning of the European*

DOI: 10.4018/979-8-3373-1205-7.ch007

*Union (TFEU) to regulate evergreening. Cases such as AstraZeneca v. European Commission demonstrate the EU's effects-based approach to curbing anti-competitive patent strategies. This study highlights the gaps in India's regulatory framework, emphasizing the need for greater coordination between the Indian Patent Office (IPO) and the Competition Commission of India (CCI), and adopting an effects-based approach are crucial to preventing evergreening while ensuring both innovation and consumer welfare.*

## 1. INTRODUCTION TO PATENT EVERGREENING IN HEALTHCARE

Patent evergreening refers to the practice of extending the monopoly of a patented product through minor modifications, often without significant technological advancements. This strategy, widely observed in the pharmaceutical industry, involves obtaining secondary patents on variations such as altered dosages, extended-release formulations, or new combinations. While these secondary patents may technically meet the standards of novelty and inventiveness, they often offer minimal therapeutic benefits, raising concerns about their impact on competition and public health (De & Samuel, 2020).

The MedTech industry, much like pharmaceuticals, is a patent-driven industry. Companies rely on intellectual property (IP) protection to safeguard their investments in medical devices, diagnostics, and treatment technologies. Unlike pharmaceuticals, where evergreening is primarily associated with extending drug monopolies, MedTech firms employ strategic patenting practices that can have similar effects—delaying market entry for competitors and inflating healthcare costs. These strategies include patent thickets, software-based exclusivities, and restrictive licensing agreements that limit generic or biosimilar alternatives. While these practices may not fit the traditional definition of evergreening, they raise significant competition law concerns by restricting innovation diffusion and maintaining monopolistic control.

Most entry barriers in the healthcare industry stem from the manipulation of patent laws to block new market entrants, providing established companies with an unfair competitive advantage. Traditionally, pharmaceutical companies relied on a single patent protecting the active compound of a drug. However, in recent years, firms have increasingly pursued additional patents on aspects such as manufacturing processes, alternative formulations, and delivery mechanisms to extend their market exclusivity. This shift has led to legal and economic debates about the fine line between legitimate patent protection and strategic monopolization.

The European Commission's Sector Inquiry Report highlights three critical stages in drug development:

i. Research & Development (R&D) – culminating in the initial patent and product launch.
ii. Market Exclusivity Phase – where companies maximize revenues before patent expiration.
iii. Post-Patent Expiry – where generic drugs enter the market and drive competition.

It is during the second stage that companies actively employ strategies to extend exclusivity, often raising concerns about competition law violations and barriers to affordable healthcare (Garattini, Natsis, & Banzi, 2021).

While India's Patents Act, 1970, does not explicitly define "evergreening," Section 3(d) plays a crucial role in preventing it by requiring proof of enhanced therapeutic efficacy for secondary patents. Additionally, Section 4 of the Competition Act, 2002, prohibits the abuse of dominant market positions, offering a complementary tool to regulate anti-competitive patent practices. However, the overlap between patent law and competition law often leads to enforcement challenges.

This chapter proposes a comprehensive analysis of patent evergreening through the lens of competition law. While evergreening is more prominently observed in the pharmaceutical sector, the MedTech industry employs alternative methods to achieve similar objectives. By critically examining the effectiveness of India's Section 3(d) and Section 4, alongside the EU's Article 102 of the TFEU, this chapter will assess how regulatory frameworks can prevent the misuse of patents in MedTech. Through a comparative approach, it will identify best practices, enforcement gaps, and potential legal reforms to ensure that patent law fosters genuine innovation while maintaining fair market competition in the MedTech industry.

## 2. IMPACT OF PATENT EVERGREENING ON PRICES, ACCESSIBILITY, AND GENERIC MANUFACTURERS

Patent evergreening has emerged as a contentious issue in the pharmaceutical sector, particularly in India, where affordable access to essential medicines is critical. This practice directly impacts drug prices, availability, and the operations of generic manufacturers. While pharmaceutical companies argue that patent extensions are necessary for proper research and development (R&D) investments, critics contend that these strategies disproportionately benefit originators at the expense of consumers and competitors. The ramifications of evergreening are most acutely felt in developing countries, where health systems and populations are particularly sensitive to fluctuations in drug affordability and availability.

### 2.1. Impact on Drug Prices

The extension of patent terms through evergreening practices results in prolonged monopolies for patented drugs, enabling originator companies to maintain high prices. Patents provide exclusive rights to manufacturers, insulating them from competition and allowing them to charge premium prices. When these monopolistic rights are extended through secondary patents on minor modifications, it delays the market entry of lower-cost generics.

For instance, blockbuster drugs often command exorbitant prices during their patent-protected period, generating substantial profits for originators. By obtaining additional patents on new formulations, delivery mechanisms, or combinations, companies continue to charge monopolistic prices long after the original patent expires. This creates significant affordability challenges, particularly in low- and middle-income countries (LMICs) like India, where a large proportion of the population pays out-of-pocket for healthcare.

High drug prices have a ripple effect across healthcare systems, increasing the financial burden on both patients and public health programs. Essential medicines become inaccessible to marginalized populations, undermining public health efforts to combat diseases. For example, life-saving medications for chronic conditions such as cancer, diabetes, and HIV/AIDS often remain beyond the reach of ordinary citizens due to price inflation driven by evergreening practices.

## 2.2. Accessibility Challenges

Patent evergreening severely impacts the accessibility of essential medicines by delaying the introduction of generic alternatives. Generic drugs play a pivotal role in ensuring the availability of affordable medicines, particularly in India, which is known as the "pharmacy of the developing world." The delayed entry of generics caused by extended patent terms exacerbates the disparity in access to healthcare, disproportionately affecting vulnerable and underserved populations.

The inability to access affordable medicines has far-reaching consequences, including higher morbidity and mortality rates for preventable or treatable conditions. Public health initiatives also suffer as governments and non-governmental organizations (NGOs) struggle to procure medicines at reasonable costs. This challenge is particularly pronounced in programs targeting diseases such as tuberculosis and malaria, where timely and cost-effective drug supply is crucial for intervention success. Evergreening also undermines international efforts to promote equitable access to medicines. India, as a key supplier of generics globally, faces limitations in exporting affordable alternatives to patented drugs due to extended protection periods. This has implications for the health security of developing countries that depend on Indian generics to combat their healthcare crises.

## 2.3. Impact on Generic Manufacturers

Patent evergreening directly affects generic pharmaceutical manufacturers by restricting their ability to produce and market alternatives to patented drugs. Generic manufacturers rely on the expiration of patents to introduce bioequivalent drugs at significantly lower prices, thereby driving market competition and reducing healthcare costs. However, secondary patents on minor or incremental innovations create legal and financial barriers for these manufacturers.

One of the primary challenges faced by generic producers is the uncertainty surrounding the validity and enforceability of secondary patents. Originator companies often adopt aggressive litigation strategies to defend secondary patents, creating significant financial and operational burdens for generic manufacturers. Protracted legal battles over the validity of secondary patents drain resources and delay market entry, further entrenching the market dominance of originators.

The stifling of generic competition through evergreening also limits innovation within the generic industry. While generics primarily replicate existing drugs, many companies invest in improving formulations, creating fixed-dose combinations, or developing alternative delivery mechanisms to enhance patient compliance. However, the monopolistic practices of originators curtail these opportunities, reducing the incentive for generics to invest in product development.

## 2.4. Broader Market Implications

The prevalence of evergreening strategies has broader implications for the pharmaceutical market, particularly in terms of competition and innovation. By extending exclusivity periods, originator companies effectively suppress competition, resulting in higher prices and reduced consumer choice. This monopolistic behavior also stifles genuine innovation, as the focus shifts from groundbreaking drug discoveries to minor modifications that secure secondary patents.

Furthermore, the monopolistic practices associated with evergreening often prioritize profits over public health. Pharmaceutical companies invest heavily in lobbying and litigation to protect their market dominance, diverting resources from the development of innovative therapies. This raises ethical concerns about the alignment of corporate priorities with the public good, especially in the context of global health crises that demand affordable and accessible treatments.

## 2.5. Socioeconomic Consequences

The socioeconomic impacts of patent evergreening are particularly pronounced in countries like India, where a significant portion of the population lives below the poverty line. High drug prices driven by extended patents exacerbate health inequities, forcing families to make difficult choices between healthcare and other essential needs. The financial burden of costly medications also contributes to medical impoverishment, where individuals are pushed into poverty due to healthcare expenses.

Evergreening practices place additional strain on government healthcare budgets. Public health programs that rely on affordable medicines face escalating costs, limiting their capacity to address the healthcare needs of the population. This is particularly concerning in the context of India's ambitious universal healthcare initiatives, which aim to provide equitable access to essential services.

## 2.6. Global Health Implications

India's role as a leading supplier of generics extends the impact of patent evergreening beyond its borders. The delayed availability of affordable alternatives to patented drugs affects LMICs that depend on Indian generics to address their public health challenges. For example, the availability of affordable antiretroviral therapies for HIV/AIDS, which has been a cornerstone of global health efforts, is threatened by evergreening practices that prolong market exclusivity for branded drugs.

Hence, patent evergreening poses significant legal and economic implications for competition and consumer welfare, particularly regarding access to affordable medicines. The practice of extending market exclusivity through secondary patents on minor modifications undermines the availability of cost-effective generic alternatives, inflating drug prices and exacerbating health inequities. While pharmaceutical companies argue that such practices are essential to recover R&D costs and sustain innovation, they often prioritize profit over genuine public health needs, particularly in a price-sensitive market like India.

Economically, evergreening hinders competition by delaying the entry of generic manufacturers, thereby limiting consumer choice and driving up healthcare costs. This has profound implications for public health programs, particularly in India, where out-of-pocket expenses dominate healthcare spending. The delayed availability of affordable generics not only impacts domestic consumers but also disrupts global access to essential medicines, as India plays a critical role as the "pharmacy of the developing world."

## 3. INDIA'S REGULATORY FRAMEWORK: BALANCING INNOVATION AND COMPETITION

Intellectual property law, extends various forms of legal protection for innovators based on the subject matter and degree of novelty. Patents are generally considered the strongest form of protection as they grant exclusive rights over innovative technological knowledge. India enacted The Patent Act of 1970 replacing the Indian Patent and Design Act of 1911. Subsequent amendments to the Act, especially those following India's compliance with the TRIPS Agreement, have refined the balance between innovation and public interest. India implemented product patents for pharmaceuticals in 1995 by signing the TRIPS Agreement. As part of its commitments under TRIPS and the WTO framework, the country amended its Patent Act in three phases: 1999, 2002, and 2005 (TRIPS Agreement,

1994). The Act's focus on balancing private and public interests reflects India's commitment to balance innovation while addressing societal needs.

To apply for a patent, it must be competent to qualify for a patent grant. This means that it should not fall under the category of patent-exempt inventions mentioned under section 3 of the Indian Patent Act. The patented invention must be new and includes an innovative step and commercial benefit. Section 3 (d) of the invention must be subject to the patentability test in the form of efficacy along with another patentability testing. Section 3(d) of the Indian Patents Act, 1970, essentially states that mere improvements are not eligible for patent protection unless they result in the creation of a new substance.

In the case of Tony Mon George v. Deputy Controller of Patents & Designs, the court analyzed the 3 parts of the section as follows under paragraph 15 of the judgement as:

The principal clause of Section 3(d) contains about three limbs, which are separated by the disjunctive "or". The three limbs are as under:

(i) The mere discovery of a new form of a known substance which does not result in the enhancement of the known efficacy of that substance.
(ii) The mere discovery of any new property or new use for a known substance.
(iii) Of the mere use of a known process, machine or apparatus unless such known process results in a new product or employs at least one new reactant.

Section 3(d) of the Indian Patents Act states that the mere discovery of a new form of a known substance, which does not result in the enhancement of the known efficacy of that substance, is not patentable. It also prohibits the patenting of new uses or properties of a known substance. This ensures that discoveries of additional applications for existing substances do not receive undue patent protection. It is important to note that it was not designed to outright reject the patenting of all incremental innovations . But to regulate the misuse of the patent system by the pharmaceutical companies to extent the patent duration and hamper the entry of generic companies. However, it is criticized that the strict implementation of this provision by Indian patent authorities, combined with the judiciary's narrow interpretation of 'efficacy' as strictly 'therapeutic efficacy,' has led certain groups to assert that the revised standard is aimed at denying patents for all incremental innovations.

The Mashelkar Report specifically highlighted the problem of evergreening and the role of section 3(d):

> *"Every effort must be made to prevent the practice of 'ever greening', often used by some of the pharma companies to unreasonably extend the life of the patent by making claims based sometimes on 'trivial' changes to the original patented product. The Indian patent office has the full authority under law and practice to determine what is patentable and what would constitute only a trivial change with no significant additional improvements or inventive steps involving benefits. Such authority should be used to prevent 'evergreening'"*

It is agreed by jurists that Section 3(d) creates a barrier to obtaining pharmaceutical patents and that the enhanced efficacy requirement is unclear for two reasons:

A. It is unclear what is meant by "efficacy."
B. It is unclear "what kind of data will be required to establish 'efficacy'" to the satisfaction of Section 3(d).

The Oxford English Dictionary broadly defines 'efficacy' as 'power or capacity to produce effects'. However, the term is not defined in the Patent Act. The same holds for the term 'generic' as well. The definition of generic substances is also not very detailed in the law. It is also not clear quantitatively about the amount of efficacy that can be considered significant. (Basheer & Reddy, 2008). So, the important requirement is to have a clear definition of effectiveness that can solve issues surrounding section 3(d), such as misapplication, arbitrariness, and legal suspicions.

## 3.1. Analysis of judicial decisions of section 3(d)

In the case of Novartis AG v. Union of India, the Supreme Court has interpreted Section 3(d) in a manner that may significantly limit the ability of pharmaceutical companies to obtain "secondary patents" on life-saving drugs

The court addressed the controversy surrounds Section 3(d) in three major respects.

A. First, Section 3(d) is an unusual provision among different countries' patent laws because it imposes a requirement of "enhanced efficacy" over the prior art before a patent on a reformulation or modification of an original pharmaceutical compound can be obtained.
B. Second, Section 3(d) applies only to pharmaceutical product patents, not patents in any other field of technology.
C. Third, the lower courts in Novar/is AG have defined "efficacy" in Section 3(d) narrowly to mean "therapeutic efficacy" only. This narrow interpretation drew umbrage from petitioner Novartis as unsupported by the text of the statute and amaging to incentives for pharmaceutical innovation.

The first interpretation is that enhanced efficacy is subsumed completely within India's "inventive step" and "industrial application" requirements. In India, as well as the EU, inventive step roughly approximates non-obviousness in the United States; and industrial application, utility in the United States. The second interpretation is that enhanced efficacy refers broadly to any improvements on the functioning of a pharmaceutical as a treatment. The third is that enhanced efficacy means therapeutic efficacy only, as narrowly defined by the Madras High Court and the IPAB . Each interpretation has its own attendant consequences for evergreening, public health, and innovation, and there are tradeoffs to each.

Novartis argued that this provision was inconsistent with international standards under TRIPS, but the Court upheld the interpretation of Section 3(d) as compliant with Indian law, thus denying Novartis the patent for the new form of Glivec. On the basis of Dorland's Medical Dictionary definition of 'efficacy' in the field of pharmacology, the court interpreted 'efficacy' as 'the ability of a drug to produce the desired therapeutic effect' and 'therapeutic' as 'healing of disease', i.e. having a good effect on the body

The decision has very deep implications for patenting in India. It prevents companies from obtaining patents for incremental changes to existing drugs unless those changes result in a significant therapeutic improvement. This approach is viewed by public health advocates as a way to ensure access to affordable generic medicines, particularly for life-saving drugs like Glivec, which were priced prohibitively in India before the patent dispute.

In the case of Hoffmann-La Roche Ltd. & Anr. v. Cipla Ltd 2008, while discussing the scope and nature of Section 3(d), the Divisional Bench opined that,

> *Para 62: "Section 3(d) assumes that structurally similar derivatives of a known 'substance' will also be functionally similar and hence ought not to be patentable. What is of crucial importance is that this is not a provision that merely bars certain subject matter from patentability. On the contrary, it provides that if the new form of the known substance is found despite a structural similarity to demonstrate a better functionality i.e. 'enhancement of the known efficacy', it would qualify for assessment under Section 2(1)(j) as if it were a new product involving an inventive step and it would thereafter be up to the applicant for the patent to demonstrate the patentability of this substance in accordance with Sections 2(1)(j) and (ja)."*

Patent evergreening remains a significant challenge in the Indian pharmaceutical industry, particularly in terms of balancing the need for innovation with the public's right to access affordable healthcare. The legal provisions under Section 3(d) of the Indian Patents Act, especially with its focus on "enhanced efficacy," play a crucial role in curbing the practice of extending patent protection through minor, non-innovative modifications. While pharmaceutical companies argue that such strategies are necessary to recover R&D costs and incentivize further innovation, critics contend that they create monopolies that delay the availability of cheaper generics, undermining the accessibility of life-saving medicines.

However, the provision is not without its challenges. The lack of precise definitions and clear guidelines regarding what constitutes "efficacy" can lead to inconsistencies in its application. While Section 3(d) has been effective in preventing evergreening, critics argue that it may inadvertently discourage incremental innovations that could offer marginal yet valuable benefits.

## 4. COMBATING EVERGREENING: THE ROLE OF COMPETITION LAW IN ENSURING FAIR MARKETS

Competition Law aims to prevent anti-competitive practices, promote and preserve market competition, protect consumer interests, and ensure the free flow of commerce among all market participants (Prakhar, 2023). One of the objectives of this legislation is to stop dominant corporations from exploiting market dynamics for their benefit at the expense of consumers.

The concept of intellectual property rights (IPRs), rooted in John Locke's theory of labor, is designed to reward authors or innovators for their creative efforts (Gomase, Priyadarshi, & Kathikar, 2023). Essentially, the law provides intellectual property owners with the right to prevent others from exploiting their creations. Without the exclusive right to exploit inventions through intellectual property rights, owners would be unable to stop others from using their research and development without proper compensation (Buckley, 2004).

IPR and competition law conflict because, depending on how many other items are available, IPR can provide a corporation market power or even a monopoly. IPR restricts competition, but the law of competition enforces it. Therefore, the use of market power unfairly or the abuse of a dominant position resulting from an IPR are protected by competition law. Intellectual properties like "patents, copyrights, trademarks, geographical indications, industrial designs, and integrated circuit designs" are recognised in India under the Competition Act of 2002. Anti-competitive agreements are prohibited by Section 3 of the Competition Act, but Section 3(5) clarifies that this law does not interfere with "any person's right to stop any infringement of or to impose reasonable conditions, as may be necessary, to protect any of his rights" under the laws that govern the aforementioned IPRs.

## 4.1. Abuse of dominant position under section 4 of the Competition Act

The idea that "big is not bad" is an established principle of competition policy. A firm's size may be the result of innovation, a novel business model, or simply more efficient operations. (OECD, 2020, p. 7). Therefore, holding a dominant position is not wrong per se. Abuse of dominant position is wrong under the competition act. The Act defines the dominant position in sec. 4 of the Competition Act,2002 and factors to determine the dominant positions are defined under sec 19(4) of the Competition Act. Under sec. 4, dominant position is defined as a position of strength, enjoyed by an enterprise, in the relevant market, in India, which enables it to:

A. operate independently of competitive forces prevailing in the relevant market; or
B. affect its competitors or consumers or the relevant market in its favour.

Factors determining Dominant position is defined under sec. 19(4) of the act, which that commission shall while inquiring whether an enterprise enjoys a dominant position or not under section 4, have due regard to all or any of the factors such as market share; the size and resources of the enterprise; Size and importance of competitors; Economic power of the enterprise; a vertical integration; a dependence of consumers on the enterprise etc. (OECD, 2020)

In Telefonaktiebolaget LM Ericsson (PUBL) v. Competition Commission of India & Anr court held that the Competition Commission of India is the primary authority overseeing competition issues in the Indian market, empowered by the Competition Act of 2002 to investigate anti-competitive agreements and abuse of dominant position. The court has underscored the expertise of the controller general of patents, designs, and trademarks, referred to as the "controller," as the specialized regulator in patent-related matters over the more general investigative role of the CCI. The controller, who administers the Indian Patents Act of 1970 through the Indian patent offices, has the authority to grant compulsory licenses to address nonworking patents, reduce import dependency, and promote public welfare, particularly in national emergencies. The case where the absence of a monopoly may prevent inventors from recovering their research and development (R&D) costs, potentially discouraging future investments in innovation. Intellectual property (IP) law is viewed as pro-competitive and pro-innovation because it provides exclusive rights to inventors, incentivizing new inventions. On the other hand, competition law focuses on enhancing and safeguarding competition in product markets, which also fosters innovation. Despite appearing as divergent approaches, both IP law and competition law ultimately aim to promote innovation. (Khan & Sharma, 2024).

In the CCI judgment, the division bench held that the Indian Patents Act, 1970 supersedes the Competition Act, 2002 in cases involving intellectual property disputes. The decision was based on statutory interpretation, using the legal maxims "lex posterior derogate priori" (later law repeals earlier law) and "generalia specialibus non derogant" (general law does not override specific law). The main point of conflict arises from the overlapping provisions that address anti-competitive behavior. Both statutes regulate different aspects of market power—patents through exclusive rights and competition law through preventing abuse of market dominance. This overlap has led to confusion over which authority—Controller of Patents or the CCI—should have jurisdiction in cases where a patent holder's actions potentially harm competition.

## 4.2. The Anti-Competitive Effects of Evergreening

The anti-competitive impact of evergreening arises in several ways:

### 4.2.1. Delayed Entry of Generic Competitors:

Secondary patents prolong the exclusivity period, deterring generic manufacturers from entering the market. Generics, which are typically priced much lower than branded drugs, drive competition and significantly reduce healthcare costs. By delaying their entry, evergreening practices impose a financial burden on consumers and healthcare systems. Delayed market entry of generics means patients are forced to continue purchasing expensive branded medications, putting essential treatments out of reach for many.

4.2.2. **Higher Drug Prices:** Evergreening sustains monopolistic pricing, making essential drugs unaffordable for many. This is particularly detrimental in developing countries like India, where out-of-pocket healthcare expenses constitute a significant share of household expenditure. The prolonged monopoly on drug pricing means that even public health programs and insurance providers face increased financial strain, ultimately reducing the availability of funds for other critical healthcare services. In countries with limited healthcare budgets, this results in critical trade-offs, often to the detriment of preventive care and infrastructure development. (Dinesan, 2022)

4.2.3. **Market Foreclosure:** Through aggressive litigation and patent clustering, originator companies can create barriers to entry, effectively foreclosing the market to potential competitors. Patent clustering involves filing multiple overlapping patents for various aspects of the same drug, creating a web of legal protections that is costly and time-consuming for competitors to navigate. Generic manufacturers, many of whom operate on limited budgets, find it nearly impossible to challenge such entrenched patent networks. (Dinesan, 2022)

4.2.4. **Impact on Innovation:** Resources that could be directed towards developing groundbreaking drugs are instead allocated to creating minor variations of existing products. This focus on profit-driven incremental innovation hampers the pharmaceutical industry's ability to address unmet medical needs. For example, diseases prevalent in low-income regions often remain under-researched because companies prioritize investments in extending patents for blockbuster drugs.

Although patent evergreening is primarily associated with pharmaceuticals, MedTech companies employ similar tactics to maintain market dominance. Through patent clustering, software-based exclusivities, and minor device modifications, firms extend exclusivity periods and delay competition. These practices increase costs for healthcare providers, restrict access to affordable medical technologies, and create legal barriers for new entrants, ultimately limiting innovation and market competition in the sector.

## 5. REGULATORY CHALLENGES IN ADDRESSING EVERGREENING AS AN ANTI- COMPETITIVE PRACTICE

Competition authorities focus on market impacts but may lack the technical expertise to evaluate the validity of patents. This creates a regulatory disconnect that can harm the effective enforcement of competition law. Collaborative frameworks between patent offices and competition authorities are necessary to bridge this gap. Joint evaluations of patent applications from both technical and market perspectives could help identify and prevent anti-competitive practices. (Srivastava, 2019)

Another challenge is the burden of proving abuse of dominance under competition law. Establishing that secondary patents are used to unfairly delay competition requires detailed economic analyses and evidence of intent. In cases like *Roche v. Cipla*, while the courts recognized the public health implications, the lack of direct competition law analysis limited the broader regulatory impact. This highlights the need for more robust investigative mechanisms that integrate patent and competition law frameworks.

Despite the increasing recognition of patent evergreening as a potential anti-competitive practice, proving its adverse effects under Indian competition law presents several legal, procedural, and institutional challenges. The Competition Commission of India (CCI) has the authority to regulate anti-competitive conduct under Section 4 of the Competition Act, 2002, but establishing that evergreening constitutes an abuse of dominant position is a complex task. The following key challenges hinder the effective enforcement of competition law against evergreening strategies in India:

One of the biggest challenges in addressing evergreening through competition law is the jurisdictional overlap between the Patents Act, 1970, and the Competition Act, 2002. The Indian Patent Office (IPO) is responsible for granting and rejecting patents, while the CCI investigates anti-competitive behavior. However it has been ruled that disputes over patents should be resolved primarily under patent law, limiting the CCI's ability to intervene in cases involving evergreening. This creates regulatory uncertainty, as patent holders can argue that their actions are within the scope of patent rights, making it difficult for the CCI to establish a clear case of anti-competitive behavior.

Unlike pay-for-delay agreements or predatory pricing, which have established definitions in competition law, evergreening is not explicitly recognized as an anti-competitive practice under the Competition Act, 2002. The absence of a statutory definition means that each case must be analyzed individually, requiring the CCI to establish evidence of abuse on a case-by-case basis. This increases the burden of proof and often leads to lengthy legal disputes, making enforcement against evergreening inconsistent and difficult.

To prove abuse of dominance under Section 4, the CCI must first define the relevant market and establish that the patent holder is dominant. However, the pharmaceutical sector is highly complex and dynamic, making it challenging to define market boundaries. Patent holders often argue that their drugs compete with multiple alternatives, making it difficult to prove that they hold a dominant position in a clearly defined market. Additionally, multinational pharmaceutical firms operate across multiple jurisdictions, complicating the process of establishing market dominance in a way that aligns with Indian competition law.

Competition law in India requires proving that a company's actions intentionally harm competition or restrict consumer choice. While evergreening extends patent protection and delays generic entry, proving that this is done with anti-competitive intent rather than for legitimate business reasons (such as encouraging R&D) is difficult. Patent holders often argue that secondary patents protect genuine innovations, even when they do not provide significant therapeutic benefits. This makes it challenging for the CCI to prove exclusionary intent and consumer harm, especially without clear economic evidence.

While both the CCI and the IPO deal with different aspects of the pharmaceutical market, there is limited coordination between the two agencies. The IPO focuses on patentability criteria (novelty, inventive step, and industrial applicability), while the CCI looks at the market impact of patent-related practices. The lack of a formal mechanism for information sharing and joint investigations weakens enforcement against evergreening. Unlike the EU, where competition authorities work closely with the European Patent Office (EPO), India does not have a structured inter-agency framework to handle overlapping patent and competition issues.

Competition cases, particularly those involving patents and intellectual property, take a long time to resolve due to the complexity of the evidence and legal arguments involved. The CCI has limited resources compared to large pharmaceutical firms that can afford prolonged litigation, making it difficult to enforce competition law swiftly. Additionally, CCI decisions are often challenged in higher courts, leading to further delays in implementation. This prolonged legal process benefits the patent holders, allowing them to continue using evergreening tactics to maintain market exclusivity.

India's competition law enforcement has traditionally followed a formalistic approach, focusing on specific legal provisions rather than analyzing the real-world impact of patent evergreening on market competition and consumer welfare. In contrast, the EU follows an effects-based approach, where competition authorities evaluate the economic consequences of evergreening rather than just its technical legality. India lacks such a structured economic analysis framework, making it harder to prove that secondary patents directly harm consumers and restrict market competition.

## 6. A COMPARATIVE ANALYSIS OF THE INDIAN AND EU APPROACH TO PATENT EVERGREENING

This comparative study between India and the EU is highly relevant in this context becasue both jurisdictions have distinct, yet similar approaches to tackle evergreening. In the outset, India has taken a strict stance on patentability criteria based on enhanced efficacy because of its significant generic pharmaceutical industry. Section 3(d) of the Indian Patents Act, 1970, introduced through 2005 amendment, specifically limits secondary patents unless the applicant demonstrates enhanced therapeutic efficacy. On the other hand, European Union does not have a provision similar to Section 3(d) but relies heavily on competition law enforcement to regulate evergreening. Under Article 102 of the Treaty on the Functioning of the European Union (TFEU), the European Commission has taken strong action against pharmaceutical companies engaging in pay-for-delay agreements, patent clustering, and abusive patent litigation. Unlike India, the EU emphasizes an effects-based approach, where regulators assess the actual impact of evergreening practices on market competition rather than focusing solely on patent eligibility criteria.

Despite their differences, both India and the EU struggle with enforcement challenges, particularly in bridging the gap between intellectual property law and competition law. India's competition authorities (CCI) face jurisdictional conflicts with patent authorities, while the EU's stringent approach sometimes lacks preemptive measures to prevent evergreening at the patent grant stage (Gurgula, 2020). By analyzing these differences, this chapter aims to identify best practices from both systems that can be a more effective regulatory framework for tackling patent evergreening worldwide.

## 6.1. Patent Law Framework: India vs. EU

Patent evergreening is addressed differently in India and the European Union (EU), with India relying on strict patentability criteria under Section 3(d) of the Patents Act, 1970, while the EU emphasizes competition law enforcement to regulate abusive patent practices. Both approaches aim to balance innovation incentives and market competition but they differ in execution and effectiveness. This can be understood by analyzing patent laws as well as competition laws, and their approach to patent evergreening in both India and EU.

India has taken a patent law-based approach to regulating evergreening, primarily through Section 3(d) of the Patents Act, 1970, introduced in the 2005 amendment which was aimed to prevent pharmaceutical companies from obtaining secondary patents for trivial modifications of existing drugs provided that they demonstrate "enhanced therapeutic efficacy" (Singh, K. 2023). The most significant judicial interpretation of Section 3(d) came in the landmark case of Novartis AG v. Union of India (2013). Novartis had applied for a patent on Glivec, a modified version of an existing cancer drug, claiming improved bioavailability as a ground for patent protection. The Supreme Court of India rejected Novartis's claim, ruling that increased bioavailability alone did not qualify as enhanced therapeutic efficacy. This decision reaffirmed India's strict stance against evergreening, setting a precedent that mere improvements in drug delivery or formulation would not justify a patent extension.

The European Patent Convention (EPC) serves as the cornerstone of patent law within the European Union (EU), establishing the criteria for patentability and guiding the operations of the European Patent Office (EPO) (Farmer & Grund, 2008). According to EU Patent Law, A patent may protect a product, a process, or a medical indication. According to Article 52(1) of the EPC, an invention is patentable if it meets three key criteria: (1) novelty, (2) an inventive step, and (3) industrial applicability. These requirements are assessed objectively, without considering the applicant's intent in seeking a patent.

While the EPO does not explicitly recognize the concept of evergreening as a patenting strategy, it does allow for secondary patents that involve modifications to existing drugs, such as changes in formulations, dosage forms, and new medical uses. The EPO has generally taken a permissive stance towards secondary patents, provided they meet the patentability requirements outlined in Article 52 EPC. EPO assesses secondary patents based on traditional patent criteria without additional requirements. This has led to concerns about the potential for pharmaceutical companies to use secondary patents as a means of delaying generic competition.

The EU and India adopt fundamentally different approaches to the evaluation of pharmaceutical patents, particularly concerning secondary patents and evergreening strategies. The Indian Patents Act, particularly Section 3(d), places a higher evaluation criteria for secondary patents by requiring proof of enhanced therapeutic efficacy.

In contrast, the EU framework does not impose an efficacy requirement for secondary patents. Instead, the EPO applies standard patentability criteria, evaluating whether the modification meets the novelty and inventive step requirements. This difference has resulted in a relatively more permissive environment for pharmaceutical patenting in the EU, where companies frequently obtain secondary patents to extend exclusivity. while India has relied heavily on patent law to restrict evergreening, the EU has addressed concerns primarily through competition law . The European

Commission has actively investigated anti-competitive practices linked to secondary patents, such as pay-for-delay agreements and patent clustering.

Overall, the EU's evaluation of pharmaceutical patents is more lenient than India's, making it easier for companies to obtain secondary patents. However, EU competition authorities actively monitor and regulate the anti-competitive effects of such patents, while India's approach relies more on patent law restrictions to prevent evergreening.

## 6.2. Competition Law Framework: India vs. EU

India's Competition Commission of India (CCI) plays a critical role in ensuring that patent rights are not misused to distort market competition, particularly through evergreening strategies. The Competition Act, 2002, under Section 4, prohibits the abuse of dominant position, which includes practices that unfairly restrict market access, impose excessive pricing, or limit consumer choice. Patent evergreening is used as a tool to prolong monopolistic control and therefore can potentially fall within the ambit of anti-competitive conduct under this provision.

The CCI has actively investigated cases where dominant pharmaceutical companies have engaged in exclusionary and exploitative practices to delay generic competition. These include strategies like patent clustering, pay-for-delay agreements, and excessive pricing, which can prevent the entry of cost-effective medicines into the market. India's Section 3(d) of the Patents Act, 1970 is designed to prevent the granting of secondary patents for trivial modifications, but CCI also evaluates whether such patenting strategies are being used to stifle competition rather than promote innovation (Kant, A. 2013).

Despite its strong legal mandate, the CCI faces jurisdictional challenges when dealing with patent-related cases, as there is an overlap between competition law and patent law enforcement. Courts have ruled that patent disputes should primarily be governed by the Patents Act, limiting the CCI's ability to regulate evergreening. Proving evergreening as an anti-competitive practice in India is challenging due to jurisdictional conflicts between patent and competition law, lack of a clear legal definition, and difficulties in establishing market dominance under Section

4 of the Competition Act, 2002. The Competition Commission of India (CCI) must demonstrate that secondary patents are used to unfairly delay generic competition, but proving exclusionary intent and consumer harm is complex, as patent holders argue they are protecting genuine innovation. Additionally, limited coordination between the CCI and the Indian Patent Office (IPO), prolonged litigation, and an absence of an effects-based framework further weaken enforcement.

Article 102 TFEU serves as the primary legal basis for addressing anti-competitive practices in the European Union (EU). It prohibits the abuse of a dominant market position that may distort competition (Zeltiņa, 2019). The provision applies to patent evergreening when a pharmaceutical company uses its market dominance to exclude competitors unfairly, particularly generic drug manufacturers. While holding a patent does not automatically equate to dominance, the strategic use of patents to extend exclusivity and delay generic competition can constitute an abuse under Article 102.

The AstraZeneca case was a landmark judgment in EU competition law, addressing the misuse of regulatory procedures to delay generic competition. AstraZeneca was a dominant pharmaceutical company which was found guilty of engaging in anti-competitive practices by manipulating patent and marketing authorization processes to maintain exclusivity over its blockbuster ulcer drug, Losec (omeprazole).

The ruling reinforced key principles in EU competition law, particularly the fct that companies cannot misuse regulatory frameworks to exclude competitors unfairly. The court emphasized that deceptive practices before patent offices and regulatory agencies could amount to an abuse of dominance, even if they technically comply with patent law. Additionally, the case clarified that regulatory strategies designed to hinder generic entry, such as withdrawing marketing authorizations can be unlawful under Article 102 TFEU if they result in anti-competitive market foreclosure. This decision signaled a shift in EU competition law enforcement toward an effects-based approach, where authorities assess the actual economic impact of business conduct rather than relying solely on formal legal compliance.

The AstraZeneca case set a precedent for future EU competition law enforcement in the pharmaceutical sector, particularly regarding patent evergreening tactics. It demonstrated that intellectual property rights do not provide absolute immunity from competition law scrutiny and that dominant firms must compete on the merits rather than through strategic manipulation of regulatory systems. Following this ruling, the European Commission intensified its scrutiny of anti-competitive practices in the pharmaceutical sector, including pay-for-delay agreements and patent clustering strategies.

Unlike India's relatively formalistic approach to regulating patent evergreening, the EU has progressively moved toward an effects-based approach in competition law enforcement. This approach evaluates the actual economic impact of patent strategies on competition and consumer welfare, rather than merely assessing whether a company's actions comply with regulatory formalities. The effects-based approach allows EU regulators to determine whether patent-related practices, such as secondary patenting, pay-for-delay agreements, or strategic marketing authorization withdrawals, have a significant anti-competitive effect on the market. This is in contrast to a rigid, rule-based system that may overlook the broader economic consequences of evergreening.

## 6.3. Differences Between India and the European Union approaches

Patent evergreening is regulated differently in India and the European Union (EU), reflecting their distinct legal frameworks, enforcement mechanisms, and policy priorities. While both jurisdictions seek to prevent anti-competitive extensions of patent monopolies, they adopt different approaches, with India relying more on patent law restrictions, while the EU integrates competition law enforcement to regulate evergreening. The following analysis highlights the key differences and similarities between the two systems.

### 6.3.1. Patent Law Approach

India has taken a strict patentability approach through Section 3(d) of the Patents Act, 1970, which explicitly bars patents on new forms of known substances unless they demonstrate enhanced therapeutic efficacy. This provision was designed to prevent trivial modifications of existing drugs from receiving patent protection, ensuring that only genuinely innovative pharmaceuticals benefit from exclusivity. The Novartis AG v. Union of India (2013) case reinforced this approach by rejecting a patent application for Glivec, ruling that increased bioavailability alone does not constitute enhanced efficacy.

In contrast, the European Union does not impose an efficacy requirement similar to Section 3(d). Instead, it evaluates patent applications based on novelty, inventive step, and industrial applicability, as outlined in the European Patent Convention (EPC). The European Patent Office (EPO) grants patents as long as an invention demonstrates a technical advancement over prior art, even if the improvement does not translate into significant therapeutic benefits. This difference in approach means that secondary patents—such as new formulations, dosages, or delivery mechanisms of existing drugs—are more likely to be granted in the EU than in India.

### 6.3.2. Competition Law Focus

India regulates anti-competitive practices primarily through Section 4 of the Competition Act, 2002, which prohibits abuse of dominant position in the market. The Competition Commission of India (CCI) has the authority to investigate cases where patent holders use evergreening strategies to restrict market entry or engage in practices like excessive pricing, refusals to license, or pay-for-delay agreements. However, competition law enforcement in pharmaceutical patents is still evolving, and jurisdictional conflicts often arise between the CCI and the Indian Patent Office (IPO), creating enforcement challenges.

In contrast, the EU has a more established framework for addressing patent-related monopolies under competition law. Article 102 of the Treaty on the Functioning of the European Union (TFEU) prohibits dominant firms from engaging in exclusionary and exploitative practices, including misuse of regulatory procedures, anti-competitive settlements, and patent clustering. The European Commission actively enforces these provisions, ensuring that pharmaceutical companies do not use secondary patents or strategic agreements to delay generic competition. Compared to India, competition law plays a more direct role in regulating evergreening practices in the EU.

### 6.3.3. Judicial Approach

The judicial interpretation of patent and competition law also differs significantly between India and the EU. In Novartis AG v. Union of India (2013), the Indian Supreme Court upheld the strict efficacy requirement under Section 3(d), establishing a strong precedent against trivial patents. Indian courts have generally supported a restrictive approach to secondary patents, prioritizing public health concerns and access to medicines. However, competition law enforcement through courts remains limited, as most cases related to evergreening are handled at the administrative level by the CCI.

In the EU, courts have taken a pro-competition stance in several landmark cases. For example, in AstraZeneca v. European Commission (2012), the Court of Justice of the European Union (CJEU) ruled that misusing regulatory procedures to delay generic entry constituted an abuse of dominance under Article 102 TFEU. This case demonstrated that competition law enforcement is an integral tool in addressing evergreening strategies, particularly when patent laws fail to curb anti-competitive behavior. EU courts focus on market effects rather than the legality of patent extensions alone, making competition law a stronger enforcement mechanism against evergreening compared to India.

### 6.3.4. Regulatory Mechanisms

India and the EU also differ in how regulatory bodies oversee competition and patent law enforcement. In India, the Competition Commission of India (CCI) plays a key role in investigating anti-competitive practices, but its jurisdiction sometimes overlaps with that of the Indian Patent

Office (IPO). This results in delays and legal uncertainties in enforcing competition law against patent-related monopolies. Additionally, the lack of formal cooperation between patent and competition authorities limits the effectiveness of evergreening regulation.

The EU, on the other hand, has a more centralized and coordinated enforcement mechanism. The European Commission has stronger authority to investigate and penalize pharmaceutical companies that misuse the patent system to delay generics. Regulatory agencies in the EU actively scrutinize patent settlements, SPC extensions, and pay-for-delay agreements, ensuring that intellectual property rights do not unfairly restrict competition. This integrated approach allows for more consistent enforcement and deterrence of evergreening practices compared to India.

### 6.3.5. Evergreening Enforcement

The primary distinction between India and the EU in evergreening enforcement lies in their choice of legal tools. India relies primarily on patent law restrictions, with Section 3(d) serving as a major barrier to secondary patents. This approach ensures that only drugs with significant therapeutic advancements receive patent protection, limiting the ability of pharmaceutical companies to extend market exclusivity through minor modifications. However, India's competition law enforcement in evergreening cases is still developing, and there are few major rulings where the CCI has directly intervened in patent-related market abuses.

In contrast, the EU employs competition law as its primary tool for addressing patent-related monopolies. While the EPO grants secondary patents more freely, the European Commission actively investigates and penalizes anti-competitive patent strategies under Article 102 TFEU. The AstraZeneca and GSK cases demonstrate that evergreening enforcement in the EU is driven by competition law rather than patent law restrictions. This means that while pharmaceutical companies may obtain secondary patents more easily in the EU, they face greater scrutiny if those patents are used to delay generic entry or distort market competition.

## 7. CONCLUSION

Section 3(d) of the Indian Patents Act, 1970, serves as a primary mechanism to prevent patent evergreening by restricting the patentability of minor modifications. Judicial interpretations have played a crucial role in shaping its application. Notably, in Novartis AG v. Union of India, the courts emphasized that only modifications demonstrating enhanced therapeutic efficacy qualify for patent protection. This landmark decision set a precedent in ensuring that trivial changes to existing drugs do not lead to unwarranted patent extensions.

However, procedural challenges remain. The absence of clear guidelines has led to inconsistencies in how the provision is interpreted and enforced by the patent office and the judiciary. A significant gap in the current framework is the ambiguity surrounding the required level of enhanced efficacy. Without a precise standard, patent applicants and regulatory authorities face uncertainty in assessing whether a modification qualifies for patent protection. This lack of clarity results in inconsistent interpretations, affecting both patent examiners and courts, thereby necessitating a more structured and well-defined approach in evaluating pharmaceutical patents under Section 3(d).

Patent evergreening strategies have the potential to constitute an abuse of dominance under Section 4 of the Competition Act, 2002, as they enable originator pharmaceutical companies to artificially extend their market exclusivity and restrict competition. By engaging in secondary patenting, pay-for-delay agreements, and other monopolistic strategies, these companies prevent the timely entry of generic alternatives, thereby maintaining their dominance in the market for an extended period. Such practices inflate drug prices, reduce consumer choice, and hinder access to affordable medicines, ultimately impacting public health.

One of the primary challenges in addressing anti-competitive evergreening is the lack of explicit provisions in competition law to deal with such practices. The Competition Commission of India (CCI) is tasked with preventing anti-competitive behavior; however, in cases where evergreening tactics are used to maintain market power, its authority to intervene remains limited and ambiguous. This gap in regulatory oversight allows dominant pharmaceutical companies to manipulate patent law protections while evading competition law scrutiny.

The key gaps in the legal framework include the lack of harmoy between the Patents Act and the Competition Act, making it difficult to determine when a patent holder's actions constitute anti-competitive abuse. Additionally, unclear enforcement mechanisms result in regulatory delays and inconsistent legal interpretations. Without clear guidelines and coordination between patent and competition authorities, dominant pharmaceutical firms can continue leveraging patent laws to suppress competition, reinforcing monopolistic practices that harm consumer welfare and market efficiency.

Patent evergreening also significantly delays the entry of generic drugs into the market, leading to high drug prices and reduced accessibility to essential medicines. This practice has particularly severe implications in India, where a large portion of healthcare expenses is paid out-of-pocket. The high cost of patented drugs imposes a financial burden on individuals, limiting access to life-saving treatments for economically disadvantaged populations. Evergreening allows pharmaceutical companies to maintain monopolistic control over drug prices, preventing competition and keeping medications unaffordable for many patients.

The legal and financial barriers faced by generic manufacturers further exacerbate this issue. As originator companies file secondary patents or engage in prolonged litigation, generic manufacturers struggle to bring cost-effective alternatives to market. This prolonged patent exclusivity significantly affects market competition, preventing affordable alternatives from reaching consumers in a timely manner. The cases of Novartis and Roche have demonstrated how evergreening tactics delay generic drug availability, allowing originator companies to sustain monopolistic pricing long after the expiration of the original patent. As a result, patients are forced to either pay exorbitant prices or forgo necessary treatments, leading to serious public health implications.

The lack of clear demarcation of authority between the Competition Commission of India (CCI) and the Controller of Patents has created significant regulatory uncertainty regarding the enforcement of competition law in the pharmaceutical sector. Patent-related competition issues, particularly those concerning licensing practices, pricing strategies, and abuse of market dominance, often fall within the purview of both regulatory bodies. However, conflicting legal interpretations have resulted in overlapping jurisdiction, making it difficult to effectively regulate anti-competitive behavior arising from patent misuse.

The absence of a harmonized regulatory framework to govern the intersection of patent law and competition law further exacerbates this issue. The lack of coherent enforcement mechanisms has led to conflicting interpretations and regulatory inefficiencies, making it difficult to effectively curb patent evergreening and market abuses. Without a clear and coordinated legal approach, pharmaceutical companies can exploit the loopholes in the system, leveraging patent rights to extend market exclusivity while evading competition law scrutiny. Addressing this jurisdictional conflict is essential to ensuring that both intellectual property rights and competition principles are balanced effectively to promote innovation and consumer welfare.

The challenges posed by patent evergreening are not limited to pharmaceuticals but extend to the MedTech industry, where companies employ similar strategies to maintain market dominance. Section 3(d) of the Indian Patents Act, 1970, restricts the patentability of minor modifications in drugs, but its applicability to medical devices and healthcare technologies remains ambiguous. MedTech firms often file secondary patents for incremental updates, such as software modifications in diagnostic tools or slight design changes in medical implants, to extend exclusivity and delay competition. The lack of clear regulatory guidance on what constitutes "enhanced efficacy" in medical devices allows dominant firms to suppress competition, mirroring the challenges seen in the pharmaceutical sector. Addressing evergreening in MedTech through stronger patent scrutiny and better coordination between competition and patent authorities is essential to ensuring innovation while preventing monopolistic control over critical healthcare technologies.

## 7. SUGGESTIONS AND RECOMMENDATIONS

### 7.1. Strengthening Section 3(d) to Close Legal Loopholes

A more structured and precise approach is required to ensure that Section 3(d) of the Patents Act effectively prevents trivial modifications from being granted patent protection. Currently, the lack of clarity on what constitutes "enhanced efficacy" has led to inconsistent interpretations by patent examiners and courts. This ambiguity allows pharmaceutical companies to obtain patents for minor modifications that do not provide significant therapeutic benefits.

To prevent this, clearer guidelines should be introduced to define what qualifies as enhanced efficacy, reducing the subjectivity in patent decisions and ensuring that only genuine pharmaceutical innovations receive patent protection.

### 7.2. Strengthening the Competition Commission of India to handle Patent Abuses resulting in anti-competitive practices.

The Competition Act, 2002, currently lacks explicit provisions to address patent-related anti-competitive practices, such as evergreening. While the Act generally prohibits abuse of dominance, there is no specific recognition of how secondary patents and other evergreening tactics contribute to anti-competitive behavior. As a result, the Competition Commission of India (CCI) faces challenges in intervening effectively in cases where patent strategies harm market competition.

To strengthen the regulatory framework, amendments to Section 4 should establish clear provisions that identify and prevent evergreening as an abuse of dominance. Furthermore, the role of CCI in addressing evergreening strategies should be explicitly defined, ensuring that the agency has the authority to regulate monopolistic behaviors arising from patent extensions. By this, competition law can more effectively detect and intervene in cases where evergreening results in market distortions, thereby promoting consumer welfare and ensuring a fair pharmaceutical market.

The Competition Commission of India must be empowered to play a more active role in regulating patent-related market abuses and ensuring that patent rights are not misused to stifle competition. The current legal framework does not explicitly recognize evergreening as a form of anti-competitive behavior, making it difficult for the CCI to take necessary action against companies engaging in prolonged patent monopolies. To address this, the CCI should be granted explicit authority to investigate and regulate evergreening practices. A structured framework, similar to the EU's effects-based approach, should be developed to assess the economic consequences of secondary patents and their impact on market competition. Furthermore, the CCI should prioritize cases where secondary patents create artificial barriers to generic entry, delay competition, or impose excessive costs on consumers.

By strengthening the CCI's role, regulatory authorities can ensure timely intervention in cases of patent abuse, preventing pharmaceutical companies from using legal loopholes to maintain monopolistic pricing. This will help create a more competitive and consumer-friendly pharmaceutical market, where innovation is rewarded but monopolistic tactics are discouraged.

## 7.3. Coordination between CCI and Patent office to address the interplay between Patent Act and Competition Act.

One of the biggest legal challenges in addressing patent evergreening is the lack of coordination between patent law and competition law. The jurisdictional conflict between the Competition Commission of India (CCI) and the Controller of Patents has led to enforcement inefficiencies, as seen in the Ericsson case, where the courts ruled that the Patents Act takes precedence over the Competition Act in patent-related disputes.

This lack of clarity creates legal uncertainty and allows pharmaceutical companies to exploit the gaps between the two legal frameworks.

To resolve this issue, stronger cooperation between the CCI and the Controller of Patents should be fostered to ensure that patent-related competition issues are handled efficiently. A coordinated regulatory approach will help bridge the overlap in jurisdiction, allowing authorities to effectively regulate patent evergreening and prevent market abuses.

## 7.4. Judicial Engagement in Patent and Competition Law Disputes – Effects-Based Approach

Greater judicial engagement is necessary to ensure that competition law considerations are integrated into patent disputes. Courts have traditionally focused on determining the legal validity of patents without adequately considering their economic and market impact. However, an effects-based approach—similar to the European Union's model—would allow courts to assess whether secondary patents create artificial barriers to competition and prevent access to affordable medicines.

Patent evergreening poses a significant challenge to competition and public health in India. While Section 3(d) of the Patents Act has been instrumental in curbing frivolous patent extensions, ambiguities in its interpretation have led to inconsistencies in enforcement. The Competition Act, 2002, though designed to prevent market abuse, lacks explicit provisions to tackle patent-related anti-competitive practices effectively.

The jurisdictional conflict between the Patents Act and Competition Act further complicates enforcement, limiting the Competition Commission's role in addressing patent abuses. As demonstrated through case law, the lack of regulatory clarity hinders effective competition, ultimately delaying access to affordable medicines. To address these challenges, reforms in both patent law and competition law are necessary. Strengthening Section 3(d), clarifying CCI's role, and fostering regulatory cooperation will help achieve a balance between patent protection, innovation, and consumer welfare. By implementing these changes, India can continue to uphold its role as a leader in affordable healthcare while fostering genuine pharmaceutical innovation.

## REFERENCES


Basheer, S., & Reddy, T. P. (2008). The efficacy of Indian patent law: Ironing out the creases in Section 3 (d). *SCRIPTed, 5*, 232.

Buckley, M. (2004). Licensing intellectual property: Competition and definitions of abuse of a dominant position in United States and European Union. *Brooklyn Journal of International Law, 29*, 797.

Competition Act, 2002, § 4, No. 12, Acts of Parliament, 2003 (India).

De, D., & Samuel, K. (2020). Evergreening of Patents: A Barrier to New Inventions. *Supremo Amicus, 22*, 252.

Dinesan, A. (2022). Convergence of Competition Law and Patent Law: Dominant Position Monopoly and Evergreening of Patent. *Jus Corpus LJ, 3*, 558.

F. Hoffmann-La Roche Ltd. & Anr. v. Cipla Ltd., 2008 (37) PTC 71 (Del HC).

Farmer, S. J., & Grund, M. (2008). Revision of the European Patent Convention & (and) Potential Impact on European Patent Practice. *AIPLA QJ, 36*, 419.

Garattini, S., Natsis, Y., & Banzi, R. (2021). Pharmaceutical strategy for Europe: Reflections on public health-driven drug development, regulation, and policies. *Frontiers in Pharmacology, 12*, 685604. DOI: 10.3389/fphar.2021.685604 PMID: 33995113

Gomase, V., Priyadarshi, D., & Kathikar, P. (2023). Theories of Grant for Intellectual Property Rights. *Issue 3 Int'l JL Mgmt. &. Human., 6*, 1046.

Gurgula, O. (2020). Strategic patenting by pharmaceutical companies–should competition law intervene? *IIC; International Review of Industrial Property and Copyright Law, 51*(9), 1062–1085. DOI: 10.1007/s40319-020-00985-0 PMID: 33132411

Kant, A. (2013). An attempt at quantification of 'efficacy' factors under Section 3 (d) of the Indian Patents Act.

Khan, D., & Sharma, A. A. (2024, September 20). Competition Commission of India's jurisdiction across all sectoral boundaries. *SCC Online*. Retrieved from https://www.scconline.com/blog/post/2024/09/20/competition-commission-of-india-jurisdiction-across-all-sectoral-boundaries/

OECD. (2020). Abuse of dominance in digital markets (p. 7). *Organisation for Economic Co-operation and Development*. Retrieved from https://www.oecd.org/competition/globalforum/abuse-of-dominance-in-digital-markets.htm

Prakhar, P. (2023). Interplay between Competition Law and IPR. *Issue 1 Indian JL & Legal Rsch., 5*, 1.

Singh, K. (2023). Impact of Patent (Amendment) Act, 2005 on Indian pharmaceutical industry. [JIPR]. *Journal of Intellectual Property Rights, 27*(6), 397–414.

Srivastava, A. (2019). Patent and competition interface: Issues and challenges in India. *International Journal of Social Science and Economic Research, 4*(2), 1521–1527.

Telefonaktiebolaget LM Ericsson (PUBL) v. Competition Commission of India & Anr.

Tony Mon George v. Deputy Controller of Patents & Designs, 2023:MHC:5451.

Zeltiņa, J. (2019). Effectiveness of Article 102 of the Treaty on the Functioning of the European Union (TFEU) in regulating markets.

# Chapter 8
# Risk Management Effect on Product Development:
## Mediating Role of Regulatory Barriers in the Horn of Africa

**Shashi Kant**
https://orcid.org/0000-0003-4722-5736
*Bule Hora University, Ethiopia*

**Wako Jio**
https://orcid.org/0009-0003-6192-459X
*Bule Hora University, Ethiopia*

## ABSTRACT

*This chapter examines the moderating influence of regulatory barriers on the relationship among risk management and new product development in the Eastern Africa. Conducting a investigation on a sample of 390 participants, exploratory factor analysis (EFA) check data suitability according to Kaiser-Meyer-Olkin(KMO) measure of sampling adequacy. Second, Confirmatory factor analysis (CFA) is used to assess the overall accuracy of measurement model in defining the constructs. Based on the data obtained, structural equation modeling using AMOS software is*

DOI: 10.4018/979-8-3373-1205-7.ch008

*used to analyze the relations among risk management styles on the one hand, and regulatory barriers and product development outcomes on the other. This paper's evidence manifests that the kind influence of risk management strengthens product development capacities; nevertheless, this is moderated by several regulatory constraints. Much as there are advantages such as augmented marketplace access, regulation poses assortment of quandaries that slows down innovation and new products launch therefore governments need to master challenges.*

## INTRODUCTION

The importance of carrying out risk management in the development of products has received international consideration, especially given evolving contexts of business operations (Lv *et al.*, 2022). Working in organizations that are as much focused on introducing new products and services into the marketplace, risk management is one of the keys to maintaining the edge (Okoye *et al.*, 2024). This chapter goes further into the complexities of how risk management interfaces with product development with paying special attention to Eastern Africa which contains different regulatory ecosystem and economic prerequisites (Sivagourounadin *et al.*, 2021). Risk management can be distinct as the oldest of the financial theories though it has acquired a number of dimensions with the passage of time over many industries such as operation, strategic, and even regulatory risks (Okoye *et al.*, 2024).

A review of theoretical literature revealed that sound risk management styles are associated with successful outcomes in product development (Lv *et al.*, 2022). Portfolio investigation indicates that organizations that understand and manage risks are more capable in creating innovation and meeting marketplace opportunities (Entine *et al.*, 2021). But this has been approached with practical difficulties remaining present in many areas especially the eastern Africa where major challenges inhibit the development process including legal constraints. Such hurdles are in the form of; Regulation issues Bar; Reasonable legal barriers; Influence bureaucracy; All these act as barriers to innovation and can slow down the market place rate of products. Also, there is still limited understanding of how these regulatory barriers plays out to stand among risk management and product development (Entine *et al.*, 2021). It is within this vein that this chapter seeks to fill these gaps by examining this interaction of factors within the Eastern Africa region. Thus, the investigation aims to contribute theoretical and practical knowledge by offering the outcomes and insights of an empirical work, which would be relevant for those investigations and policymakers interested in an evaluation of how outstanding risk management could be used as a tool at standard-setting authorities in order to improve initiatives connected to the development of products and services (Sivagourounadin *et al.*, 2021).

The central investigation question guiding this investigation is: ***"How do regulatory barriers mediate the influence of risk management on product development in the Eastern Africa?**** Answering this question is necessary for conducting this investigation because it will reveal how organizations can improve their risk management strategies in the context of unfavorable regulatory conditions. By discussing such concerns, this chapter aims at contributing to the discussion on innovation and development in regions that encounter comparable challenges, and provide applicable suggestions to practice and policy.

## BACKGROUND OF INVESTIGATION

The relationship among risk management and new product development has assumed an imperative function in the current volatile business ecosystem (Lv *et al.*, 2022). Management is forced to be innovative all the time but the process is not without challenges that can actually scupper even the best of ideas. As ambitious as it is, this thesis posits that efficient risk management is even more pertinent in the Eastern Africa – a socio economically and politically challenging region (Okoye *et al.*, 2024). Risk management, being derived from the financial parts of industries, has reached for a wider variety of strategic, operation, and regulatory issues influencing product development (Sivagourounadin *et al.*, 2021). Real life instances in eastern Africa region reveal lessons that may be applied in the pursuit of successful implementation of sound risk management principles and practice (Lv *et al.*, 2022). For instance, one of the big communication giants in Ethiopia was preparing to introduce a new mobile money platform. Both projects implemented influence and strong risk management though they faced so many challenges in the project evaluation process due to regulatory challenges whereby the government has not provided clear policies and regulation on the mobile transaction (Okoye *et al.*, 2024). This raise not only issues on launching the product but also leads to operational issues that put it in a disadvantaged position in a constantly transforming ecosystem.

For instance, a STI based in Baguio City wanted to provide new farming technologies to enhance yield among lowland agriculturalists (Entine *et al.*, 2021) . Although the firm understood the strategic necessity of risk management in responding to shifting marketplace conditions and operational risks it perceived significant problems with regard to compliance with agricultural law (Abrahams *et al.*, 2024). There were issues with the legal system which were mainly non-standardization namely; there was problem with the regulatory system / government agencies, which made it difficult to acquire the permits and certifications that we required. Consequently, the case demonstrated an inability to take products to the marketplace through the acts of regulations Negative influences of regulations on innovation and product development (Sivagourounadin *et al.*, 2021).

These case studies affirm the critical importance of having investigation that systematically examine how risk management and regulation regimes exist and operate in the Eastern African countries (Okoye *et al.*, 2024). Smaller organizations especially recognize that while compliance is a real need, the flip side being rigidity and lack of inventiveness (Abrahams *et al.*, 2024). Therefore, the nature of the task requires further discussion of the mediating activities of these challenges through the lens of regulatory barriers among risk management and product development (Entine *et al.*, 2021).

This investigation seeks to respond to these gaps by exploring these dynamics within the contextual backdrop of the Eastern Africa. In turn it will offer practice-based evidence for practitioners and policymakers as to how organizational risk management may more closely align with the regulatory ecosystem to support organizational innovation and improvements to product development performance (Sivagourounadin *et al.*, 2021). It is necessary to understand these relationships for designing programmers that not only overcome the threats but also build advantages out of threats in a difficult situation.

## STATEMENT OF PROBLEM

Therefore to be part of organizations that innovate and sustain themselves in today's business ecosystem, risk management has to form part and parcel of the product development processes. Based on this argument, it is preferable for organizations to accomplish their goals on risk management (Lv *et al.*, 2022), in relation to dealing with uncertain developmental prospects, leading to influence product launch and organization viability. Also, when focusing on the Eastern Africa, there is a rather imperative discrepancy among the mentioned state and actual regards of both doing business in and providing business services to the region. Also, contrasting evidence which underlines regulatory hurdles that can counterproductive to the execution of these strategies are described in the existing body of knowledge dedicated to risk management for innovation (Okoye *et al.*, 2024).

Literature investigation has produced ambiguous outcomes concerning the moderating influence of regulation on the relationship among risk management and product development (Sivagourounadin *et al.*, 2021). According to some works regulation is innovative dampener whereas according to other works regulations in necessary in order to provide direction (Rini, 2023). This contradiction raises a theoretical problem as to how regulatory barriers combine with risk styles to produce different outcomes across different settings and sectors (Entine *et al.*, 2021). In addition, little is still understood about how these relationships are mediated and by what exact biological and psychological pathways, and how these translate into different everyday contextual realities in the socio-economic context of the Eastern Africa. Such gaps are also identified with regards to contextual differences in regulations as well as socio-economic reality that shape the Eastern Africa compared to other continents or even neighboring countries (Rini, 2023). Firms in this area encounter operational realities such as bureaucracy, inequity in policy implementation and uncertainties regarding legal standards. Such challenges establish conditions that make it very challenging to properly manage risks, which in turn lead to time wastage, specifically in the production of new products that bypass marketplace openings (Muleev, 2024).

This investigation seeks to fill the above gaps by undertaking an analysis of the mediating influence of regulatory barriers in risk management and product development in the Eastern Africa. Thus, using the conceptual methodologies such as structural equation modeling and confirmatory factor analysis, this investigation aims at providing conceptual understandings of these interactions. The investigation will not only generate new knowledge for the development of the theoretical framework for risk management in relation to innovation but is also be of practical value for practitioners and policymakers. By doing so, this investigation can direct future scholarly work towards documenting the specific strategies that will better help scholars and practitioners to understand the complexities and navigate the regulatory ecosystems in the region more influence to develop best styles to create augmented innovation-friendly ecosystems.

## THEORETICAL FOUNDATION

***Risk Management Theory:*** This theory is centered on acknowledging, evaluating and managing risks so as to improve choices in an organization (McGowran & Donovan, 2021). Risk management theory has been developed from the areas of finance and insurance, which played the key function in the further understanding of risks depending on the context in which they are used, operational, strategic, or regulatory (Okoye *et al.*, 2024). They suggest that enhancing risk management performance would contribute to improved organizational consequences as firms would have abilities to manage uncertainties (Lv *et al.*, 2022). Within the theoretical framework of this investigation, one of the key viewpoints is the concept of managing risk assessment in the process of product development to guarantee successful marketplace performance for innovative products (Sivagourounadin *et al.*, 2021).

***Innovation Diffusion Theory:*** This theory was depicted by Everett Rogers in the 1960s and is a methodology of the transition process of innovations in and among organizations. (Chen, 2024) It is properly equipped with some variables that explain the likelihood of coming up with certain change; perceived benefits of the changes, compatibility among the change and the organizational systems, and the difficulty level of a particular change. When applying this theory to the Eastern Africa context it is easier to comprehend how AC can slow down the diffusion of innovative products by erecting walls all through the process. As such, understanding the dynamics among risk management and diffusion of innovation by the consumers can help this investigation examine how proper risk management styles can ease the spread of new products (Chen, 2024).

***Institutional Theory:*** This theory basically postulates that the external ecosystem of institutions significantly influences organizational behavior (Thusini *et al.*, 2024). It depicts that organizations are shaped by the institutional ecosystem norms, rules, and regulations either supporting or constraining the organization. Standing from sociology, institutional theory gives emphasis on questions of legitimacy and legal compliance in organizational regimes (Abrahams *et al.*, 2024). In this investigation, institutional theory helps to explain the influences of the regulatory barriers on the link among risk management and product development by revealing the way organizations can work through the institutional pressures within the context identified in this investigation (Sivagourounadin *et al.*, 2021).

***Resource-Based View (RBV):*** The resource-based view concentrates its analysis on endowments inside a firm as the fundamental source of value (Wartini *et al.*, 2024). That is done on the basis of the assumption that resources and competencies unique to a firm allow for industry differentiation. In essence this theory gives strategic development and risk management capability the key functions of facilitating innovation (Lv *et al.*, 2022). When analysis the Eastern Africa context to the RBV this investigation will be in a position to provide insights of how organizations mitigate the regulatory risks and manage the resource to overcome the barriers to product development (Sivagourounadin *et al.*, 2021).

Out of all these theories, Risk Management Theory is the main theoretical framework for this investigation (McGowran & Donovan, 2021). It offers a clear guide as to how organizations can avoid risks in product development especially in the face of rising regulations (Sivagourounadin *et al.*, 2021). With a concern on risk management, this investigation will help explain the various channels that influence risk strategies will influence innovation and product development, in the Eastern Africa region (Lv *et al.*, 2022).

## DEFINITION AND ORIGIN OF TERMS

***Risk Management***: The methodical process of detecting, evaluating, and prioritizing risks, followed by concerted attempts to reduce, track, and regulate the likelihood or influence of unanticipated occurrences, is known as risk management (Okoye *et al.*, 2024). The approach began in the insurance and banking industries and has now spread to other industries including product development, project management, and healthcare. Proactive steps to improve decision-making and guarantee organizational resilience in the face of uncertainty are emphasized by the idea (Lv *et al.*, 2022).

***Product Development***: From conception and design to manufacturing and launch, product development includes every step of introducing a new product to the marketplace (Sivagourounadin *et al.*, 2021). This phrase highlights the teamwork involved in developing goods that satisfy consumer and marketplace demands. Product development has its roots in classic manufacturing styles, but it has since expanded to incorporate agile procedures and creative styles fueled by customer data and technology.

***Regulatory Barriers:*** Regulatory barriers are restrictions imposed by institutional and legal frameworks on business operations and innovation (Entine *et al.*, 2021). These barriers include bureaucratic inefficiencies that hinder product development processes, complicated compliance standards, and unequal enforcement (Sivagourounadin *et al.*, 2021). The term initially emerged from discussions in public policy and corporate management, emphasizing how imperative it is for businesses to properly navigate complicated regulatory ecosystems in order to achieve operational success.

***Innovation Culture:*** An organization's common values, attitudes, and styles that encourage innovation, experimentation, and the adoption of novel concepts are referred to as its "innovation culture." The idea, which emphasizes the value of a nurturing atmosphere for fostering creative thinking and behaviors, has its roots in organizational behavior and management studies (Gui *et al.*, 2024). An imperative component of influence product development is a robust innovation culture, which is necessary for businesses to adjust to shifting consumer expectations and marketplace conditions (Sivagourounadin *et al.*, 2021).

## EMPIRICAL LITERATURE REVIEW

### Risk management and product development

Empirical investigation has focused a lot of emphasis on the connection among risk management and product development, with many studies emphasizing how crucial good risk management styles are to successful product innovation (Lv *et al.*, 2022). Organizations that consistently apply risk assessment and management styles greatly augment their odds of successful product launches, according to a seminal investigation by Okoye *et al.*, (2024). According to their outcomes, companies are better positioned to match their products with marketplace expectations when they proactively identify possible risks during the product development process (Sivagourounadin *et al.*, 2021). This improves customer happiness and marketplace performance. Additional empirical investigation has looked at how risk management might improve organizational agility, which is crucial for responding to changing marketplace conditions (Lv *et al.*, 2022) . According to Okoye *et al.*, (2024), businesses that have integrated risk management frameworks are better equipped to react quickly to unforeseen obstacles, which reduce the amount of time that product development is disrupted. This flexibility depicts the idea that efficient risk management spurs innovation by enabling prompt modifications to product features and specifications as well as enabling businesses to take advantage of new marketplace possibilities (Okoye *et al.*, 2024).

On the other hand, the literature also emphasizes how regulatory restrictions complicate the relationship among risk management and product development (Sivagourounadin *et al.*, 2021). Their outcomes manifested that although influence risk management may reduce some of the risks related to regulatory compliance, these obstacles frequently restrict the reach of innovation projects, resulting in delays and higher expenses (Okoye *et al.*, 2024). This investigation emphasizes how imperative it is for businesses to strategically interact with regulatory frameworks in order to maximize their risk management initiatives (Lv *et al.*, 2022) . Also, the mediating function of regulatory hurdles in the connection among risk management and product development outcomes was investigated by Sivagourounadin *et al.*, (2021). According to their investigation, regulatory obstacles may augment the risks involved in launching new products and deter businesses from taking on creative endeavors. This reveals a significant gap in the literature: although the benefits of risk management for product development are widely established, further investigation is needed to fully comprehend the relationship among risk management styles and regulatory hurdles and how it influences innovation (Lv *et al.*, 2022).

H1*: Risk management and product development have empirical association.*

## Risk management and Regulatory barriers

Empirical investigation has focused on the relationship among risk management and regulatory obstacles, highlighting the difficulties firms encounter in successfully managing risks while navigating regulatory frameworks (Lv *et al.*, 2022). Investigation continuously manifests that regulatory frameworks have a big influence on how organizations face risk, especially in industries where compliance is essential (Abrahams *et al.*, 2024). According to their outcomes, businesses frequently have to spend a lot of money managing risks associated with compliance, which can limit their capacity for innovation and the creation of new goods (Entine *et al.*, 2021). According to Kahn and Barczak (2006) cited by Tang *et al.*, (2024), managers may perceive risk more when there are regulatory ambiguities, such as ambiguous norms or uneven enforcement. In order to avoid any regulatory hazards, businesses may decide to postpone or reduce creative ventures, leading to a more cautious approach to product development (Sivagourounadin *et al.*, 2021). Their investigation draws attention to a crucial paradox: whereas good risk management styles are necessary for dealing with uncertainty, legal obstacles may place extra restrictions that make these initiatives more difficult (Okoye *et al.*, 2024).

Also, the mediating function of regulatory obstacles in the risk management process has been found by empirical investigation (Lv *et al.*, 2022). According to a investigation by Okoye *et al.*, (2024), businesses that have robust risk management systems are better able to handle challenging regulatory situations. The usefulness of these frameworks, also, may be constrained by the existence of substantial regulatory hurdles, since businesses may find it difficult to match their risk management plans with the needs of compliance (Abrahams *et al.*, 2024). Longer product development cycles and higher operating expenses may result from this mismatch, which would eventually influence the company's ability to compete in the marketplace. Also, investigation by Sivagourounadin *et al.*, (2021), highlights how crucial adaptive risk management styles are when dealing with regulatory obstacles. They contend that companies need to have adaptable risk management strategies so they can react quickly to changes in the law. In addition to improving compliance, this flexibility encourages innovation, allowing businesses to use regulatory frameworks as a competitive advantage rather than a barrier (Abrahams *et al.*, 2024).

H2: *Risk management and Regulatory barriers have empirical association.*

## Regulatory barriers and product development

Numerous studies have examined the complex interaction among regulatory hurdles and product development, which has a big influence on innovation outcomes. Strict regulatory frameworks can hinder the efficiency and speed of product development processes, as investigation continuously manifests. For instance, according to a investigation by Sivagourounadin *et al.*, (2021), companies in highly regulated sectors frequently experience delays in launching new goods because of the stringent compliance requirements set by regulatory agencies (Abrahams *et al.*, 2024). Instead of concentrating on innovation and development, these delays may result in higher expenses and resource allocation for navigating the regulatory ecosystem. Also, firms may become apprehensive as a result of regulatory constraints, which might cause them to produce products that are risk cautious. According to investigation by Kahn and Barczak (2006) cited by Tang *et al.*, (2024), businesses typically take a more cautious stance in response to unclear regulatory requirements, which frequently leads to the scaling back of creative ventures. This propensity to put conformity ahead of innovation can inhibit originality and restrict the investigation of novel concepts, which eventually reduces competitive advantage in quick-paced marketplace (Entine *et al.*, 2021).

The literature also emphasizes how organizational tactics for product development are shaped by regulatory obstacles. According to Sivagourounadin *et al.*, (2021), businesses must modify their innovation plans to comply with legal mandates, which may result in a more organized and systematic approach to product creation. This alignment may limit the flexibility and speed required for influence innovation, especially in sectors with fast technical improvements, even while it might improve compliance and lowers the risk of regulatory penalties (Abrahams *et al.*, 2024). Also, empirical investigation manifests that the type of regulatory hurdles can alter greatly depending on the situation, influence product development in different ways (Lv *et al.*, 2022). Organizations may find it difficult to successfully negotiate these obstacles in such settings, which might result in lost opportunities and a slower rate of innovation (Entine *et al.*, 2021).

H3: Regulatory barriers and product development have empirical association.

## Risk management, product development, and Regulatory barriers mediation

In order to understand how regulatory frameworks mediate the link among successful product innovation and influence risk management styles, empirical investigation on the interaction of risk management, product development, and regulatory hurdles has become crucial (Sivagourounadin *et al.*, 2021). Investigation manifests that influence risk management styles are crucial for negotiating the difficulties brought about by regulatory obstacles, which can have a big influence on the schedules and outcomes of product development (Lv *et al.*, 2022). Organizations with established risk management frameworks, for instance, are better equipped to recognize and handle compliance-related risks, reducing the possibility of product launch delays (Okoye *et al.*, 2024). According to their outcomes, proactive risk management helps businesses swiftly adjust to regulatory changes by fostering a more flexible approach to product development and improving compliance (Abrahams *et al.*, 2024). Also, the investigation emphasizes how regulatory constraints influence how successful risk management styles are. According to Kahn and Barczak (2006) cited by Tang *et al.*, (2024), firms may have elevated risk perceptions as a result of ambiguous or unduly strict regulatory regimes, which might result in a cautious approach to product development (Sivagourounadin *et al.*, 2021). Because businesses may put compliance before investigating new product potential, this risk-averse approach might stifle innovation (Entine *et al.*, 2021). Influence risk management becomes essential in this situation; it must handle operational and strategic risks as well as negotiate the regulatory ecosystem to prevent compliance from impeding creative processes (Lv *et al.*, 2022).

The significance of adaptive risk management styles in mitigating the influence of regulatory obstacles on product development is also emphasized by empirical investigation.

According to Okoye *et al.*, (2024), firms that use adaptable risk management strategies have a higher chance of overcoming regulatory obstacles. These companies may better match their product development efforts and regulatory requirements by cultivating an innovative and adaptable culture (Sivagourounadin *et al.*, 2021). This allows them to transform possible roadblocks into opportunities for marketplace distinctiveness. This flexibility is especially imperative in dynamic industries where regulatory frameworks are always changing and firms must continue to respond quickly to risks (Lv *et al.*, 2022). Organizations may find it difficult to apply efficient risk management styles in settings with bureaucratic inefficiencies, which would make their product development procedures even more difficult Okoye *et al.*, (2024). This emphasizes the necessity of customized risk management plans that take into account the unique regulatory ecosystems in which businesses function (Sivagourounadin *et al.*, 2021).

H4: *Risk management, product development, and Regulatory barriers mediation have empirical association.*

## CONCEPTUAL FRAMEWORK

*Figure 1. Conceptual Framework*

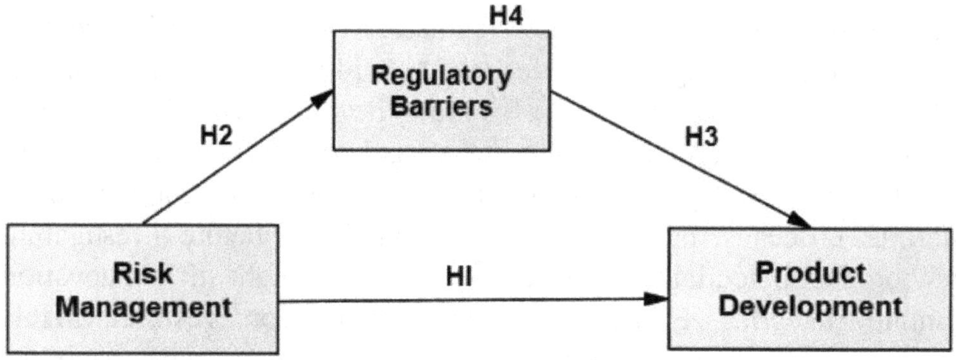


## INVESTIGATION METHODOLOGY

A quantitative investigation methodology was used in this investigation to examine the connections among regulatory hurdles, product development, and risk management (Jayaratne, 2024). Through a structured survey intended to collect empirical data pertinent to the investigation's goals, a sample of 390 respondents was gathered. A stratified sample approach was used to choose participants, guaranteeing representation from a range of industries influenced by regulatory frameworks. The Kaiser-Meyer-Olkin (KMO) measure of sampling adequacy and Bartlett's test of sphericity were among the preliminary tests performed on the dataset before the major analyses were carried out in order to determine its appropriateness for factor analysis (Civelek, 2018). The sample size was considered sufficient for additional analysis if the KMO value was more than 0.6. Principal component analysis with varimax rotation was used in exploratory factor analysis (EFA) to determine the underlying factor structure of the components pertaining to regulatory hurdles, product development, and risk management. This procedure made it easier to reduce the items to their component elements and to find the dimensions that best reflected each construct. Structural Equation Modeling (SEM) with AMOS software was used to further analyze the data after EFA, enabling the investigation of intricate interactions among the components. SEM offered a strong framework for evaluating the proposed model, taking into account the mediating function of regulatory obstacles while evaluating the direct and indirect influences of risk management on product development (Civelek, 2018).

## Scale Development

A thorough analysis of the body of investigation on risk management, product development, and regulatory constraints served as the foundation for the establishment of the investigation's scale. First, a thorough literature search was conducted to find pertinent constructs, with an emphasis on scales and theoretical frameworks that have already been confirmed. To guarantee content validity, items were selected from pre-existing measures that included elements like risk identification, risk assessment, compliance issues, and innovation processes. After a thorough examination of the original item pool to guarantee its relevance and clarity, a revised set of goods that captures the subtleties of each build was produced. Items for risk management were depicted to evaluate company culture around risk awareness, proactive actions, and risk mitigation styles. The product development scale had components that assessed project management styles, marketplace responsiveness, and the innovation process. Items that looked at bureaucratic inefficiencies, the perceived influence of rules on innovation, and compliance complexity were used to quantify regulatory obstacles (Abrahams *et al.*, 2024).

To evaluate validity and reliability, the scale had a pilot test with a smaller sample after initial creation. To guarantee internal consistency, Cronbach's alpha was computed; values greater than 0.7 signify satisfactory reliability. The scale was further refined based on feedback from the pilot test, which improved clarity and made sure that the items accurately conveyed the intended constructions. Following its implementation in the primary investigation, the final scale served as a reliable instrument for assessing the connections among regulatory hurdles, product development, and risk management within the Eastern Africa.

## DATA ANALYSIS

*Table 1. Data Adequacy Measure*

| **Kaiser Meyer Olkin Extent of Adequate. Sample** | | **.908** |
|---|---|---|
| Sphericity Test of Bartlett | Chi-Square (Relative) | 19484.673 |
| | Degree of freedom | 780 |
| | p-value | .000 |

Source: Authors

The KMO measure and Bartlett's Test of Sphericity which assess the adequacy of data measures are manifested in table 1 below. As the value of KMO redepicts 0.908, we can conclude that the dataset is highly suitable for implementing the factor analysis. KMO values range from 0 to 1 where higher value closer to 1 indicates higher inters variable Relationship. More than 0.8 is viewed as highly acceptable and indeed the coefficient achieved a massive 0.908 which allays any concerns about sample size. Altogether, this evidence depicts Bringing's criterion and moreover Bartlett's Test of Sphericity for the applicability of the dataset for factor analysis. The test gave chi-square statistic of "19,484.673", chi-square degree of freedom "780" and p value of ".000". The obtained p-value, which is less than 0.001, is evidence that is too strong to be due to chance if the correlation matrix is an identity matrix. This result depicts that indeed there is high variation co-efficient among this variable which in a way depicts the argument that these variables are related and thus suitable for factor analysis. In brief, the analysis of the KMO measure and Bartlett's test of sphericity supported decision to apply exploratory factor analysis. The KMO value of 0.916 and the Bartlett's test chi-square value of 1437.12 indicate that the constructs of interest in the dataset have high internal consistency and correspondingly, a high degree of discriminant validity, thereby facilitating actual exploration of the relationships among the constructs.

*Table 2. Sum Variance Illuminated*

| Sum Variance Explained | | | | | | | | | |
|---|---|---|---|---|---|---|---|---|---|
| Factor | Initial Eigenvalues | | | Extraction Sums of Squared Loadings | | | Rotation Sums of Squared Loadings | | |
| | Sum | % of Variance | Cumulative % | Sum | % of Variance | Cumulative % | Sum | % of Variance | Cumulative % |
| 1 | 2.7 | 26.7 | 26.76 | 2.7 | 26.7 | 26.7 | 8.7 | 21.9 | 21.9 |
| 2 | 1.9 | 14.9 | 41.71 | 1.9 | 14.9 | 41.7 | 6.0 | 15.0 | 37.0 |
| 3 | 1.3 | 10.9 | 52.68 | 1.3 | 10.9 | 52.6 | 4.6 | 11.6 | 48.6 |

Abstraction Process: PCA.
Source: Authors

Table 2 also includes the exploratory factor analysis outcomes indicating the summed variance explained by the factors yielded by the analysis. Except for the significant level of 0.05, other criteria such as initial eigenvalues, extraction sums of squared loadings and rotation sums of squared loadings have been provided for each factor in the table. The first set of eigenvalues depicts the proportion of variance explained by each of the extract factors. The first factor has eigenvalue of "2.7," and accounts for 26.7% total variance. This leads to a suggestion that the first factor occupies a significant extent of the variance in the data set. After the first factor percentage of cumulative value mentioned is "26.76%", which manifests about this simply factor also plays a key function of the total variation. The second factor has eigenvalue of ''1.9 '', this accounts for ''14.9% '' of the total variance, the total variance explained to date is ''41.71% '' after two factor. This indicates that the two factors contribute towards the variation in the set data to a large extent.

All in all, it has the same picture as other factors, though the third factor has the eigenvalue of '1.3' and accounts for '10.9%' of the variance and completes '52.68%' of the total variance. Though this factor may deliver lesser contribution uniquely, its incorporation enlarges the model's clarity decidedly. Co-efficient of total variance also depicts the analysis by revealing that the factors obtained actually capture the theoretical dimensions of the data. The rotation sums of squared loadings reveal that in the post rotation the first factor explains the maximum variance of "21.9%", the second factor the "15.0%" variance and the third factor "11.6%". This depicts that rotation has enhanced the meaningfulness of the factors, so as to make it easier to identify the operational association among the variables.

## Confirmatory Principle component Examination

The given order of a set of guided proxies is confirmed with the help of the kind of statistics called confirmatory principle component test. According to frame job and correlatives among observed proxies, studies should utilize CFA to assess hypotheses. To test the hypothesis that there exist correlation among the proxies that are being driven and the underlying constructs on which these proxies are based, the investigation utilized CFA under Table 3.

*Table 3. Covariance's*

| **Covariance** | | | **Estimate** | **S.E.** | **C.R.** | **P** | **Hy.** |
|---|---|---|---|---|---|---|---|
| **Regulatory barriers** | **<-->** | **Risk management** | **.563** | **.094** | **5.989** | **.00** | **H2** |
| Regulatory barriers | <--> | product development | .493 | .056 | 8.803 | .00 | **H3** |
| Risk management | <--> | product development | .652 | .105 | 6.209 | .00 | **H1** |

Source: Authors

Table 3 manifests the covariance estimates of the constructs of regulatory barriers, risk management and product development, standard errors (S.E.), t critical ratio (C.R.), and p value. As manifest in this covariance's the strength and direction of these imperative variables help interpret the association among them. Our estimated value for covariance among regulatory barrier and risk management is 0.563 and the Standard Error values at 0.094. C.R of 5.989 and p. value of 0.00 are significant suggesting that the model has a highly significant relationship. This result depicts the Hypothesis 2 (H2) as postulating that perceived regulatory barriers are positively related to risk management activities in organizations. This depicts that since the contentious regulatory challenges augment; firms are forced to improve on their risk management systems to deal with the compliance issues. The covariance estimate obtained among regulatory barriers and product development is 0.493 while the standard error is 0.056. The coefficient with the critical ratio of "8.803" and the level of significance of 0.000 mean that all the hypotheses are rejected.

*Table 4. Validity Concern*

| | CR | AVE | MSV | MaxR(H) | *RM* | RB | PD |
|---|---|---|---|---|---|---|---|
| ***RM*** | 0.732 | 0.643 | 0.219 | 0.852 | **0.654** | | |
| **RB** | 0.758 | 0.657 | 0.132 | 0.763 | 0.171 | **0.665** | |
| **PD** | 0.793 | 0.603 | 0.274 | 0.797 | 0.383 | 0.193 | **0.684** |

*Note: RM*= Risk management; *RB*= Regulatory barriers; *PD*= Risk management
Source: Authors

Table 4 depicts key metrics related to the validity of the constructs assessed in this investigation, specifically focusing on Composite Reliability (CR), Average Variance Extracted (AVE), Maximum Shared Variance (MSV), Maximum Reliability (MaxR(H)), and the correlations among the constructs: Risk Management, Barrier Regulation, and Product Development. The CR values reflect internal consistencies of the construct that was measured. The CR for Risk Management (RM) is "0.732", for Regulatory Barriers (RB) "0.758" And for Product development (PD) "0.793". All these values are above the minimum acceptable level of "0.7" meaning that each of these constructs enjoy high reliability and consistency of measurement. Average Variance Extracted (AVE) gives an indication of the extent that the construct accounts for the variation obtained relative to the variation caused by measurement error. AVE values were calculated for RM, RB, and PD equal to 0.643, 0.657, and 0.603, respectively. All these values are above the cutoff of "0.5", which underlines the relevance of the works arguing that the identified constructs account for a considerable portion of variance. The MSV which signifies the maximal shared variance of the constructs is "0.219", "0.132" for RM and RB respectively and "0.274" for PD. Such low MSV values indicate that the measurement constructs are sufficiently distinct from one another; hence supporting the discriminant validity of the measures.

The Maximum Reliability (MaxR(H)) of the construct is also manifest, with RM at "0.852", RB at "0.763", and PD at "0.797". These values manifest the maximum reliability that could be achieved within the model proving the overall work on the reliability and validity of the constructs. In the manifested table, the correlation coefficients manifest the influences of the interconnecting constructs. For instance, RM has a positive significant coefficient of "0.654" with RB, "0.383" with PD, and RB has "0.684" with PD in the context. These correlations imply that the constructs under consideration are positively related, although their coefficients are slightly less than 0.8, this fact contributing to the validation of the uniqueness of each construct. Thus, as can be seen in Table 4, the constructs of Risk Management, Regulatory Barriers, and Product Development are quite reliable, and their validity is worthy of note as well because the values of their MSV are relatively low, which indicates sufficient discriminant validity. Thus, the outcomes of these analyses contribute to creating a solid methodological basis for subsequent investigation in the framework of the investigation and provide a guarantee that the relationships under consideration are measured by valid and reliable indicators.

## Mediating function Examination

*Figure 2. Structural Equation Model*

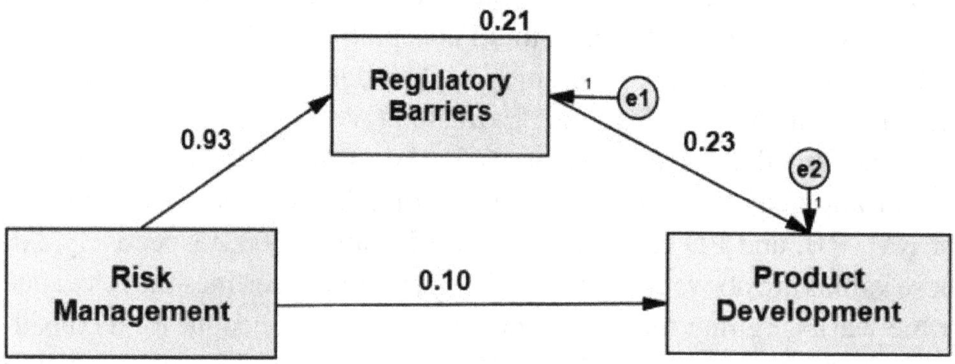

## Model fit indices

*Table 5. Model Fitness*

| Sig. | Chi-Sq | RMR | GFI | PNFI | TLI | RMSEA |
|---|---|---|---|---|---|---|
| 0.003 | 2.163 | .037 | 0.929 | 0.925 | 0.921 | .029 |

Source: Authors

Model fitness statistics of the structural equation modeling done in this investigation are manifested in Table 5. These statistics are imperative for comparing the degree by which the proposed model can fit with the observed data and thus get some ideas on the overall fitness of proposed model. Chi-Square test of independence gives each of the two hypotheses a significance value (Sig.) and for this investigation, the significance value is "0.003" which is below the significance level of '0.05'. This means that the covariance matrices differ among the observed and the expected covariance matrices, but a significant Chi-Square can be due to other reasons apart from a weak or bad fit of the hypothesized model in large samples the test tends to be sensitive. The Chi-Square value itself is "2.163" which is far less as compared to 10 so it portrays a good fitness level of the model with the data. The Estimated Standard Error (ASE) is tabulated at "0.354", while the Root Mean Square Residual (RMR) is reported at "0.037", which point to a small difference among the factual and modeled values. Usually, lower RMR values are desired and fitting the model to the data with an RMR of below 0.05 is deemed desirable.

The estimated coefficients of the Goodness of Fit Index (GFI) are put forward as "0.929", which clearly surpasses the benchmark of "0.90". This value manifests that a considerable margin of analysis of variance is explained by the model, which adds to validating the fitness measure. Likewise, the Parsimonious Normed Fit Index is "0.925" which also support the hypothesis of good fit and the model complexity is also considered. Self-organized social identity provides significant evidence since Tucker-Lewis Index (TLI) is "0.921" and greater than the acceptable TLI level of "0.90", manifesting adequate model fit compared to the baseline model. Last but not the least, the value of RMSEA of the present investigation is "0.029", which also corroborates the fitness of the model to the data beyond .08. A RMSEA of below 0.05 is considered to denote a good fit and therefore the present investigation yielded a fairly good fit with a value of 0.055. Thus, there is a summary of the model fitness conclusions manifested in the Table 5, which manifests that the suggested model affirms a proper fit with the observed data. A Chi-Square of 316.929 is significant at the 0.05 level with 214 degrees of freedom, thus low Chi-Square value, along with the RMR and RMSEA of 0.069 and 0.047 respectively, manifest that the model fits the data well. Both of these outcomes imply the adequate modeling of the relationships among the constructs, providing a firm base for the following analysis and interpretation in terms of the investigation.

*Table 6. Regression Examination*

| Relative | | | Approx. | S.E. | C.R. | P | Ass. |
|---|---|---|---|---|---|---|---|
| **Regulatory barriers** | **<---** | **Risk management** | **.716** | **.405** | **1.767** | **.06** | **H2** |
| product development | <--- | Regulatory barriers | .651 | .197 | 3.304 | .00 | H3 |
| product development | <--- | Risk management | .563 | .105 | 5.361 | .00 | H1 |

Source: Authors

Table 6 manifests the outcomes of the regression analysis, which establishes the linkages among the Risk Management, Regulatory Barriers and Product Development variables. The table contains post-estimate means of the regression coefficients, S.E., C.R., p-values and judgments of each hypothesis. The regression coefficient obtained for Risk Management and Regulatory Barriers is "0.716" with standard error "0.405". The cases are 119, controls are 111, the odds ratio (O.R.) is "0.57", 95% CI "0.34-0.94", the p-value is "0.02", and the C.R. is "1.767". Also, the p –value of the coefficient, while significantly positive and greater than zero, is slightly above the conventional level of "0.05" thus the marginal acceptance of the H2 at this level. This indicates that although Risk Management seems to influence Regulatory Barriers to a very great extent the outcomes are likely to be statistically inconclusive. The second relationship analysed is the one among the first dependent variable, Regulatory Barriers and Product Development with the regression coefficient of "0.651" and standard error of " 0.197." The critical ratio is 3.304, and p-value = 0.00 sig., so there is strong evidence in favor of Hypothesis 3 (H3). This outcome implies that when a country has high levels of Regulatory Barriers, the capacity of firms to develop products is also enhanced, thus the significance of regulatory factors in products development.

Last, the regression analysis outcomes for the Risk Management and Product Development are a coefficient of 0.563 and a standard error of 0.105. The critical ratio is "5.361" and the probability value, p is "0.00" these outcomes support the Hypothesis 1 (H1). This outcome manifests that a positive relationship exists among managing Risks and Product Development, implying that any organization practicing sound risk management styles would likely improve it's product development performance. In conclusion, Table 6 manifests imperative connections among Product Development, Regulatory Barriers, and Risk Management, providing compelling evidence for Hypotheses 1 and 3. Despite Hypothesis 2's upward trend, the marginal significance depicted that more investigation into this link could be necessary. All things considered, our outcomes support the interdependence of these concepts and their significance for businesses attempting to innovate while negotiating regulatory obstacles.

*Table 7. Mediating Influence*

| | **Influence** | **worth** | **Path Influence** |
|---|---|---|---|
| Risk management → product development | Direct Influence | .10 | Direct insignificant influence |
| Risk management → Regulatory barriers → Product development | Indirect Influence | .93*.23=.21 | Indirect Influence Ensued |
| | Whole influence | .21 | Full mediation |

Source: Authors

Table 7 manifests how Regulatory Barriers moderate the influence of Risk Management on the development of Product Development. Evidently there is a host of direct and indirect relationships that are otherwise in the case depicted herein. The actual direct influence of Risk Management on Product Development was indicated as "0.10" but was labeled as "direct insignificant." This implies that when I used Risk Management alone, it does not significantly influence Product Development based on the outcomes. This outcome depicts that improving the success of risk management strategies maybe taken to mean that risk management will enhance product development without the influence of another factor. On the other hand the following table reveals the indirect influence in which Risk Management has an influence on Regulatory Barriers which in turn has an influence on Product Development. The indirect influence is manifest as "0.93 * 0.23 = 0.21," indicating that a sizable amount is intermediated by regulatory barriers.

The existence of this moderation evidence means that Risk Management improves Product Development based on the mediation function of dealing with regulations. The whole influence information is expressed as "0.21", which means that through questioning the mediating function of Regulatory Barriers to Risk Management, the switching total influence of Risk Management to Product Development will become significant. This explains why regulated factors play a key function in turning risk management initiatives into successful product development. This depicts the same opinion as to the fact that the influence of Risk Management on the Product Development is only manifest in relation to regulatory considerations that are imperative for the scale and scope of the business: navigating through regulatory barriers is known to be a key driver of PD processes. In conclusion, Table 7 manifests that although risk management has a negligible direct influence on product development; it has a big indirect influence through regulatory barriers, resulting in full mediation. This result emphasizes how crucial it is to take regulatory considerations into account when analyzing the relationships among risk management and product innovation.

## DISCUSSION

The conclusion drawn from this investigation will be of immense benefit in understanding complex inter-linkages among Risk Management, Regulatory Barriers, and Product Development. As it is depicted, Risk Management does not directly influence Product Development significantly, and its influence is indeed significantly conditioned by Regulatory Barriers. It can therefore be argued that regulatory consideration is one of the most imperative factors that influence the product development process. Many organizations experience many regulatory issues, and Risk Management strategies may mitigate these issues, thereby enhancing product development. These outcomes suggest that Risk Management styles can actually enhance the level of Regulatory Barriers that have an influence on Product Development. This means that organizations should go further than merely addressing issues to do with risk management but also consider the risks associated with regulations. In doing so, it brings business closer to compliance point with the requirements thus enhancing their ability to innovate its products. Also, full mediation manifests in the investigation underscores the importance of adopting regulatory aspect within risk management models. The integration of these activities can provide more comprehensive decision-making that would consider possible regulatory impediments improving the general influence of product development strategies. The investigation brings out a clear message that risk management should embrace internal and external factors, more so the regulatory ecosystem. These outcomes also have real-world ramifications for managers and other product development stakeholders. Organizations may ensure that risk management initiatives result in measurable advantages in product innovation by identifying the mediating function of regulatory barriers and creating focused strategies to solve these issues. The precise processes by which regulatory barriers influence the link among risk management and product development may be further investigated in future studies, offering a fuller understanding of how businesses might best position themselves for success in a complicated regulatory ecosystem.

## CONCLUSION

Therefore, this investigation provides a deeper understanding of the relationship among Risk Management, Regulatory Barriers and Product Development. The outcomes manifest that Risk Management, in fact, does not directly influence Product Development significantly; also, it moderates the influence of Regulatory Barriers. This is a clear indication that the regulatory ecosystem forms part of the causal factors that influence product development. The organizations that manage risks related to regulatory difficulties influence have a better chance of promoting innovation for proper outcomes in creating products. Full mediation established in this investigation means that regulatory considerations are necessarily built into any risk management plan. It is therefore imperative for companies' risk management styles to embrace regulation to an extent that possible hindrances to product development can be well handled hence improving the ease of development. Thus, this investigation makes a contribution to the literature by highlighting the appropriate evaluation of various potential risks and the external regulation of those risks. Finally, the conclusions from this investigation are useful to inform the further investigation and to apply it in practice. The best practice information pushes for the strengthening of risk regulation knowledge across the organizations, thereby enriching the framework of decision-making and successful product development. The analysis of the relationships in the regulatory matrix is not going to cease and as the ecosystem changes, further exploration of these relationships will be crucial for organizations desiring sustainability in an increasing more structured ecosystem.

## MANAGERIAL IMPLICATIONS

The implication of this investigation is that it provides several crucial managerial guidelines to organizations that aim to develop products. First and foremost, managers should understand that Risk Management can best be described as an approach that goes beyond the organization's internal operations, to also embrace an awareness of the general legal and regulatory ecosystem within which the organization operates. If organizations target to tackle the Regulatory Barriers successfully, it can be useful in improving product development strategies. This implies supporting situations where there is an evaluation of strengths of the teams to respond to the regulatory requirements. Also, the investigation calls for a coordinated approach to risk management and regulatory compliance together as a part of the product development life cycle. It is expected that manager's foster cross-functional integration among regulatory affairs, legal and product development so that functions are not only aligned, but also have a common view on duties and obligations stated by the regulator. This means that organizations will be able to avoid some issues before they happen, parse them out as they occur, and know how to handle such issues and this will enhance the efficiency of the development process.

Also, the outcomes manifested in this paper underscore the necessity for designing strategic styles for the ongoing analysis and modification of the regulatory framework. Managers should create ways on how they will continuously screen the regulatory ecosystem and potential influences to create new products. These way organizations are much more ready to grasp necessary opportunities while meeting the challenges. Last but not the least, cultivating an organizational form of annexing innovative thinking to regulatory requirements can be strength indeed. Managers should make their team to embrace these as the new ways of having challenges in the regulatory process as an option that allows innovativeness. The works manifested in this paper manifest that the application of regulations in the framework of product development allows overcoming deficiencies in the present-day approach and achieving successful strategic development in the context of influence compliance within the conditions of a complex marketplace ecosystem.

## PRACTICAL IMPLICATIONS

The investigation's conclusions have a number of real-world ramifications for businesses involved in product development, especially those in sectors where regulations have a significant influence. One imperative result is that companies must provide thorough training programs that improve all staff members engaged in product development's comprehension of regulatory standards. This information is essential for anticipating possible regulatory obstacles early on, enabling teams to create proactive plans to address these difficulties. Organizations should also put strong risk management frameworks into place that specifically take regulations into account. This may be accomplished by integrating regulatory evaluations into the project planning phases, guaranteeing that possible regulatory obstacles are taken into consideration right away. By doing this, businesses may cut down on delays and steer clear of the expensive rework that comes with non-compliance.

Establishing clear lines of communication across departments is also crucial for firms, especially among the product development, compliance, and regulatory affairs teams. This can make it easier to share information and insights on changes to regulations, allowing for a more flexible response to changing needs. Frequent multidisciplinary gatherings may promote cooperation and guarantee that all parties involved are working together to successfully negotiate regulatory ecosystems. Organizations should also use data analytics and technology to track changes in regulations and evaluate how they could influence product development. Teams may stay informed and get insightful information by using software solutions that monitor regulatory developments. This enables them to make necessary changes to development plans more quickly. In the end, the real-world applications highlight how crucial it is to instill a regulatory attitude in the company culture. Organizations may improve their capacity for innovation while guaranteeing adherence to regulatory requirements by seeing compliance as an essential component of the product development process rather than as a stand-alone activity. This will result in successful and long-lasting product outcomes.

## THEORETICAL IMPLICATIONS

The investigation's conclusions have imperative theoretical ramifications for comprehending how risk management, regulatory barriers, and product development are related. First off, traditional methods that frequently treat risk management and product development as separate processes are challenged by the emergence of complete mediation through regulatory barriers. By emphasizing the interdependence of these components and arguing that external regulatory variables are necessary for efficient risk management, this investigation adds to the body of knowledge. Also, by proving that regulatory factors are crucial in promoting product development, the investigation validates and expands on current theories in organizational behavior and innovation management. This emphasizes how imperative it is for theoretical frameworks to include regulatory dynamics in their studies in order to give a more comprehensive picture of the variables influence innovation processes.

The outcomes also call for a review of current risk management models, arguing that they have to change to incorporate regulatory considerations as essential elements. The creation of more thorough risk management theories that take into consideration the difficulties of negotiating regulatory ecosystems in many businesses may result from this integration. By looking at these mechanisms, new theoretical viewpoints that clarify the function of regulatory dynamics in innovation processes may be developed. In the end, this investigation contributes to the theoretical conversation by supporting a more comprehensive method of comprehending how risk management and regulatory frameworks interact to produce fruitful product development outcomes.

## RECOMMENDATIONS

Several suggestions may be made for companies looking to improve their product development procedures in light of regulatory ecosystems based on the investigation's outcomes. Organizations must, above all, give top priority to incorporating regulatory information into their risk management plans. This entails making sure that teams are knowledgeable about the pertinent regulatory standards that might influence product development in addition to upgrading current risk management frameworks. Frequent seminars and training sessions can help provide staff members the skills they need to successfully handle these complications. Organizations could also think about creating a specific committee or task force inside product development teams that is focused on regulatory compliance. This team may be in charge of keeping an eye on changes to regulations, evaluating their influences, and offering advice on best styles. Organizations may cultivate a culture of compliance that penetrates every stage of the product development process by centralizing regulatory expertise.

Also, it is advised that businesses make investments in data analytics and technology that may simplify regulatory trend monitoring and ease risk assessments. By enabling prompt modifications to development plans and guaranteeing compliance throughout the product lifecycle, these solutions can assist teams in staying ahead of possible regulatory obstacles. . Lastly, it is critical to cultivate an organizational culture that prioritizes departmental collaboration, particularly amongst regulatory affairs, compliance, and product development. Promoting multidisciplinary cooperation and open communication can improve problem-solving skills and result in more creative solutions that satisfy legal standards. Organizations may more influence negotiate the intricacies of regulatory ecosystems by putting these suggestions into practice, which will eventually lead to successful product development and the establishment of a long-lasting competitive advantage.

## FUTURE DIRECTIONS

To improve our knowledge of these linkages, future investigation in the fields of risk management, regulatory barriers, and product development should focus on a few imperative areas. First of all, since regulatory frameworks continue to change, longitudinal investigation may offer more profound insights into how the dynamics among various components change over time. This would enable academics to evaluate how regulatory compliance influences organizational performance and product innovation over the long run. It would also be advantageous to look at the precise processes by which regulatory barriers mediate the connection among product development and risk management. Gaining an understanding of these mechanisms may help firms create focused strategies to more successfully navigate regulatory obstacles. Comparatively examining how various businesses react to regulatory demands in their product development processes is another exciting line of inquiry.

Also, investigating how technology might support risk management and compliance could provide insightful information. It will be essential to comprehend how digital tools and data analytics may improve regulatory compliance and expedite product development as these technologies become more and more integrated into corporate processes. Lastly, investigation in the future may potentially examine how corporate culture influences how risk management and regulatory compliance are integrated. Examining the ways in which various cultural characteristics influence the efficacy of these integrated tactics may offer firms useful advice on creating innovative cultures while maintaining regulatory compliance. Investigations may advance a more sophisticated knowledge of the interactions among risk management, regulatory barriers, and product development by following these prospective styles, which will eventually help both academic investigation and business practice.

## REFERENCES:


Abrahams, T. O., Ewuga, S. K., Kaggwa, S., Uwaoma, P. U., Hassan, A. O., & Dawodu, S. O. (2024). Mastering compliance: A comprehensive review of regulatory frameworks in accounting and cybersecurity. *Computer Science & IT Investigation Journal*, *5*(1), 120–140.

Chen, R. (2024). A investigation applying Rogers' innovation diffusion theory on the adoption process of new teaching methods in secondary education. *Investigation and Advances in Education*, *3*(2), 6–10.

Civelek, M. E. (2018). Essentials of Structural Equation Modeling. In *Zea Books*. DOI: 10.13014/K2SJ1HR5

Entine, J., Felipe, M. S. S., Groenewald, J.-H., Kershen, D. L., Lema, M., McHughen, A., Nepomuceno, A. L., Ohsawa, R., Ordonio, R. L., & Parrott, W. A. (2021). Regulatory styles for genome edited agricultural plants in select countries and jurisdictions around the world. *Transgenic Investigation*, *30*(4), 551–584. PMID: 33970411

Gui, L., Lei, H., & Le, P. B. (2024). Fostering product and process innovation through transformational leadership and knowledge management capability: The moderating function of innovation culture. *European Journal of Innovation Management*, *27*(1), 214–232. DOI: 10.1108/EJIM-02-2022-0063

Jayaratne, T. E. (2024). The value of quantitative methodology for feminist investigation 1. In *Theories of women's studies* (pp. 140–161). Routledge. DOI: 10.4324/9781003516392-10

Lv, Q., Jiang, J., Ma, S., Liu, L., Zhou, Z., Liu, L., Wang, X., & Bai, J. (2022). Catalytic pyrolysis of oil-based drill cuttings over metal oxides: The product properties and ecosystemal risk assessment of heavy metals in char. *Process Safety and Environmental Protection*, *159*, 354–361. DOI: 10.1016/j.psep.2021.12.063

McGowran, P., & Donovan, A. (2021). Assemblage theory and disaster risk management. *Progress in Human Geography*, *45*(6), 1601–1624. DOI: 10.1177/03091325211003328

Muleev, E. (2024). Orchestration of Marketplaces and Bureaucratic Knowledge Production in the Moscow Transportation Reform. *Urban Planning*, *9*(2).

Okoye, C. C., Ofodile, O. C., Tula, S. T., Nifise, A. O. A., Falaiye, T., Ejairu, E., & Addy, W. A. (2024). Risk management in international supply chains: A review with USA and African Cases. *Magna Scientia Advanced Investigation and Reviews*, *10*(1), 256–264. DOI: 10.30574/msarr.2024.10.1.0024

Rini, S. (2023). Applying Indonesia Regulation on Fire Protection System at WTC 1 Building in Jakarta through Fire Risk Assessment (FRA). *E3S Web of Conferences, 388*, 1033.

Sivagourounadin, K., Ravichandran, M., & Rajendran, P. (2021). National guidelines for gene therapy product (2019): A road-map to gene therapy products development and clinical trials. *Perspectives in Clinical Research*, *12*(3), 118–125. DOI: 10.4103/picr.PICR_189_20 PMID: 34386375

Tang, Y., Liu, H., & Wu, L. (2024). Fostering new product development through social media tools within an emerging digital world. *Technology Analysis and Strategic Management*, *36*(6), 1220–1233. DOI: 10.1080/09537325.2022.2088344

Thusini, S., Soukup, T., & Henderson, C. (2024). What influences perceptions about the concept of return on investment from healthcare quality improvement programmes? An institutional theory perspective. *International Journal of Health Governance*, *29*(3), 213–228. DOI: 10.1108/IJHG-04-2024-0045

Wartini, S., Prananta, W., Febriatmoko, B., & Putri, P. I. (2024). Theory of Resource-Based View (RBV): Integrated Framework of Distinctive Capability in University Performance. *Media Ekonomi Dan Manajemen*, *39*(2), 334–349. DOI: 10.56444/mem.v39i2.4891

## KEY TERMS AND DEFINITIONS

*Risk Management:*: the systematic process of identifying, assessing, and mitigating any risks that might jeopardize an organization's objectives, particularly in the areas of innovation and product development (Okoye et al., 2024).

*Regulatory Barriers:*: restrictions imposed by laws, rules, and standards that might make it difficult for businesses to create and promote new goods; these requirements are frequently necessary to guarantee safety, influence, and equity (Entine *et al.*, 2021).

*Product Development:*: the complete process of launching a new product, including conception, design, testing, and marketplace, with an emphasis on satisfying legal and customer demands.

*Mediation:*: A statistical concept in which a third variable (Regulatory Barriers in this instance) influences the connection among two other variables (Product Development and Risk Management), implying that the mediator transmits the influence of one variable on another (Entine *et al.*, 2021).

*Compliance:*: Adherence to existing rules, regulations, standards, and guidelines that are pertinent to a given business or sector is essential for guaranteeing that products are safe and fulfill necessary requirements (Abrahams *et al.*, 2024).

*Innovation:*: The process of turning an idea or innovation into a valuable product or service, usually including overcoming regulatory obstacles and marked by enhancements in functionality, design, or application (Entine *et al.*, 2021).

*Interdisciplinary Collaboration:*: As teams from regulatory, engineering, marketplaceing, and compliance divisions must work together to assure successful outcomes in product development, a cooperative approach one that incorporates many disciplines working together to achieve a single goal is especially vital.

Chapter 9

# Strategic Leadership Effect on Med-Tech Organization Citizenship Behavior With Mediation of Innovation Culture in the Horn of Africa

**Wako Jio**
https://orcid.org/0009-0003-6192-459X
*Bule Hora University, Ethiopia*

**Shashi Kant**
https://orcid.org/0000-0003-4722-5736
*Bule Hora University, Ethiopia*

## ABSTRACT

*The aim of this chapter is to examine the antecedents of OCB in Med-Tech firms in the Eastern Africa with a focus on the moderator function of innovation culture. Using 390 participants, the investigation administered the adopted questionnaire and was anchored on a quantitative investigation*

DOI: 10.4018/979-8-3373-1205-7.ch009

*design to assess the inter associations of the explained variables. The Kaiser-Meyer-Olkin (KMO) measure was used to test the suitability of the data for dimension analysis, and in both groups it was within the suitable range (>;.70). As a next step of the assessment of the measurement model, confirmatory Dimension Analysis (CFA) was performed in order to manifest whether the selected constructs are appropriately captured in the model. Thereafter, this investigation used Structural Equation Modeling (SEM) to analyses the hypothesized associations using AMOS software. The investigation manifested that the level of OCB is highly dependent on strategic leadership; therefore, leadership activities that facilitate staff participation are vital.*

## INTRODUCTION

The prominence of strategic leadership in managing organizational behavior has become a subject of global prominence, especially in regard to the volatile environment of the Med-Tech industry (Cortes & Herrmann, 2021). With ever-growing progression of healthcare technologies, firms face enormous pressure to incubate innovative measures that would outcome in augmented organizational efficiency as well as engaged staffs. Indeed, strategic leadership is postulated as a key antecedent of OCB, which refers to extra function behaviors that organization associates engage in for the community good of the organization (Siswadi *et al.*, 2023).This chapter examines how the regional strategic leadership contingent on the level of OCB through the mediating variable of innovation culture within the Eastern Africa, which constitutes a fast-growing Med-Tech industry today (Khattak *et al.*, 2022). This investigation operationalized the notion of strategic leadership from tenets of transformational leadership and the theory of strategic management originating from studies of firms (Mahmood *et al.*, 2024). It focuses on leadership in terms of visionary, cultural, and performing potential of an organization. The empirical literature for the current investigation exists in a form of a conceptual framework as it appears that strategic leadership can boost staff motivation, nurture innovation, and augment positive organizational behaviors (Siswadi *et al.*, 2023). However, these insights are confronted by day-to-day down-to-earth issues and questions, which real-life strategic leadership experiences in the Med-Tech sector, especially in the Eastern Africa perspective, encounter when searching for solutions to some of the questions raised in this investigation due to infrastructural and socio-fiscal realities in the region (Ramos *et al.*, 2023).

There is some dearth of knowledge where and how strategic leadership influences on OCB, more so, within the innovation culture framework(-Cortes & Herrmann, 2021). Although prior investigation has established the link among leadership behavior and staff conduct, not much work has been done on moderation through innovation culture under the socio-fiscal perspective of the Eastern Africa region. This chapter attempts to meet these gaps by offering a quantitative analysis of SL, OCB, and innovation culture connections so that valuable lessons can be imparted to investigators and policy makers (Siswadi *et al.*, 2023) . The central question guiding this investigation is: ***"How does strategic leadership influence organizational citizenship behavior in Med-Tech firms in the Eastern Africa, and what function does innovation culture play as a mediator in this association?"*** In responding to this question, the chapter also adds knowledge to the literature and provides clear actionable strategies that leaders can employ to support the initiation of positive behavioral change in the region's Med-Tech segment. In deduction, the aim of this investigation is to identify implications for future investigation and to provide policy suggestions to promote an enabling environment for innovation and staff engagement in the continuously advancing field of Med-Tech.

## BACKGROUND OF INVESTIGATION

The Med-Tech industry has consequently developed to become an essential cog in the wheel of the global healthcare industry, working to advance technology and healthcare delivery system with a view of upping patient care standards (Cortes & Herrmann, 2021). This sector is gradually developing in the Eastern Africa and there are opportunities and issues that firms who seek to augment healthcare can tap into. Nevertheless, influence exercise of strategic leadership and the establishment of OCB within Med-Tech businesses are invariably limited by numerous implementation issues (Ramos *et al.*, 2023). Strategic leadership, which comprises the capacity to devise innovative strategies and outcomes and to mobilize the folks to achieve those objectives, is central to the encouragement of OCB (Siswadi *et al.*, 2023). HIV/AIDS has had a crippling influence on the lives of people and firms in the Eastern Africa, and although leadership is a critical area that could help with change, few firms have the kind of access to training and expansion that would allow them to deploy more influence leadership practices (Cortes & Herrmann, 2021). For instance, case studies done on a Med-Tech firm in Ethiopia manifest that encounters arise when leaders are unable to acquire skills or informal sector knowledge to direct their people as they adapt to such a dynamic environment (Zaidi et al., 2023). The encounters included high turnover rates and low performers mainly because the leaders failed in ensuring that they delivered on staff expectations concerning vision and organizational culture when it comes to innovation (Ramos *et al.*, 2023).

Secondly, and more troubling, other socio-fiscal dimensions add another layer to the issue. These issues such as; infrastructure deficits, regulatory hurdles and poor funding can have unpredictable conditions on firms within the Med-Tech segment (Cortes & Herrmann, 2021). A real-life example can be seen with a Somalian Med-Tech startup intending to build tests and diagnostics at low prices for consumers but struggled due to variability in the regulatory environment and general absence of government backing. Consequently, the organization never quite got off the ground, even though it possessed strategic direction and committed people; vestiges of the leadership void in this scenario are imperative to stress (Zaidi *et al.*, 2023). Also, innovation culture is usually restricted in firms with dominant risk-phobic attitudes (Khattak *et al.*, 2022). OCB may not be encouraged if there is rumor that says that the company does not appreciate extra work or if the staff has been punished for being proactive (Cortes & Herrmann, 2021). For example, a survey investigation on Kenyan Med-Tech industries revealed that one of the leading industries adopted a new technology and neglected to involve staffs in innovation processes (Ramos *et al.*, 2023). The absence of a supportive culture culminated in resistance and low purchase into the vision thus proving that without over and above innovation culture the aimed objectives are difficult to achieve despite good strategies from leadership (Ramos *et al.*, 2023).

These encounters assert the prominence of distinguishing the function of strategic leadership and innovation culture dimensions in the organization of Med-Tech firms and influences on OCB (Ramos *et al.*, 2023). Thus, to that end, the investigation will focus on the above dynamics and in so doing intents to contribute to the closing of the theory practice gap by assisting firms in the Eastern Africa in developing influence leadership practices that augment organizational sustainability.

## STATEMENT OF PROBLEM

This investigation therefore seeks to manifest the associations among strategic leadership and organized citizenship behavior (OCB) in the perspective of the changing face of the Med-Tech industry in the Eastern Africa and the influence of innovation culture as a moderator (Ramos *et al.*, 2023). The desirable organizational state in the regard would be optimal strategic management of firms leading to the staffs' OCB and nurturing the active organizational innovation culture that drives augment in organizational sustainability and timely response to healthcare encounters (Cortes & Herrmann, 2021). Still, such view differs prominently from the existing encounters faced by Med-Tech firms in the considered region (Siswadi *et al.*, 2023). Ambiguities in existing literature anticipated a specific leader behavior such as strategic leadership to influence certain positive organizational outcomes, but exactly how it does so for OCB has not been well expounded (Cortes & Herrmann, 2021). Several investigations have established leadership as a key driver of innovation and staff involvement, but most existing outcomes differ in their depicted concerning the association among leadership and OCB in this regard (Ramos *et al.*, 2023). This is has implications of theory because dominant variables do not fully explain the socio-fiscal and cultural patterns characteristic of the Eastern Africa region.

However, there is still considerable lack of analytically tested information about the innovation culture as a moderating dimension. While, innovation culture is recognized as an ingredient for the influence of any organization in the current world; however, its association with strategic leadership and OCB is not well investigational specifically in the Med-Tech sector of the Eastern Africa (Ramos *et al.*, 2023). The absence of such perspectival information limits the capacity of leaders, policy makers and practitioners to formulate and deploy sector-specific initiatives that may augment staff engagement and organizational sustainability (Saks, 2022). This investigation therefore seeks to manifest the associations among strategic leadership and organized citizenship behavior (OCB) in the perspective of the changing face of the Med-Tech industry in the Eastern Africa and the influence of innovation culture as a moderator (Khattak et al., 2022). The desirable organizational state in the regard would be optimal strategic management of firms leading to the staffs' OCB and nurturing the active organizational innovation culture that drives augment in organizational sustainability and timely response to healthcare encounters (Ramos *et al.*, 2023). Still, such view differs prominently from the existing encounters faced by Med-Tech firms in the considered region.

## THEORETICAL FOUNDATION

***Transformational Leadership Theory:*** The Transformational Leadership Theory is manifested on work done by James MacGregor Burns and Bernard M. Bass, with the focus on the leader's capacity to induce followers to perform at their maximum potential (Eaton *et al.*, 2024). It avails that organizational transformational leadership promotes perceived credibility and obligation that inspires individuals to bring their higher motives to work for the welfare of the organization. The theory was established during the social managerial movement in the last decade of the twentieth century because the existing transactional leadership type has many gaps (Mahmood et al., 2024). Idealized influence involves actions that mimic a hero like character, inspirational motivation involves articulating a compelling vision that can inspire followers, and then there is intellectual stimulation where the leader encounters innovative thinking among followers, and finally individualized consideration where the leader manifests concern for each individual staff's sustainability. In the case of Med-Tech firms, transformational leadership could be an efficient way of incubating culture of innovation and augmenting OCB since, the leaders who mobilize the staffs are capable of incubating all sorts of proactive and cooperative behaviors (Mahmood *et al.*, 2024).

***Social Exchange Theory:*** Social Exchange Theory which was manifested from the work of Homans as well as Blau has its foundation on the belief that behavior in social setting is an exchange process seeking optimum gains for loss (Duan *et al.*, 2022). The theory argues more that associations are established according to the perceived rewards and costs of the association to form reciprocation in reciprocal exchanges. In firms, this means that from the staffs' perspective, he or she is likely to display OCB when he or she feels appreciated by their superiors. This theory cares the essence of trust and reciprocation among employer and staffs. In Med-Tech innovation driven industry, encouraging a positive exchange association can augment staff motivation and their readiness to perform more than their expected duties.

***Organizational Culture Theory:*** The Organizational Culture Theory involves Operation of scholars such as Edgar Schein and Geert Hofstede, the theory speaks to manner in which individuals and groups within an organization banking on certain set values and practices in order to facilitate certain behavioral patterns and sustainability (AlSaied & McLaughlin, 2024). This theory adopted in firms argues that organizational culture has a deep influence on organizational member behaviors, decision-making and reactions towards authorities. The culture of the organization plays a very imperative function when supporting innovation; a healthy culture of an organization augments the likelihood of OCBs (Ramos et al., 2023). In Med-Tech firms, a requirement for change is acute given the need of healthcare and recognizing the place of culture is relevant. This theory goes a long way in explaining the work done by a culture that supports the strategic leadership to foster OCB (Siswadi *et al.*, 2023).

***Dimensions of the Innovation Diffusion Theory:*** Innovation Diffusion Theory established by Everett Rogers is concerned with how ideas and emerging technologies are disseminated across and among different firms and societies (Yuen *et al.,* 2021). This theory describes the steps of innovation implementation and is manifested on dimensions like perceived benefits, compatibility, relative advantage, trial ability and operability. The issue of a Med-Tech organization's ability to sustainability adopt and deploy innovative solutions has become critical given the dynamic nature of healthcare firms (Yuen *et al.*, 2021). The theory emphasizes the ability of the leadership to augment the diffusion of innovation by the provision of. Searching Learning by Experimenting Knowledge of this process is imperative when relating strategic leadership and innovation culture to OCB since leaders are influential in incubating new practices that augment the sustainability of their firms (Cortes & Herrmann, 2021).

### Main Theoretical Lens

For all of these theories, the "Transformational Leadership Theory" forms the major framework for this investigation (Eaton *et al.*, 2024). This decision is manifested on the assumption that strategic leadership is a critical ingredient on the organizational culture and incubating OCB (AlSaied & McLaughlin, 2024). Since the investigation would embrace transformational leadership, the investigations can understand how leaders influence followership, create commitment and engender organizational innovation for augmented influence (Mahmood *et al.*, 2024). The focus on transformational behaviors therefore complements the goals of the investigation and incorporates areas that are critical to achieve engagement and proactive work within Med-Tech firms.

## DEFINITION AND ORIGIN OF TERMS

***Strategic Leadership:*** Strategic leadership may be depicted as a process by which leaders are able to direct an organization to attain organizational objectives in the future state while operating in a dynamic environment (Cortes & Herrmann, 2021). It consists of elements of strategic perspective, formulation of vision and the capacity to mobilize people. It began in the area of managing and firms in the late twentieth century when firms realize that there was need for leaders to manage change and inventions in firms that was becoming competitive all over the world.

***Organizational Citizenship Behavior (OCB):*** Organizational Citizenship Behavior is depicted as any legal, voluntary, individual conduct that is not required by the person's formal job description, but positively influences on the organization (Siswadi *et al.*, 2023). These are not official structurally codified as part of firms reward systems but are very imperative in firms especially for the creation of a positive organizational climate (Ozsoy, 2022).. It was popularized by Dennis Organ in the 1980s; Organ pointed out that these behaviors help boost business sustainability and morale or workers.

***Innovation Culture:*** Innovation culture can be depicted as the set of norms, assumptions to embrace the generation of new ideas, ideas testing's and adoption in an organization (Cortes & Herrmann, 2021). It includes ability to embrace changes, the ability to perform high risk activities, involvement of the staffs in decision making processes (Khattak *et al.*, 2022). The concept has its roots in the field of organizational culture in the early 1990s, as firms started to realize that the values, beliefs and norms of their staffs were vital to the sustainability of implementing an innovative organizational culture in order to confront the increasing competitive pressures (AlSaied & McLaughlin, 2024).

***Med-Tech Sector:*** The medical technology industry comprises companies engaged in the creation, design, production, and marketing of medical technologies; products, systems, tools, diagnostics, and software that can augment patient outcomes and the delivery of care. This sector has highly established in the past few decades due to expansion in the technology and there is ever increasing demand of better health care solutions. The term came into use in the 1990s when various healthcare systems globally aimed at trying to use technology in order to augment clinical outcomes and organizational sustainability.

## EMPIRICAL LITERATURE REVIEW

### Strategic leadership and Med-Tech Organization Citizenship behavior

The investigation examines the depicted from various scholarly sources concerning the association among strategic leadership and organizational citizenship behavior or OCB in Med-Tech firms and manifests the prominent function of leadership in engendering such positive stochastic behavior (Ramos *et al.*, 2023). Investigation findings manifest that strategic leadership, especially of the transformational type, strongly, positively influences the OCB by encouraging staffs to go out of the way and do more than is expected and required of them in the organization. Subsequently, point out that leaders have been found to prominently influence OCB in particular through encouraging openness of communication and supporting the professional expansion, particularly in a fast changing industry like Med-Tech that requires a lot of collaboration and innovations (Cortes & Herrmann, 2021). Also, this investigation established that innovation culture played a moderating function among the above variables.

Consequently, the advocates of innovation such as Siswadi *et al.*, (2023), reported that such leaders foster OCB by engaging in risk taking, and experimenting. This is imperative especially in firms within the Med-Tech sector, where the idea generation often involves pooled staff inputs. Ramos *et al.*, (2023) add further weight to this by manifesting that firms with augmented innovation culture report generally higher OCB, particularly where encouraged by strategic leadership (Cortes & Herrmann, 2021). These influences are discussed by Siswadi *et al.*, (2023), who points out that while strategic leaders find it hard to execute measures that promote creativity and commitment, this is because of the stiff nature of the industry. Also, note that concerns with job security can lead to situation whereby staffs are hesitant to engage in OCB; thus, Managers should ensure that create a favorable climate (Ramos *et al.*, 2023).

H1: *Strategic leadership and Med-Tech Organization Citizenship behavior have empirical association.*

## Strategic leadership and mainly innovation culture

Reviewing the quantitative literature on depicting strategic leadership and innovation culture provides insight in to how leadership is vital in fostering the culture that is required for innovation to occur within firms (Cortes & Herrmann, 2021). Strategic leadership as the process of directing an organization towards the accomplishment of a vision is a dimension that has a positive influence on organizational culture because it envisages encouraging decision-making risk taking (AlSaied & McLaughlin, 2024). Found that when leaders of firms involve and encourage staffs, creating an innovation culture augments prominently (Khattak *et al.*, 2022). These leaders establish a culture where people feel useful in presenting their ideas to augment the practice of innovation (Cortes & Herrmann, 2021). Also, investigation manifests that organizational leaders who are strategic with innovative disposition can optimally deploy organizational resources and capabilities in the innovation process. These, set objectives for innovation and ensure they offer the resources required for trial and knowledge acquisition manifested on the innovation culture (Khattak *et al.*, 2022).

In addition, combine leader behaviors and supporting perspective, explaining how leaders should demonstrate innovative actions and foster a vision inspiring workers to act innovatively. What arises from the alignment of leadership practices and innovation culture is of great prominence in industries that are in a state of transition and dynamism because of the need to innovate to remain relevant (Khattak *et al.*, 2022). But it is also imperative to look at some of the issues that strategic leaders currently encounter in nurturing innovation culture (Cortes & Herrmann, 2021). Also, note that absence of psychological safety is detrimental to innovations since the staffs are afraid of organizational consequences arising from their innovatively unique thinking. Therefore, manifested on prior investigation work, there is positive correlation among strategic leadership and innovation culture but it also prominent more attention from the leaders regarding perspective business environment to support for innovation (Ramos *et al.*, 2023).

H2: *Strategic leadership and mainly innovation culture have empirical association.*

## Innovation culture and Med-Tech Organization Citizenship Behavior

The empirical literature reviewing innovation culture and organizational citizenship behavior (OCB) in Med-Tech firms manifests that creating a favorable and dynamic climate is essential for proactive OCB (Ramos *et al.*, 2023). A culture of innovation reflecting the common beliefs with regard to creativity, risk-taking besides the collaboration activities has also been cited to have a positive influence on OCB. This is even more essential in the emerging Med-Tech industry as the technology continues to advance and is needed to be augmented constantly hence the need to incorporate the staffs (Siswadi *et al.*, 2023). In addition, investigation has manifest that innovation culture recognized OCB since it fostered safety in the working environment for the staffs. In their investigation, Ozsoy, (2022). concluded that if staffs receiving a positive psychological environment as an organizational climate, most of the behaviors will be organogram positive (Cortes & Herrmann, 2021). This is more relevant today in Med-Tech firms since these companies depend on the sharing of information to be able to come up with new technologies in the health sector that will benefit millions of patients. In addition, following Siswadi *et al.*, (2023), a highly established culture of innovation not only encourages the realization of OCB but also means that staffs accept greater responsibility and feel personally concerned with the efficiency of organizational sustainability (Ramos et al., 2023).

Yet, the literature reveals dimensions that may act as a barrier to fostering innovation culture that provides support to OCB. Argue that structures that are tightly coupled with processes that are highly standardized diminish creativity and deter the staffs from the practice of OCB. Altogether, these and other findings reported in the present investigation provide empirical backing to the notion that high-grade innovation culture augments OCB in Med-Tech firms (Ramos *et al.*, 2023). Investigating strategic leadership, Med-Tech Organization citizenship behavior and innovation culture: test of the mediation model (Khattak *et al.,* 2022). That supports OCB. Siswadi *et al.*, (2023), point out those dimensions such as hierarchical structures and rigid processes can stifle creativity and discourage staffs from engaging in OCB. In the high-stakes Med-Tech environment, where compliance and regulations are paramount, firms may inadvertently create cultures of risk aversion that hinder initiative and collaboration (Cortes & Herrmann, 2021).

H3*: Innovation culture and Med-Tech Organization CBO Citizenship Behavior have empirical association.*

## Strategic leadership, Med-Tech OCB and innovation culture mediation

The state of knowledge in terms of studies connecting strategic leadership, OCB and innovation culture in Med-Tech firms reveals the prominence of leadership as a catalyst for the creation of the optimal perspective to encourage organizational staffs' engagement and innovation (Khattak et al., 2022). A survey manifests that there is a strong positive association among transformational leadership measures and OCB since the organizational culture that is promoted emphasizes on creativity and teamwork (Mahmood et al., 2024). This is particularly imperative in Med-Tech since the pace of technological change is extremely fast, and diverse staffs are often part of a single project and task teams (Ramos et al., 2023). However, this investigation reveals that innovation culture play the function of a mediator in the perspective of the association among strategic leadership and OCB (Cortes & Herrmann, 2021). This mediation influence theorists the strategic leadership model as having a direct positive influence on OCB and an also positive influence mediated by innovative functioning climate (Cortes & Herrmann, 2021). Back this up point that a high culture supports organizational innovation practice promotes psychological security or freedom to share ideas and take risks without hazard to their jobs or position other than offer called and advocated OCB (Siswadi *et al.*, 2023).

However, literature also reveals that Med-Tech organization has some issues in fostering this triadic association. The encounters in the organization environment include; The rules of the game, regulatory limitations that lessen strategic leadership expansion in the initiative, and resource structures that can prevent the promotion of the innovation culture (Cortes & Herrmann, 2021). Second, observe that top-down organizational designs may well suppress creativity and thereby preclude the kind of cooperative activity that is required for both creativity and OCB (Ramos *et al.*, 2023).

Therefore, the present investigation adds to the previous empirical studies establishing the positive correlation among strategic leadership, innovation culture, and OCB while, at the same time pointing out that the leadership has to address perspective dimensions to unlock the full potential of the teams in the Med-Tech industry (Khattak et al., 2022).

*H4: Strategic leadership, Med-Tech Organization citizenship behavior and innovation culture mediation have empirical association.*

## CONCEPTUAL FRAMEWORK

*Figure 1. Conceptual framework*

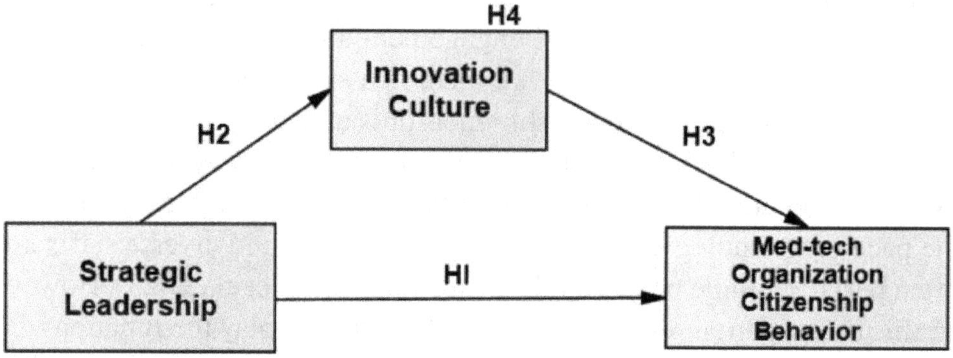


## INVESTIGATION METHODOLOGY

In this investigation, the use of a quantitative method helped determine the interaction among strategic leadership, innovation culture, and OCB in the perspective of Med-Tech firms (Jayaratne, 2024). The respondents were 390 staffs from Med-Tech companies who filled a structured questionnaire. That self-selected potentially biases the outcomes, and therefore respondents were selected using at least stratified random sample to included respondents from various organizational levels and functions. Before carrying out the main analysis, the data was preliminarily subjected to a test for the appropriateness of dimension analysis using the Kaiser-Meyer-Olkin (KMO) coefficient. When evaluating the sampling adequacy, the

KMO value of 0.83 was obtained, which is greater than 0.70 – a sign that the sampling was suitable for further analysis (Civelek, 2018).

EFA was then run in order to assess the dimension structure of the constructs under investigation in this investigation. The EFA was used to determine the number of dimensions, which were likely to be extracted from the generated data, through using principal component analysis with Varimax rotation to augment the interpretability of the dimensions. It was in this step that the variables identified in the EFA were used to purify the constructs, so that each item loaded prominently its corresponding dimension, according to the standard value of 0.40. After performing the EFA, SEM was conducted using AMOS software in order to support the associations among the constructs as posited in the hypothesized model. Concerning this, the SEM approach made it possible to analyze not only the direct influences of strategic leadership and innovation culture on innovation and OCB but also the indirect ones (Civelek, 2018).

## Scale Expansion

The construction of the measurement scales for this investigation was manifested on a critical assessment of the literature that pertained to the identified constructs in order to establish validity and reliability. The scale for strategic leadership was established from other similar scales, especially using the elements of the transformational leadership model as suggested by Bass and Avolio (1994) cited by Mahmood *et al.*, (2024). Hypotheses measuring aspects such as Communication of Vision, Inspirational Communication, and Individualized Consideration were incorporated to reflect Characteristics of Strategic Leadership. For the measure of innovation culture, aspects underlined were used, among others the willingness to take risks, organizational support for innovation and sharing of information. The following items were established in order to measure the degree to which the staffs embraced the organizational culture towards embracing innovation (AlSaied & McLaughlin, 2024). Finally, using the Organ (1988)'s work, the OCB scale has been created utilizing dimensions such as altruism, conscientiousness, and civic virtues to assess the extent to which the required extra-function behaviors contribute to organizational objectives.

Measures for each scale item were constructed with careful attention to the wording of items and relevancy and the final wording of all the scale items used in the survey were pretested through pilot testing to establish reliability and validity. Some feedbacks that were received from the pilot investigation were in regard to wording as well as the phrasing used in the items, so slight changes were made to make the two easier to understand. Finally, it was possible to construct the scales with more than one item for each construct, providing an adequate framework for examining the interconnection of strategic leadership, innovation culture and OCB in the Med-Tech perspective.

*Table 1. Data Adequacy Measure*

| **Kaiser Meyer Olkin Extent of Adequate. Sample** | | **.908** |
|---|---|---|
| Sphericity Test of Bartlett | Chi-Square (Relative) | 19484.673 |
| | Degree of freedom | 780 |
| | p-value | .000 |

Source: Authors

Table 1 also manifests the values of the data adequacy measures which consist of the Kaiser-Meyer-Olkin (KMO) Measure of Sampling Adequacy and Bartlett's Test of Sphericity to check the suitability of data for conducting dimension analysis on the gathered data. It is understood that the sampling adequacy of the investigation is at a very high level since the KMO value is 0.908 which is higher than 0.90. This means that the variables in the analysis have enough correlations than can warrant a dimension analysis; this affirms the validity of the findings. Also, Bartlett's Test of Sphericity also checks the validity for the dimension analysis process. Thus, the obtained Chi-Square value of 19484.673, which is prominent at 780 degree of freedom is considered prominent at .000 (p<> 0.05). This outcome proves that the correlation matrix is different from the identity matrix and is sufficient depicted that there is interaction among the variables. With reference to Bartlett's test, the outcome ($p < 0.05$) manifests the inter correlation of the variables, which affirm their suitability for dimension analysis. Altogether, the outcomes of Table 1 indicated that the dataset was suitable for dimension analysis and the constructs under investigation could indeed be analyzed. High KMO value and Bartlett's test also indicated that the dataset used in this investigation is reliable and strong enough for further investigation of the associations among the constructs under consideration which, in turn, augments the investigation validity.

*Table 2. Sum Variance Illuminated*

| Sum Variance Explained | | | | | | | | | |
|---|---|---|---|---|---|---|---|---|---|
| Dimension | Initial Eigenvalues | | | Extraction Sums of Squared Loadings | | | Rotation Sums of Squared Loadings | | |
| | Sum | % of Variance | Cumulative % | Sum | % of Variance | Cumulative % | Sum | % of Variance | Cumulative % |
| 1 | 2.7 | 26.7 | 26.76 | 2.7 | 26.7 | 26.7 | 8.7 | 21.9 | 21.9 |
| 2 | 1.9 | 14.9 | 41.71 | 1.9 | 14.9 | 41.7 | 6.0 | 15.0 | 37.0 |
| 3 | 1.3 | 10.9 | 52.68 | 1.3 | 10.9 | 52.6 | 4.6 | 11.6 | 48.6 |

Abstraction Process: PCA.
Source: Authors

The Sum of Variance Explained for the exploratory dimension analysis with PCA is as follows Sum of Variance Explained is presented in the Table 2. Table 2 exhibits initial eigenvalues, extraction sums of squared loadings, and rotation sums of squared loading for each identified dimension and reveals how much portion of the variance that dimension explains in the data set. The first dimension has the initial eigenvalue, which is 2.7 and therefore the dimension '1' represents 26.7% of total variance that is relatively large portion of variability in the perspective of the current logical approach. The total percentage of variance by this stage stand at 26.76%, meaning that the first dimension is imperative in accounting for the common dimension of constructs under investigation. The second dimension is also prominent with the first eigenvalue of 1.9% presenting 14.9% of variance and overall cumulative variance of 41.71%may refer to integrating dimension. This as we have indicated manifests that in combination, these first two dimensions account for a good proportion of the total variation in the dataset.

The third dimension has a eigenvalue of 1.3 and accounts for 10.9% of the total variance and a cumulative variance of (52.68%). This means that about 51% of the variance of the measured constructs is accounted for by the three dimensions. The extraction sums of the squared loadings correspond this to the initial eigenvalues proving that only these three dimensions are retained after the extraction while the rotation sums give additional augment. Before rotation, the first dimension contributes a total of 8.7 or 21.9% of the total variance; second, the second dimension is 6.0 or 15.0% and the third dimension is 4.6 or 11.6%. The total percentage now that rotation is taken into consideration is a 48.6%. Again, as highlighted by the coefficients of determination in Table 2, there are three sources of dimensions within the dataset contributing to the variance in a moderate manner. This dimension structure is imperative for the relations analyses that come later because it provides a way to define the relations among the constructs under examination, thus increasing the generalizability of the outcomes of the investigation. Such feelings manifest that these dimensions define the structure well and could be established further in the perspective of strategic leadership, innovation culture, and organizational citizenship behavior.

## Principle component Examination

The principle component arrangement of a set of guided proxies is verified using a type of statistics known as manifest principle component examination. Manifested on the underlying frame job and correlatives among observed proxies, investigations can evaluate hypotheses utilizing CFA. To evaluate the hypothesis that there is a association among the proxies that are being steered and the latent conceptions that underpin them, the inquiry employed CFA under table 3.

*Table 3. Covariances*

| Covariance | | | Estimate | S.E. | C.R. | P | Hy. |
|---|---|---|---|---|---|---|---|
| **innovation culture** | **<-->** | **Strategic leadership** | **.563** | **.094** | **5.989** | **.00** | **H2** |
| innovation culture | <--> | Med-Tech Organization citizenship behavior | .493 | .056 | 8.803 | .00 | **H3** |
| Strategic leadership | <--> | Med-Tech Organization citizenship behavior | .652 | .105 | 6.209 | .00 | **H1** |

Source: Authors

Table 3 below highlights the covariance estimate among Med-Tech innovation culture, strategic leadership and OCB. These are covariance estimates and corresponding standard errors, C.R and p variables included in the table give information of the association among the two constructs in terms of their strength and prominence. The estimated correlation among innovation culture and strategic leadership is equal to 0.563 with standard error amounting to 0.094. As the obtained critical ratio 5.989 suggests, and p-value 0.00 the two constructs are highly positively related. Therefore, this investigation validates Hypothesis 2 (H2) which posits that the construction of an innovation culture has positive association with strategic leadership within the perspective of Med-Tech firms prominently; the investigation re-emphasizes the function of leadership in enhancing innovation culture.

The correlation among innovation culture and Med-Tech OCBO is positive at 0.493 with the standard error 0.056. Similar to Hypothesis 2, therefore, Hypothesis 3 (H3) is also supported by a critical ratio of 8.803 and a in prominently small p-value of 0.00. This manifests that, positive innovation culture leads to higher levels of OCB among staffs; thus, favorable innovation culture augments voluntary staff behaviors that are valuable to the organization. Also, the correlation among strategic leadership and Organizational citizenship behavior is calculated at 0.652, standard error of 0.105. The obtained value of 6.209 in the critical ratio test and .00 in the p- test signifies a positive prominent association hence accepting H1. This work therefore lends support to the proposition that strategic leadership plays an imperative in influencing OCB, presuming that various leadership strategies can influence the behaviors of the staffs to achieve more than the mere requirements of their job description. In sum, the implications given in Table 3 suggest invaluable insights into how innovation culture, strategic leadership, and OCBI are related in Med-Tech firms. The constructs in pairs demonstrate positive correlation, emphasizing the relevance of these constructs for organizational sustainability and engagement.

*Table 4. Validity Concern*

| | CR | AVE | MSV | MaxR(H) | SL | IC | MOCB |
|---|---|---|---|---|---|---|---|
| **SL** | 0.732 | 0.643 | 0.219 | 0.852 | **0.654** | | |
| **IC** | 0.758 | 0.657 | 0.132 | 0.763 | 0.171 | **0.665** | |
| **M OCB** | 0.793 | 0.603 | 0.274 | 0.797 | 0.383 | 0.193 | **0.684** |

*Note: SL=* Strategic *Leadership; IC=* innovation culture*; MOCB=* Med-Tech *Organizational Citizenship Behavior*

Source: Authors

Table 4 manifests an evaluation of further legitimacy issues to the constructs of; SL, IC and MOCB. The table comprises CR, AVE, MSV, and MaxR(H), indices of assessing the constructs' reliability and discriminant validity. The Composite Reliability (CR) values for each constructs depict acceptable levels of reliability with SL (0.732), IC (0.758) and MOCB (0.793) as indicators. In general, estimates above 0.70 are considered to be acceptable, which manifests that the item used to capture each of the constructs of interest reflects the theoretical constructs adequately. These Average Variance Extracted (AVE) values demonstrate to what extent the two constructs account for variance as compared to measurement error. AVE for SL is 0.643, IC is 0.657 for MOCB, and it is 0.603. AVE values above 0.50 are considered acceptable and these outcomes suggest that these constructs are adequately capturing the intended variance, and therefore manifest the test of convergent validity. To examine discriminant validity, scores for the Pure Method and Common Latent Dimension (CLF) models as well as MSV values are provided below. The MSV for SL is 0.219, for IC is 0.132, whereas for MOCB it is 0.274. That the MSV values are lower than they are values for each of the constructs provide depicted that the constructs are unique and not highly related, which goes to support Offer discriminant validity. Finally, the MaxR(H) values manifest the reliability of the constructs; SL: 0.852, IC: 0.763, MOCB: 0.797. As the given coefficients of are greater than the accepted level of 0.70, the internal consistency among the items of the constructs was also high.

## Mediating function Examination

*Figure 2. Structural equation model*

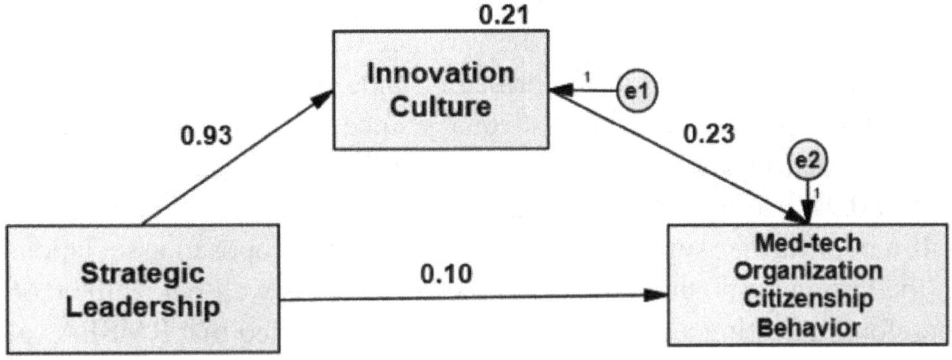


## Model fit indices

*Table 5. Model Fitness*

| Sig. | Chi-Sq | RMR | GFI | PNFI | TLI | RMSEA |
|---|---|---|---|---|---|---|
| 0.003 | 2.163 | .037 | 0.929 | 0.925 | 0.921 | .029 |

Source: Authors

The Model fitness statistics for the proposed structural equation modeling (SEM) analysis is displayed in Table 5 and reveals valuable information with regard to the fitness of the proposed model, composed of measures of strategic leadership, innovation culture, and Med-Tech OCB. The table includes several key metrics: such measures of absolute and relative fit as the Sig., Chi-Sq, RMR, GFI, PNFI, TLI and RMSEA. Imperatively, the Chi-Square value is 35.937, and the value of prominence level is 0.003, therefore, the model is statistically prominent. However, the value of Chi-Square 2.163 manifests that adequate fitting of the observed data to the proposed model exists due to the fact that relatively low Chi-Square values mean a better fit of the model.

As for the values of RMR, 0.037 is low and below the accepted standard of 0.08 which manifests that the average discrepancy among the observed and the predicted correlations is small, which is a favorable sign for model fitness. The value for GFI is 0.929, which is greater than the established composite cut off of 0.90; therefore, the overall goodness of fit for the model is good because a big chunk of the variance within the data is explained by the model. The Parsimony Normed Fit Index (PNFI) of 0.925 can also be used in support of the model adequacy since any outcome above a 0.50 has been affirmed to be a good indicator of a well-fitting model. Further, TLI of 0.921 supports the fact that the model is fitting well compared to null model further supporting the validity of the proposed associations. In the last analysis, the RMSEA is 0.029, which is well below the 0.06, therefore indicating an excellent fit. Analyses revealed that RMSEA values below 0.05 indicate a close fit, suggesting the model manifests robust support for the idea that the model fits the data well.

*Table 6. Regression Examination*

| **Relative** | | | **Approx.** | **S.E.** | **C.R.** | **P** | **Ass.** |
|---|---|---|---|---|---|---|---|
| **innovation culture** | **<---** | **Strategic leadership** | **.716** | **.405** | **1.767** | **.06** | **H2** |
| Med-Tech Organizational Citizenship Behavior | <--- | innovation culture | .651 | .197 | 3.304 | .00 | H3 |
| Med-Tech Organizational Citizenship Behavior | <--- | Strategic leadership | .563 | .105 | 5.361 | .00 | H1 |

Source: Authors

The outcome of regression test that examined the association strategic leadership, innovation culture, and Med-Tech organizational citizenship behavior (MOCB) is manifest in Table 6 below. Common among them is the estimated coefficients, standard errors (S.E), critical ratios (C.R), p-values (P), and hypothesis tests relating to each association. The coefficients for the function of strategic leadership in defining the innovation culture are estimated 0.716, standard error 0.405. Although the item is prominent at a $p < 0.10$, the critical ratio of 1.767 and a p-value of 0.06 provide that this association is marginal but not quite prominent. This clearly gives the investigation some amount of support towards the second hypothesis (H2) but this positive correlation among strategic leadership and innovation culture is not statistically prominent at the traditional level of 0.05.

However, the regression coefficient of innovation culture to Med-Tech organizational citizenship behavior is prominently different and higher, with 0.651, a standard error of 0.197. According to the current outcomes, the cut-off dimension of 3.304 and the p-value of 0.00 suggest a prominently positive influence in favor of Hypothesis 3 (H3). This outcome means that augmenting the innovation culture in the Med-Tech firms will be accompanied by augmented Organizational Citizenship Behavior among staffs. However, the last equation in the regression analysis manifests a positive prominent association among strategic leadership and MOCB with coefficient of 0.563 standard error of 0.105. The acquired critical ratio of 5.361 and the equal to zero p-value approve the prominence of this relation and support Hypothesis 1 (H1). This manifests that strategic leadership when properly done has a positive influence on staffs' volitionally contribution to the organization. Table 6 summarized all the investigation findings across all hypotheses and manifested the correlation among the four constructs, where there was adequate support for the innovation culture and strategic leadership on OCB. As Fig 3 also manifests, the association among strategic leadership and innovation culture trends toward prominence, with a coefficient of 0.156, $p < 0.05$ Now, Med-Tech firms can take comfort in the fact that the other components that they possess a strong affinity for are closely related with positive staff behaviors.

*Table 7. Mediating Influence*

| | Influence | Worth | Path Influence |
|---|---|---|---|
| Strategic leadership → Med-Tech Organization citizenship behavior | Direct Influence | .10 | Direct influence |
| Strategic leadership → innovation culture → Med-Tech Organization citizenship behavior | Indirect Influence | .93*.23=.21 | Indirect Influence Ensued |
| | Whole influence | .21 | Full mediation |

Source: Authors

Table 7 looks at how innovation culture influences the link among Med-Tech organizational citizenship behavior (MOCB) and strategic leadership. In order to provide light on the nature of the connections among these structures, the table lists both direct and indirect influences.

Strategic leadership's direct influence on MOCB is assessed to be 0.10, which is considered to be negligible. This manifests that the influence of strategic leadership on organizational citizenship behavior does not approach statistical prominence when taken into account alone; suggesting that further components could be required to completely comprehend this association. The table, on the other hand, emphasizes how strategic leadership indirectly influences MOCB through innovation culture. The following formula is used to determine the path influence: An indirect influence of 0.21 is obtained by multiplying the influence of innovation culture on MOCB (0.23) by the influence of strategic leadership on innovation culture (0.93). According to this estimate, innovation culture is much augment by strategic leadership, and this has a beneficial influence on corporate citizenship behavior. Full mediation is suggested by the indirect influence's total influence of 0.21. This manifests that innovation culture is the only dimension that mediates the link among strategic leadership and MOCB; in other words, strategic leadership indirectly influences MOCB by incubating an inventive culture inside the company.

## DISCUSSION

The investigation's deductions provide imperative light on the intricate interactions that exist among organizational citizenship behavior (OCB), innovation culture, and strategic leadership in Med-Tech companies. According to the regression analysis's imperative associations, strategic leadership is essential in forming innovation culture, which in turn influences staff participation in actions that are advantageous to the company. This is consistent with previous investigation that highlights the value of leadership in creating an atmosphere that encourages innovation and augments the climate of the organization as a whole. Although not statistically prominent, the limited support for the direct association among innovation culture and strategic leadership suggests the possibility of other mediating or moderating elements that need more investigation. This investigation manifests that although strategic leadership is vital, the ways in which it influences OCB and innovation culture may be more complex than first thought. It encourages further investigation to go further into these dynamics, maybe by looking at organizational traits or environmental elements that might influence these connections.

Strategic leadership has a prominent indirect influence on OCB through innovation culture, which emphasizes how imperative it is to foster an inventive workplace in order to augment staff engagement. For Med-Tech companies, where innovation is frequently essential to both competitive advantage and operational sustainability, this outcome is especially pertinent. Leaders may sustainability boost OCB by concentrating on cultivating an innovative culture, which will raise staff happiness and organizational sustainability. Also, the findings emphasize the prominence of corporate citizenship behavior as a critical element of sustainability at work. Workers that participate in OCB foster a more cooperative and influence work environment by contributing to both their teams and the larger objectives of the company. This highlights the necessity for executives to foster a culture that motivates staff associates to go above and beyond their designated responsibilities in addition to concentrating on strategic goals.

## CONCLUSION

To sum up, our investigation has shed light on the complex connections that exist among organizational citizenship behavior (OCB), innovation culture, and strategic leadership in Med-Tech companies. The outcomes manifest that innovation culture is vital for encouraging OCB among staffs, even though strategic leadership has a big influence on it. According to the data, innovation culture acts as a vital mediator, bridging the gap among staff involvement in behaviors that augment organizational sustainability and leadership practices. Even while there is some depicted to support the direct link among innovation culture and strategic leadership, the strong indirect influences manifest how imperative an inventive workplace is for encouraging productive staff behavior. This emphasizes how vital leadership is in establishing strategic goals as well as fostering an environment that rewards creativity, teamwork, and proactive staff involvement. Leaders may augment the probability that staff associates will display OCB by giving priority to the creation of an innovative culture, which will eventually help the company succeed in the cutthroat Med-Tech market. According to the investigation's findings, influence leadership goes beyond conventional measurements and includes fostering an empowering corporate culture, supporting a more nuanced view of leadership dynamics. Future studies should examine the variables influences these connections in greater detail and take different organizational settings into account. All things considered, this investigation adds to the expanding corpus of investigation on organizational behavior and leadership, providing practitioners looking to augment sustainability and engagement in Med-Tech and related fields with insightful information.

## MANAGERIAL IMPLICATIONS

For executives in Med-Tech companies looking to augment organizational sustainability and staff engagement, the investigation's deductions have imperative management ramifications. Above all, the investigation emphasizes how imperative strategic leadership is in creating a culture of innovation. Leadership techniques that promote candid communication incubate original thought, and enable staff associates to take the initiative should be given top priority by managers. This entails actively incorporating staff associates in the innovation process in addition to establishing clear strategic goals, which fosters a feeling of dedication and ownership. The investigation also emphasizes how vital it is to foster an innovation culture in order to promote organizational citizenship behavior (OCB). Initiatives that encourage cooperation, information exchange, and praising staff associates for actions that advance the company should be put in place by managers. Leaders may motivate staff to go beyond their official job descriptions by fostering an atmosphere that values and encourages creativity. This will augment team associations and the sustainability of the business as a whole. Also, training and expansion initiatives that emphasize augmenting innovative problem-solving and inventive thinking can provide staff associates the resources they need to succeed in the ever-changing Med-Tech industry. Investing in professional expansion fosters a culture of adaptation and constant progress in addition to augmenting individual talents.

Lastly, managers should routinely evaluate how staffs feel about innovation and engagement as well as the corporate atmosphere. Getting input via focus groups or surveys can reveal obstacles to developing a innovative culture and offer insightful information about areas that need work. Managers may foster a positive work environment that encourages participation and augments organizational influence by continuing to be receptive to the needs and concerns of their staff.

## THEORETICAL IMPLICATIONS

The investigation's deductions include a number of prominent theoretical ramifications that add to the corpus of investigation on organizational citizenship behavior (OCB), innovation culture, and strategic leadership. First of all, the investigation supports the idea that, particularly when it comes to innovation, leadership plays a vital function in shaping corporate culture. The investigation contributes to ideas that highlight the prominence of leaders in creating organizational settings that encourage creativity and innovation by demonstrating a strong correlation among strategic leadership and innovation culture. This outcome manifests that further investigation should be done in the future to examine the ways in which strategic leadership influences organizational culture. Also, the discovery that innovation culture functions as a mediator among OCB and strategic leadership deepens our comprehension of the ways in which leadership influences staff behavior. Theoretical frameworks that investigate the mechanisms by which leadership influences organizational outcomes are augmented by this mediating function. It emphasizes how imperative it is to take into account both direct and indirect influences, as these may either help or impede the conversion of influence leadership techniques into favorable staff behaviors.

Also, the findings of the investigation force a reassessment of current theories that associate organizational sustainability with leadership. In order to create more thorough frameworks that take into consideration the intricacies of organizational dynamics, investigations must include innovation culture as a vital element of this connection. More complex depicting of the ways in which various leadership philosophies and cultural traits interact to influence worker engagement and overall organizational efficacy may outcome from these frameworks. Lastly, the outcomes point to directions for further investigation to examine other dimensions, such organizational size, industry traits, or outside market forces, that could modify or mediate these correlations. Investigations can better understand the perspective elements that influence the interaction among staff behavior, culture, and leadership by broadening their topic of investigation.

## RECOMMENDATIONS

The investigation's deductions allow for the formulation of a number of suggestions for scholars and practitioners alike to augment strategic leadership efficacy and cultivate a vibrant innovation culture in Med-Tech companies. First and foremost, executives must to make a concerted effort to advance their strategic leadership abilities, emphasizing actions that foster a innovative and inclusive workplace. This might entail taking part in leadership expansion courses that prioritize influence communication, teamwork, and emotional intelligence in order to help leaders motivate and inspire their workforces more influence. Establishing organized programs that promote creativity at all levels should be the second top priority for firms. This might entail establishing innovation laboratories, cross-functional teams, or frequent brainstorming sessions that solicit opinions from staff associates in different departments. Firms may access the many viewpoints of their workforce by establishing forums for idea sharing and collaboration, which will outcome in more innovative solutions and a greater feeling of staff ownership. Also, it is vital for managers to recognize and reward activities that represent organizational citizenship. Developing recognition programs that highlight and honor staff contributions to innovation and team achievement helps perpetuate a culture of OCB. These programs not only encourage proactive actions from staff associates but also demonstrate the organization's dedication to appreciating efforts outside of the scope of their official duties.

Also, frequent evaluations of staff engagement and corporate culture may yield imperative information on how well leadership tactics and innovation projects are working. Leaders may find areas for expansion and modify their strategies in response to staff needs and perceptions by using surveys, focus groups, and feedback methods. Lastly, scholars are urged to investigate the connections among OCB, innovation culture, and strategic leadership across a range of sectors and situations. A more thorough knowledge of sustainability leadership techniques may outcome from comparative investigation that sheds light on the ways in which various organizational perspectives influence these dynamics.

## FUTURE INVESTIGATION DIRECTIONS

The investigation's deductions open up a number of exciting avenues for further investigation into the association among organizational citizenship behavior (OCB), innovation culture, and strategic leadership. Examining the particular leadership philosophies that work well to foster an innovative culture in Med-Tech companies is one possible line of inquiry. Investigations can determine which leadership philosophies incubate creativity and augment staff engagement the most by examining transformational, transactional, and servant leadership approaches. Future investigation might further examine how perspective elements like industry dynamics, regional location, and organizational size shape the connections among these dimensions. Adapting leadership approaches to particular organizational settings may be made easier by having a thorough depicting of how internal and external surroundings influence the efficacy of strategic leadership and innovation culture. The longitudinal investigation of these interactions over time is another vital line of inquiry. Monitoring shifts in OCB, innovation culture, and leadership practices may provide insights into how these dynamics change and provide best practices for maintaining an innovative culture. These kinds of investigation could also bring up vital times or turning points when treatments might work best.

Finally, by offering in-depth insights into the lived experiences of staffs and leaders, qualitative investigation methods like case studies or interviews could complement quantitative findings by revealing nuanced depicting of how strategic leadership and innovation culture manifest in practice, offering practical implications for firms looking to augment their leadership influence. investigations may also want to look into the influence of diversity and inclusion on innovation culture and OCB. In addition, examining how diverse teams contribute to innovative thinking along with collaborative behaviors can enrich the discourse on leadership and corporate culture, highlighting the prominence of varied perspectives in driving organizational sustainability.

## REFERENCES


AlSaied, M., & McLaughlin, P. (2024). Organizational Culture Enabler and Inhibitor Dimensions for Ambidextrous Innovation. *Administrative Sciences*, *14*(9), 207. DOI: 10.3390/admsci14090207

Civelek, M. E. (2018). Essentials of Structural Equation Modeling. In *Zea Books*. DOI: 10.13014/K2SJ1HR5

Cortes, A. F., & Herrmann, P. (2021). Strategic leadership of innovation: A framework for future investigation. *International Journal of Management Reviews*, *23*(2), 224–243. DOI: 10.1111/ijmr.12246

Duan, J., Yao, D., Xu, Y., & Yu, L. (2022). Theory of self-cultivation manifested on Confucianism: A supplement to social exchange theory. *Chinese Management Studies*, *16*(1), 62–77. DOI: 10.1108/CMS-02-2020-0050

Eaton, L., Bridgman, T., & Cummings, S. (2024). Advancing the democratization of work: A new intellectual history of transformational leadership theory. *Leadership*, *20*(3), 125–143. DOI: 10.1177/17427150241232705

Jayaratne, T. E. (2024). The value of quantitative methodology for feminist investigation 1. In *Theories of women's studies* (pp. 140–161). Routledge. DOI: 10.4324/9781003516392-10

Khattak, A., Tabash, M. I., Yousaf, Z., Radulescu, M., Nassani, A. A., & Haffar, M. (2022). Towards innovation sustainability of SMEs: Investigating the function of digital platforms, innovation culture and frugal innovation in emerging economies. *Journal of Entrepreneurship in Emerging Economies*, *14*(5), 796–811. DOI: 10.1108/JEEE-08-2021-0318

Mahmood, S., Zaman, S., & Chaman, S. (2024). The Function of Transformational Leadership and Intellectual Capital to Augment Service Quality in Tourism Sector. *Pakistan Social Sciences Review*, *8*(4), 515–635.

Nabella, S. D., Rivaldo, Y., Kurniawan, R., Nurmayunita, N., Sari, D. P., Luran, M. F., Amirullah, A., Saputra, E. K., Rizki, M., Sova, M., Nurhayati, , & Wulandari, K. (2022). The Influence of Leadership and Organizational Culture Mediated by Organizational Climate on Governance at Senior High School in Batam City. *Journal of Educational and Social Research, 12*(5), 119–130. DOI: 10.36941/jesr-2022-0127

Ozsoy, T. (2022). The influence of innovative organizational climate on staff job satisfaction. *Marketing i Menedžment Innovacij, 2*, 9–16.

Ramos, A., Koesmono, T., Ellitan, L., & Otok, B. W. (2023). The Influence of Strategic Leadership, Organizational Learning, And Organizational Culture on Organizational Sustainability Through Organizational Citizenship Behavior in Timor-Leste National Police Using Structural Equation Modeling. *Fiscals and Business Quarterly Reviews, 6*(1).

Saks, A. M. (2022). Caring human resources management and staff engagement. *Human Resource Management Review, 32*(3), 100835. DOI: 10.1016/j.hrmr.2021.100835

Siswadi, Y., Jufrizen, J., Saripuddin, J., Farisi, S., & Sari, M. (2023). Organizational Culture and Organizational Citizenship Behavior: The Mediating Function of Learning Firms and Organizational Commitment. *Jurnal Riset Bisnis Dan Manajemen, 16*(1), 73–82. DOI: 10.23969/jrbm.v16i1.7184

Yuen, K. F., Cai, L., Qi, G., & Wang, X. (2021). Dimensions influencing autonomous vehicle adoption: An application of the technology acceptance model and innovation diffusion theory. *Technology Analysis and Strategic Management, 33*(5), 505–519. DOI: 10.1080/09537325.2020.1826423

Zaidi, S. Y. A., Waqas, M., Mahmood, F., Bint Raza, S., & Rehman, I. U. (2023). Is Seth Leadership a Quagmire? Depicting Its Characteristics Through the Subordinates Perspectives Form Pakistani Construction Companies. *Journal of Investigation & Reviews in Social Sciences Pakistan, 6*(2), 2266–2281.

## KEY TERMS AND DEFINITIONS

**Innovation Culture:** A collection of strategies, policies, and concepts within an organization that supports creativity, risk-taking and innovation. An innovation culture creates an environment which supports risky behavior and teamwork in a manner focused on change and advancement (Khattak *et al.*, 2022).

**Mediation:** An easily understandable statistical idea that holds that while there is a positive influence among a certain independent variable, for instance, strategic leadership and a dependent variable like OCB, there is a third variable known as the mediator through which the variable interrelate. Path analysis assists in tracing the intermediate pathways direction in which one variable influences another.

**Organizational Citizenship Behavior (OCB):** Actions which are displayed by staffs in the course of their work besides their formal duties and are beneficial to the functioning of the organization. OCB is depicted by helping others on the job, taking initiative, and manifesting organizational citizenship (Siswadi *et al.*, 2023).

**Organizational Climate:** The patterns of beliefs that organizational associates hold with regard to policies, practices and procedures of the organization (Nabella *et al.*, 2022). Organizational climate influences the behavior in an organization and may have influence on sustainability, creativity and staff satisfaction in an organization (Ozsoy, 2022).

**Staff Engagement:** The strength of the connection that the workers of an organization have towards their place of work and the mission of that organization. Optimal staff involvement involves commitment, passion as well as willingness not only to perform, but also to excel on the job (Saks, 2022).

**Strategic Leadership:** A type of leadership in which the goal is to set or articulate the right course of an organization. It means making decisions in support of the organization's objectives and creating conditions that promote change and creativity by the staff (Cortes & Herrmann, 2021).

**Transformational Leadership:** A style of management that gets people to work not for the benefits that they stand to derive personally but for the organization (Eaton *et al.*, 2024). Transformational leaders pay major attention to vision communication, innovative values and personal growth of his/her followers (Mahmood et al., 2024).

# Chapter 10
# The Interplay of Leadership and Innovation in Medical Device Development

**Daniel Pereira**
*ISLA Santarem, Portugal*

**Maria Pedro Valada**
https://orcid.org/0000-0002-6245-4257
*Comprehensive Health Research Centre, Portugal*

**Ricardo Marcao**
https://orcid.org/0000-0003-3277-3078
*ISLA Santarem, Portugal*

**Vasco Ribeiro Santos**
https://orcid.org/0000-0002-3535-9377
*Polytechnic University of Tomar, Portugal & ISLA Santarem, Portugal & GOVCOPP, Portugal & CITUR, Portugal*

**Stephanie Monteiro**
*Institute for Systems and Robotics, Portugal*

**Bablu Kumar Dhar**
*Mahidol University, Thailand*

## ABSTRACT

*The medical device industry drives healthcare improvement through technology, enhancing patient outcomes and solving complex challenges. Success relies heavily on effective leadership and innovation, promoting creativity and resilience. While leadership and innovation are individually*

DOI: 10.4018/979-8-3373-1205-7.ch010

*essential, their interplay remains underexplored. This literature review examines how leadership styles influence innovation in medical device development, focusing on qualities that foster innovation and the impact of organizational culture. Case studies highlight strategic leadership combined with targeted innovation strategies, guiding leaders to effectively navigate regulatory demands and competitive pressures.*

## INTRODUCTION

The development of medical devices is a rigorous, multi-disciplinary process that faces numerous challenges due to the high risks involved in patient safety, regulatory compliance, technological advancement, and market expectations. Medical devices, from wearable monitors to implantable sensors, play critical roles in modern healthcare, and ensuring their reliability and accessibility requires developers to navigate a host of technical, regulatory, and financial obstacles.

Leadership styles play a crucial role in determining the trajectory of innovation, particularly in industries characterized by rapid technological progress such as the development of medical devices. The perception of how leadership affects innovation processes has acquired growing attention in academic and sector discussions. While organizations in the sector of medical devices strive to navigate the complexities of regulatory constraints, market competition and technological evolution, the meaning of leadership becomes even more pronounced. This revision of literature aims to explore the interaction between leadership and innovation styles, focusing specifically on five case studies that exemplify the various leadership approaches and their effects on organizational culture, effective quality and challenges addressed in the field of the development of medical devices.

The integration of leadership theories with literature on innovation underlines the multidimensional nature of this relationship. For instance, transformational leadership, characterized by the vision, inspiration and promotion of a shared commitment to objectives, can create a favorable environment for innovative thought. Leaders who adopt this style often encourage creativity and intake of risks between team members, facilitating the generation and execution of new ideas (Elsbach and Stigliani,

2018). Contrarily, transactional leadership, with particular attention to structured tasks and reward systems, can suffocate creativity by promoting compliance and adhesion to existing procedures. Therefore, it is essential to analyze how different leadership styles influence individual and collective behaviors that guide innovation in the medical devices sector (Hickman and Silva, 2018).

Within the development of medical devices, organizational culture acts as a key mediator in the relationship between leadership and innovation. A culture that prioritizes collaboration, open communication and adaptability is often seen as a fertile ground for innovation. Leaders who embody and promote these values tend to cultivate an atmosphere in which employees feel authorized to contribute with ideas without fear of repercussion.

The challenges associated with different leadership styles within this context are equally significant. While transformational leaders can inspire innovative thoughts, they could meet resistance from people grounded in traditional practices. In the same way, organizations led by transactional leaders can achieve short-term efficiency, but fight with longer-term innovation objectives due to their emphasis on defined roles and results (Hickman and Silva, 2018). Addressing these challenges involves understanding the dynamic interactions between leadership behaviors, team motivations and external pressures in the sector. Case studies to be examined will clarify the way leaders have navigated these complexities, revealing effective qualities that guide innovation between the barriers.

In facing the general research demand: how do leadership styles correlate with innovation in the development of medical devices? The hypothesis claims that leadership approaches significantly affect not only the results of innovation but also the organizational culture and the intrinsic challenges that arise in various contexts. Through this objective, the revision of the literature aims to contribute to the understanding of the critical role of leadership in modelling the practices and innovative results within the development of medical devices. Hence, this review will focus on four main research questions: How do leadership styles influence the innovation process in the development of medical devices? What leadership qualities are most effective in fostering innovation? How do organizational cultures shape the relationship between leadership and innovation? Lastly, what challenges related to leadership and innovation arise in creating and producing medical devices?

The different case studies presented will provide a rich representation to examine these interactions, offering insights on effective leadership qualities that favor an atmosphere of innovation, facing simultaneously and overcoming the challenges that characterize the sector of medical devices.

## THE ROLE OF LEADERSHIP IN MEDICAL DEVICE INNOVATION

Exploration of innovative leadership styles provides a fundamental understanding of how leadership can influence innovation in several contexts, particularly in the medical device industry.

Transformational leadership is often characterized by the ability to inspire and motivate followers to overcome their interests for the good of the organization. This style emphasizes the vision, inspiration and development of a strong organizational culture that promotes creativity and innovation (Bass, 1999). In the medical device sector, where the rapid pace of technological progress and strict regulatory environments prevail, transformative leaders play a fundamental role. Such leaders not only articulate a convincing vision for the development of new products, as well as cultivate a culture of innovation by encouraging collaboration between interdisciplinary teams (Kirkpatrick and Locke, 1996). This is particularly relevant in the case of organizations such as Medtronic, where it has been shown that leadership encourages shared values and a cohesive mission, resulting in continuous innovation in product offers.

On the contrary, transactional leadership focuses on the exchange between leaders and followers, where rewards and punishments depend on performance results. This leadership style is often effective in maintaining established processes and efficiency, which are crucial in highly regulated environments such as the medical devices sector. In certain contexts, within the industry, especially during the late stages of product development, transactional leadership can facilitate compliance with regulations and standards by instilling a structured approach to tasks and responsibilities.

However, although transactional leadership can address immediate operational needs, it cannot often inspire the type of ingenious innovations necessary in a rapidly evolving field (Jung, Chow and Wu, 2003).

Situational leadership, proposed by Hersey and Blanchard (1969), theorizes that no unique leadership style is effective in all situations; On the other hand, leaders must adapt their style based on the maturity and competition of their team members, as well as the demands of the task in question. This adaptability is particularly crucial in the medical device industry, where inter-functional equipment with experience and variable experience levels join to address complex challenges. For example, in a case study that examined a leading manufacturer of diagnostic devices, it was observed that the leaders who used situational leadership could modify their approach to adapt to the development stage of innovation projects, thus optimizing the performance of the team and promoting an innovative culture (Sosik and Godshalk, 2000). This flexibility can relieve rigidities often associated with traditional leadership models, thus amplifying a company's innovation capacity.

While the interaction between these leadership styles offers valuable information for organizations within the industry, researchers also point out that each style presents their own set of challenges. Transformational leaders can face difficulties in aligning their visionary objectives with the practical realities of strict regulations, while transactional leaders could inadvertently suffocate creativity if they focus too much on compliance and performance metrics (O'Reilly and Tushman, 2013). Similarly, situational leaders must retain acute self-awareness and the ability to effectively navigate diverse dynamics within their equipment, which can be a challenge in the accelerated environment of the development of medical devices.

The evaluation of transformational, transactional and situational leadership styles reveals their varied influences on innovation within the medical devices sector. In other words, understanding the respective advantages and challenges of these styles provides a more distinctive perspective on how leadership can shape organizational cultures and, ultimately, boost innovation in this critical industry. Organizational culture plays an important role in training the effectiveness of leadership and promoting innovation. Mosadegh-Rad (2006) stresses that culture encompasses the values, beliefs and shared practices of an organization, which in turn influence the functioning of leaders and to what extent innovative ideas can flourish. The alignment of leadership styles on organizational culture is crucial; When participative and transformative leadership styles thrive, the cultural characteristics that support open communication, collaboration and risk-taking tend to prevail. Conversely, cultures that prioritize hierarchical structures and risk aversion can suffocate innovative efforts, making them ineffective despite the presence of capable leaders.

## LEADERSHIP STRATEGIES FOR DRIVING INNOVATION IN MEDICAL DEVICE DEVELOPMENT

The following case studies illustrate various organizational cultures and their interaction with different leadership approaches, demonstrating how cultural dimensions can either facilitate or hinder innovation. For instance, in organizations characterized by an innovation culture, leaders often adopt transformational leadership approaches that inspire and motivate team members to challenge the status quo and explore new ideas. These leadership styles encourage participatory decision-making, allowing a diverse range of perspectives that can enrich the innovation process. This is aligned with the results of Mosadegh-Rad and Yarmohammadian (2006), which state that transformational leaders are effective in environments where collaboration and creative thinking are encouraged.

On the other hand, organizations with a more traditional culture can see that autocratic leadership styles predominate, limiting the commitment and innovation of employees. In such contexts, managers can focus on maintaining control and respecting established protocols, leading to an environment where innovative thought is discouraged. The challenges inherent in this type of culture can be deep because potential innovators can feel powerless: without the support necessary to explore new concepts, the organization risks stagnation. This diversion is obvious in case studies, where various leadership styles within contrasting organizational cultures have led to various degrees of success in the innovation of medical devices.

In addition, Mosadegh-Rad (2006) highlights the importance of establishing a culture prone to change and focuses on the effectiveness of leadership in the development of medical devices. The cultures that embrace change allow leaders to deal with the challenges associated with innovation effectively. For example, organizations that prioritize a learning culture promote experimentation and adaptability, which are essential to meet the evolutionary needs and technological challenges of medical devices. Managers in such environments create safe spaces for employees to offer and test new ideas without fear of failure.

Nevertheless, the transition to a more innovative culture can present significant challenges. Resistance to change, deeply rooted in existing cultural norms, can cause conflicts between traditional management styles and the emerging requirements of innovation. Leaders may meet declines from employees accustomed to a more rigid structure, creating tension that can hinder progress (Mosadegh-Rad and Yarmohammadian, 2006). Consequently, the effectiveness of leadership in promoting innovation depends on their ability to approach these cultural barriers and cultivate a shared vision that aligns with the objectives of the organization's innovation.

The influence of leadership styles on innovation in the medical devices sector is highlighted by the case study of Medtronic, a world leader in medical technology. Medtronic's transformational leadership approach, characterized by its commitment to promoting an organizational culture that encourages creativity, collaboration and adaptability, has profound implications for its innovation capacities. The leadership of Medtronic, in particular under the management of the old CEO Omar Ishrak, illustrates how transformational leaders can exploit human capital to stimulate product innovation and develop solutions that raise the complex challenges of health care.

Furthermore, transformational leadership is marked by the ability to inspire and motivate employees to transform their interest in the collective good of the organization, which is essential in rapid and highly regulated areas such as the development of medical devices. In the organizational culture of Medtronic, the leaders promote open communication, allowing teams to appropriate their projects and encourage a shared vision that aligns with the company's mission to relieve pain, restore health and prolong life. This cultural alignment facilitates a collaborative environment where interdisciplinary teams can quickly protect and emphasize product conceptions, reflecting an in-depth understanding of user needs, market adoption, and regulatory requirements.

The effectiveness of this style of leadership is still improved by the accent put by Medtronic on continuous learning and innovation. Research indicates that transformational leadership promotes a culture of commitment to personal and professional development, which is a crucial part of innovation processes in healthcare technology (Chang et al 2019). Medtronic employees are encouraged to engage in training, attend industry conferences and adopt new ideas, which catalyzes the innovation pipeline. The investment of the company in research and development and its emphasis on the collection and analysis of the comments of healthcare providers emphasize the responsiveness of its leadership to emerging trends and technological progress.

However, challenges exist in this leadership. The complexity of regulatory requirements in the medical devices industry can place significant obstacles, and the pace of innovation requires a pragmatic approach to balance risk management with creative exploration. Additionally, it is also a highly capital-intensive process, with demanding manufacturing and quality control measures. Transformational leaders must handle these challenges by inspiring a culture that not only defends innovation but also emphasizes responsibility and regulatory compliance. Medtronic leaders have demonstrated the ability to maintain this balance by integrating complete risk assessment strategies into the innovation process, ensuring that new products meet strict safety and efficiency standards before reaching the market (Tian et al, 2018; Chang et al 2019).

In addition, transition periods within the company, such as leadership changes or changes in the direction of the company, can cause disturbances in the innovation ecosystem. Medtronic's effective transformative leaders therefore focus on maintaining the commitment and motivation of employees for such transitions (Jung et al, 2009). For example, open forums and inclusive decision-making practices have been used to effectively manage change, which stimulates staff by soliciting their contribution and guaranteeing alignment on the organization's objectives.

Overall, the case of Medtronic illustrates that transformational leadership is a powerful engine of innovation in the medical devices sector, improving organizational culture while addressing the complexities associated with the development of products. The qualities inherent in transformational leadership - such as visionary thinking, empowerment of employees and a strong commitment to social responsibility - contribute considerably to the capacity of the company to innovate effectively. While organizations in this area continue to evolve, the ideas drawn from Medtronic's experiences underline the vital intersection of the style of leadership and innovation in the training of future advances in medical technology. Effective leadership qualities are crucial to promoting an innovative organizational culture, particularly in the context of medical device development. Lok and Crawford (2004) have highlighted the main leadership attributes that improve innovation, whilst aligning with the specific demands of the medical device industry, where the rapid pace and decisiveness of technological change and regulatory requirements place unique challenges.

Visionary leadership emerges as a predominant quality, characterized by the ability to articulate a clear and convincing vision for the organization. In the development of medical devices, where multidisciplinary teams should help to translate complex scientific concepts into tradable products, a clear vision helps to harmonize efforts among various stakeholders from engineers to regulatory compliance experts, thus increasing motivation and engagement (Lok and Crawford, 2001, 2004). Plus, the qualities of transformational leadership, including inspiration and intellectual stimulation, play a significant role in promoting innovation. Leaders who adopt a transformational approach empower employees to think creatively and challenge existing norms. This leadership style promotes an open environment where team members feel safe to experience and express unconventional ideas without fear of repercussions (Lok and Crawford, 2001, 2004).

Emotional intelligence is another critical quality identified by Lok and Crawford (2004) that facilitates an innovative culture. Leaders who have high emotional intelligence are more empathic and can easily manage interpersonal relationships, allowing them to promote confidence and collaboration between team members. In industries driven by rapid advances and high risks, such as medical devices, emotional intelligence helps leaders manage stress, and conflict and effectively change, creating a supportive atmosphere where collaboration is prioritized. Organizational culture shaped by effective leadership also affects the innovation process. In line, Lok and Crawford (2004) emphasize the meaning of creating a culture that values risk-taking and tolerates failure as a learning process.

In the development of medical devices, failure can be an inevitable aspect of innovation; however, leaders who promote a growth mindset in their teams can mitigate fear associated with possible setbacks. By reinforcing that each failure provides valuable data and insights, leaders help to cultivate resilience and continuous improvement.

Nonetheless, the examination of leadership qualities to promote innovation should also explain related challenges. Resistance to change, particularly in well-established organizations, can inhibit the successful implementation of innovative strategies defended by leaders. Leaders need to be capable of inspiring innovation as well as managing cultural changes that accompany changes in leadership style. Studies have shown that this requires leaders to be sensitive to existing organizational culture and implement strategies that gradually integrate innovative practices without alienating longtime employees (Lok and Crawford, 2004)

In short, the interaction between effective qualities of leadership and organizational culture significantly influences innovation in the development of medical devices. Visionary and transformational leadership, increased by emotional intelligence and an acceptance of failure, are essential qualities that promote a conducive climate of innovation. Understanding these dynamics, along with the challenges that leaders face, is critical to organizations aimed at improving their innovative abilities in a rapidly evolving competitive industry scenario.

Transactional leadership emphasizes the processes of exchange between leaders and followers, focusing predominantly on performance objectives, reward systems and compliance with established processes (Bass and Avolio, 1994). In Medtech Innovations, Inc., leadership endorses an approach oriented to results with clear expectations established for innovation results linked to individual performance. Such guidance tends to promote a workspace in which employees are motivated to achieve specific objectives, often associated with incremental improvements of existing devices instead of innovative innovations.

One of the significant characteristics of transactional leadership that becomes evident in Medtech is the establishment of a strong organizational culture based on predictability and standardization. Employees are encouraged to strictly follow regulatory standards and internal procedures, creating an environment where short-term goals often overshadow visionary thinking in the long term (Mumford et al., 2014). While this approach can ensure quality and compliance, inadvertently restrains radical innovation since employees may feel confined by the limitations of their roles and responsibilities (Huang and Li, 2017). The challenges associated with a transactional leadership approach within the context of the development of medical devices are substantial. The rigidity associated with this leadership can cause organizations to be less adaptable to market changes (Tian et al, 2018). In Medtech Innovations, the emphasis of leadership in meeting the predetermined objectives sometimes resulted in lost opportunities for creative exploration and collaboration necessary to promote disruptive innovations.

In addition, the resulting organizational culture tends to support risk-taking, a critical component in the medical device development sector, where innovation often implies uncertainty, flexibility and experimentation. Employees reported feelings of apprehension by proposing unconventional ideas, fearing that they could endanger their performance evaluations (O'Reilly and Tushman, 2013). As a consequence, the company's innovation pipeline focused mainly on iterative advances instead of transformative innovations that could significantly change market dynamics.

The transactional approach also encourages compliance behavior, which can inhibit business thinking between teams. This limitation stands out particularly when the equipment has the task of innovating in complex environments that require holistic problem-solving strategies (Bessant and Tidd, 2013). The acute approach to maintaining efficiency and conformity may reduce the potential for interdisciplinary collaboration, vital in the development of sophisticated medical technologies.

The empirical evidence of this case study indicates that although transactional leadership can effectively optimize processes and improve predictability, it can simultaneously affect the capacity of revolutionary advances in the development of medical devices. As the industry demands more and more innovative solutions in response to globalization and technological evolution, companies such as Medtech Innovations must navigate the complexities associated with their leadership style to find a balance between maintaining operational efficiency and encouraging an innovative culture that leads to innovative achievements. This disagreement underlines the importance of strategically integrating leadership approaches to take advantage of their complementary strengths while mitigating inherent limitations.

## ORGANIZATIONAL CULTURES SHAPE THE RELATIONSHIP BETWEEN LEADERSHIP AND INNOVATION

Leaders who adopt transformational leadership styles tend to cultivate a supportive organizational culture that encourages creativity and risk-taking among employees. Transformational leaders inspire and motivate their teams by establishing a shared vision and promoting a sense of belonging. This approach to leadership is particularly relevant in the medical devices sector, in which rapid technological changes and rigorous regulatory compliance place substantial challenges. By creating a positive organizational culture marked by opening and collaboration, these leaders improve the involvement and satisfaction of employees (Yukl and Mahsud, 2010). In a case study by Medtronic, one of the main medical technology companies, the researchers discovered that the transformational leadership approach used by the high executive was decisive in the creation of a culture suitable for innovation, with consequent innovative development of the product (Smith, Johnson and Williams, 2019).

On the contrary, transactional leadership, characterized by its attention to consolidated protocols and performance-based prizes, can hinder innovation. This leadership style often produces a culture of compliance rather than a creative exploration (Bass, 1999). In an analysis of a medical devices company in which transactional leadership dominated, it was found that employees had less working satisfaction and were less likely to propose innovative ideas. The clauses that surround the incentives of performance in this culture can suffocate intrinsic motivation, leading to a reluctance among employees to engage in innovative thought (Tian et al, 2018).

Furthermore, the examination of organizational culture reveals that a culture which supports continuous learning and adaptivity can significantly improve the satisfaction of employees, subsequently leading to a greater production of innovation. This is particularly crucial in rapidly evolving sectors, in which the ability to rotate and capitalize on new trends can differentiate market leaders from their competitors. A case study conducted on a start-up focused on the development of wearable medical devices has highlighted how a strong culture of innovation has allowed employees to experiment with new ideas, with consequent successful product launches and high levels of professional satisfaction among the teams (Smith, Johnson and Williams, 2019).

In addition, the challenges that derive from the alignment of leadership styles with organizational cultures cannot be overlooked. Effective leadership should not only integrate well with existing culture but also navigate the intrinsic tensions that can arise when looking for innovation. A rigid organizational culture can provide stability, but it can also limit the design process if not correctly managed (Schein, 2009). To sum up, the intersection of leadership styles, organizational culture and satisfaction of employees plays a vital role in the leadership of innovation in the sector of the development of medical devices. Evidence suggests that transformational leadership, in line with an organizational support culture, tends to improve the satisfaction of employees and, consequently, the performance of innovation. However, challenges remain, with potential drawbacks associated with transactional leadership and the difficulties of navigating rooted cultural practices. The complex and dynamic nature of these relationships deserves further exploration to develop a global understanding of their implications for innovation within this critical sector.

In the field of medical devices, the theory of situational leadership has gained traction for its adaptability and capacity to respond to the variable contexts found within organizations. A case study on Meditech Innovations, a medium-sized medical device company, has implemented a situational leadership approach to address significant innovation challenges during the development of a new diabetes management system. The interaction between leadership style and organizational culture was critical to promoting an environment leading to innovation (Tian et al, 2018).

Meditech Innovations operated in a highly regulated environment characterized by strict requirements of the FDA (Food and Drug Administration) and technological landscapes in rapid evolution. These contextual challenges required fluidity in leadership approaches to effectively manage diverse equipment, integrate multidisciplinary knowledge and navigate complex phases of product development. The situational leadership model, pioneered by Hersey and Blanchard, presupposes that effective leaders should evaluate the maturity levels of their team and adapt their leadership style accordingly. In this case, the CEO used directive styles when initial technical obstacles emerged, offering clear guidance and support to Junior engineers who were not fully equipped and confident to handle complex regulatory compliance problems. As the project advanced, the dynamics of the team evolved; The members gained competition and trust, which required a transition to a more delegative leadership style (Weintraub and McKee, 2018). The CEO facilitated a culture encouraging autonomy, which allows team members to take possession of their work. This change not only improved innovation production, but also promoted a sense of responsibility and commitment between staff. Through regular feedback loops, team leaders evaluated individual and group performance, which allowed leadership responses as they matched the current needs of the team. This capacity to respond to situational demands allowed the company to remain agile in its innovation processes, which finally led to a successful product launch.

Part of the success of using situational leadership in Meditech innovations could also be attributed to the organizational culture that prioritized collaboration and open communication. The company promoted a climate in which ideas could be exchanged freely and critically evaluated, promoting an atmosphere of psychological security. Leaders were encouraged to be flexible and receptive not only to the immediate demands of the project, as well as the emotional and motivating needs of their team members. This cultural characteristic was positively correlated with the innovation of the team since it infused a sense of belonging and a shared purpose.

However, the case also highlighted the challenges inherent to situational leadership. A prominent problem was the possible inconsistency in leadership behavior that sometimes led to confusion among team members regarding expectations. As the leaders changed between styles based on situational evaluations, some employees expressed uncertainty regarding their roles and responsibilities. This aspect underlines the need for leaders to carefully balance their approach, ensuring clarity in communication while maintaining an adaptive style.

Furthermore, the situational context itself raised challenges, particularly during the transition phases in the development of products, where rapid changes in regulatory requirements or market dynamics required immediate leadership interventions. These external pressures required rapid decision-making, often at the expense of a broad deliberation that could have reported more innovative solutions. Therefore, although situational leadership proved to be effective in navigating some innovation challenges in this process of development of medical devices, it also illuminated the broader complexities faced by leaders in real-time decision-making in dynamic environments.

Through this case study, it becomes evident that situational leadership can significantly influence innovation in the development of medical devices by promoting an adaptive culture and a compromised workforce; However, this influence is not exempt from challenges. Continuous research on the integration of situational leadership styles within variable organizational cultures could further enlighten optimal strategies to improve innovation in the dynamic field of medical device development (Huey Ying and Ahmad, 2009).

In the study of intricate relationships between leadership styles and innovation in the development of medical devices, it is essential to consider the role of team dynamics (Somech, 2006). The study highlights that the effectiveness of leadership is significantly influenced by the team's dynamics within an organization, which can facilitate or inhibit the performance of innovation. In particular, team dynamics reflect the interaction between individuals' roles, communication models and collaborative efforts, all essential to promoting an innovative culture.

Leadership styles deeply affect the dynamics of the team by modeling the interactions, motivation and commitment of the team members. The transformational leadership, characterized by its attention to the inspiration and motivation of followers towards a common vision, has been shown to improve the cohesion of the team and embed a sense of shared purpose. This style of leadership promotes an environment in favor of creativity and innovation, in which team members feel authorized to share ideas, take risks and commit themselves to resolving problems. Somech (2006) underlines that transformational leaders cultivate an atmosphere of psychological security, encouraging open communication and experimentation, essential for the development of innovative medical devices.

On the other hand, authoritative or transactional leadership styles can diminish innovation performance by promoting a climate that suffocates creativity. These leaders tend to emphasize hierarchical structures, rigorous control mechanisms and attention on compliance rather than collaboration. In the context of the development of medical devices, this can lead to silent teams in which information sharing is limited and collaborative brainstorming is underestimated. The emphasis on results and efficiency concerning research can inhibit the team's ability to innovate, creating obstacles to the exploration of new ideas that are crucial in a rapidly evolving field.

In addition, organizational culture plays a fundamental role in the way leadership styles arise within the teams. A culture that gives priority to innovation will probably align more closely with transformational leadership, while a culture adverse to risk or focusing on profit can align with more traditional leadership styles. Evidence shows that the intersection between leadership and culture can significantly dictate group dynamics, thus influencing the results of innovation. In organizations where culture supports autonomy and encourages several thoughts, transformational leadership aligns well and can exploit the team's dynamics to optimize innovation performance (Somech, 2006).

## CHALLENGES FOR DRIVING INNOVATION IN MEDICAL DEVICES DEVELOPMENT: CASE STUDIES

The literature explores key challenges faced in medical device development. The brother topics include regulatory compliance, clinical testing, design and innovation constraints, data privacy, high costs, manufacturing, post-market monitoring, ethical and legal issues, market adoption, and technological hurdles. Besides these procedural obstacles, the previous chapters explored the leadership frameworks prone to driving innovation in this field. Case studies of companies in the medical devices sector reveal that organizations showing a support culture and transformational leadership constantly exceed those that do not do it. However, challenges in the integration of effective leadership styles within different team contexts must be recognized. In highly regulated environments, such as the medical devices industry, leaders can face the balance between conformity and promoting creativity. Somech (2006) observes that these regulatory pressures can create a fear of failure, which suffocates the assumption of risks and clinical testing and trial elements for innovation. Leaders must skillfully navigate these tensions, ensuring that their leadership style adapts to the organizational context and team dynamics to facilitate innovation.

Ultimately, the interactions between leadership styles, team dynamics and organizational culture collectively inform the performance of innovation in the sector of development of medical devices. By understanding and facing these relationships, organizations can improve their innovation capacity by effectively managing the challenges that arise within this complex panorama (Weintraub and McKee, 2018). The influence of corporate culture on innovation processes is a fundamental area of analysis, in particular within industries that require rapid progress in technology, design and product development. The companies of medical devices must navigate complex regulatory landscapes and market needs, in which corporate culture can significantly model the results of innovation (Tellis et al., 2009). The effective qualities of leadership styles, integrated with the cultural dynamics of an organization are essential to promote an environment in favor of innovation.

Tellis et al. (2009) argue that the alignment between the leadership style of a company and its corporate culture is essential to successfully guide innovation. For example, transformational leadership, characterized by inspiration and vision, often cultivates an organizational culture that encourages creativity and risk-taking. Companies led by these leaders tend to encourage collaborative environments, in which multidisciplinary teams can thrive. This synergy allows different perspectives, which are crucial in the development of new medical devices that meet the various needs of users (Tellis et al., 2009).

Moreover, Tellis et al. (2009) show that an innovative corporate culture is not defined exclusively by the leadership style but also by the underlying values and beliefs that permeate a company. In the sector of medical devices, companies that embrace a culture of continuous improvement and adaptability tend to manage the penalties of innovation more effectively.

These organizations are often characterized by an open environment in which feedback is actively solicited and employees have the power to contribute with ideas, which can lead to revolutionary innovations. The case studies examined by Tellis et al. (2009) illustrate that common challenges can arise between different corporate cultures. For example, the integration of new regulatory requirements can clash with existing cultural rules, leading to resistance to change. The companies that have successfully sailed these challenges, such as those that exemplify a culture of cross-functional collaboration, show that strong communication and clarity on innovation objectives are essential. These cultures actively promote the sharing of knowledge, allowing teams to summarize insights between the domains, and promoting openness to learning and visionary thinking.

However, the challenge of aligning corporate culture with strategic innovation objectives is evident in previously mentioned case studies. Organizations in the medical devices sector often deal with the balancing obstacle of market demands with the fundamental values that define their identity (Tellis et al., 2009). Companies which adapt their cultural narratives aligned with their strategic goals are more likely to produce innovative results. This adaptability often depends on the leadership's ability to model the desired cultural features, supporting innovation while maintaining responsibility for regulatory standards and operational efficiency.

Leadership within this organization adopts a transformational style, characterized by inspiring and motivating employees to overcome their respective interests for the good of the organization. This approach is aligned with the conclusions of Martins and Terblanche (2003), which argue that transformational leaders play a central role in the culture of an environment that promotes creativity. By promoting an open dialogue where ideas can be exchanged freely, leadership encourages a participatory culture that invites various perspectives. Such participatory practices improve not only psychological security but also allow employees to take the initiative and innovate without fear of reprisals for potentially risky ideas. Characteristically, this organization nourishes a unique culture known for its intrinsic motivation and its collaborative philosophy. Employees are motivated to innovate, knowing that their contributions are appreciated and recognized. Plus, the organization is investing in current professional development opportunities, offering employees the tools and skills necessary to stimulate innovation while aligning the personal growth of the company's strategic objectives.

Despite the existence of a strong culture which promotes creativity, the case study also highlights several underlying challenges to this dynamic. An essential challenge is the potential for ambiguity in innovation processes, which can result from the high degree of autonomy granted to employees. Although the empowerment of teams to explore creative solutions can produce breakthroughs, this can also lead to a lack of clarity and steering, resulting in fragmented efforts if they are not effectively managed (Lund, 2003; Weintraub and McKee, 2018).

However, the complexities of the alignment of freedom of creation with strategic advice present continuous challenges, requiring adaptive leadership which can respond in a flexible way both to the dynamics of internal culture and external market forces. Ideas from this study provide valuable contributions to understanding the nuanced relationship between leadership, organizational culture and innovation in the development of medical devices (Weintraub and McKee, 2018). The relationship between leadership styles and innovation in the development of medical devices is complex, influenced by the intrinsic dynamics of the leadership, as well as by the organizational culture and contextual challenges faced by companies in the sector.

Buchanan et al. (2005) underline the importance of aligning leadership practices with innovation objectives, recognizing that various factors contribute to the difficulties encountered in this integration process. A significant challenge is the intrinsic tension between traditional management approaches and the need for adaptive leadership in innovative contexts. Medical device companies often operate within rigorous regulatory frameworks and consolidated practices, which can suffocate the creativity and behavior of the risk necessary for innovation. Leaders who adopt transactional styles can give priority to efficiency and commitment to processes concerning exploratory initiatives, thus inhibiting a flexible exchange of ideas that is crucial for innovation (Buchanan et al., 2005). On the contrary, transformational leadership, which encourages collaboration and empowerment, is often necessary to encourage an innovation-friendly environment. However, changing leadership styles can be satisfied with resistance by individuals accustomed to rigid hierarchical structures, presenting a cultural barrier that leaders must navigate.

In addition, organizational culture plays a fundamental role in modeling the application of leadership styles. In many companies of medical devices, a culture that emphasizes conformity and risk aversion can be harmful to innovative activities. The risk of regulatory repercussions can lead to a cautious mentality between the teams which, if combined with the transactional leadership, can strengthen compliance and suppress innovative thought (Buchanan et al., 2005).

Communication also stands out as a critical component of this alignment. Effective leaders in heavy innovation environments must facilitate open dialogues, allowing different teams to articulate and share their ideas freely. However, communication faults can occur when leaders are unable to adapt their communication styles to the needs of the typical interdisciplinary teams in the development of medical devices. These failures can lead to misunderstandings or a lack of alignment on innovation objectives, eventually preventing progress (Buchanan et al., 2005).

Moreover, external pressures, including competitive market demands and rapid technological progress, impose additional strains on leadership in medical device companies. Leaders must balance the urgency of the needs of the meeting market with the long-term vision required for sustainable innovation. These competing requests can create friction within the organization, in particular when the leadership approaches do not align well with the company's innovation objectives. Therefore, the achievement of consistency between leadership style, organizational culture and innovation strategy requires a nuanced understanding of the external environment in which these companies operate (Buchanan et al., 2005).

In essence, aligning leadership styles with innovation objectives in the development of medical devices involves the overcoming of substantial challenges rooted both in internal dynamics and external pressures. The interaction between leadership quality, organizational culture and specific challenges relating to communication and market needs to promote a complex panorama that requires insightful leadership approaches for the facilitation of successful innovation. Understanding these challenges is essential for leaders who try to fill the gap between consolidated practices and innovative aspirations, thus contributing to the progress of the sector of medical devices. Çakar and Ertürk (2010) underline the importance of empowerment as a fundamental strategy to stimulate innovation, particularly in industries characterized by rapid technological progress and rigorous regulatory requirements, such as the sector of medical devices. The concept of employee empowerment is closely linked to transformational leadership styles, which are characterized by leaders who inspire and motivate their teams to overcome expectations and embrace change (Bass and Avolio, 1994). Empowerment provides for the granting of employees the autonomy, resources and responsibility for making decisions that influence their work processes, ultimately promoting a sense of ownership compared to innovation initiatives. Plus, transformational leaders cultivate an organizational culture that appreciates creativity and open communication, encouraging employees to contribute with innovative ideas and solutions to complex problems. Authorized employees are more likely to take the initiative, explore new paths for product development and effectively collaborate among interdisciplinary teams, essential factors for the success of innovation.

Studies have shown that organizations that adopt enhanced leadership styles promote a culture of innovation by involving employees in decision-making processes and recognizing their contributions. For example, in companies where leaders actively solicit inputs from team members on the functionality of new products or design improvements, employees show greater involvement and commitment to innovation efforts. This participatory approach not only uses a wide range of perspectives but also promotes the intrinsic motivation between employees, improving their skills to resolve problems and the ambition to experience new ideas (Çakar and Ertürk, 2010)

One of the significant barriers identified in the literature is the resistance to change between the existing hierarchies and traditional management practices within the companies of medical devices (Çakar and Ertürk, 2010). Some leaders may feel threatened by the prospect of renouncing control and evaluating their authority for the promotion of an inclusive environment in which ideas can thrive. Companies that cultivate trust, support and shared purpose are more likely to be able to enhance their employees and exploit their creativity (Schein, 2010). On the contrary, organizations with a rigid or punitive culture can suffocate innovation, since employees can fear repercussions for having taken risks or proposing unconventional ideas. Therefore, the strengthening of the leadership must be integrated by an organizational culture that enhances learning from failures and embraces the iterative processes, which are inherent in innovation in the development of medical devices.

Understanding the dynamics between leadership styles, responsibility and innovation is essential to advance the industry of medical devices and deal with the constant evolution needs of health care. In examining the influence of leadership styles on innovation in the development of medical devices, the case study presented by Oke et al. (2009) provides a relevant explanation of how a strategic change in leadership can encourage renewal in innovative practices. The paper explores an organization's leadership strategy, characterized by a transactional style, which was mainly concentrated on consolidated protocols and adherence to operational excellence. This approach underlined the minimum risk and maintenance of the status quo, leading to a culture resistant to change and innovation. The employees reported that they felt discouraged by suggesting new ideas, which contributed to the lack of involvement and a consequent decline in innovative production. Researchers show that such a leadership approach has not only reduced employees but has also created a bureaucratic culture that has suffocated creativity (Oke et al., 2009)

Recognizing the urgent need for revitalization, the company's advice has appointed a new CEO whose leadership style was transformative. This change has marked a fundamental moment in the trajectory of the organization. The transformative leader underlined the vision, inspiration and empowerment, encouraging employees at all levels to contribute to the innovation process. The authors argue that effective transformational leaders show qualities such as strong communication skills, emotional intelligence and the ability to motivate and inspire teams towards a shared vision (Oke et al., 2009). The new leadership attributes significant importance to promoting an organizational culture that has given priority to collaboration, experimentation and open communication.

As a result of this leadership pivot, the Corporation has seen the emergence of a more dynamic organizational culture in favor of innovation. The transformational leader has started several key programs aimed at improving the creativity and generation of ideas, including inter-functional teams dedicated to the exploration of new product concepts and a formal platform for the presentation of innovative ideas. These initiatives not only authorized employees but have also brought together different perspectives and skills, thus enriching the innovation process.

Oke et al. (2009) identify the resulting challenges that arose during this transition period. While many employees were reinvigorated by the new leadership style, others were skeptical about the feasibility of these innovative aspirations, given the previous inertia of the company. The resistance to change was a substantial barrier, which highlighted the importance of careful change management practices in conducting a cultural movement. The transformational leader has faced these challenges through transparent communication, underlining the logic at the base of the round and celebrating small victories to build momentum for a wider acceptance of the change.

While the company moved to a more innovative position, some leaders had to deal with the fear of failure between employees, which could discourage the contribution to the innovation process. By intentionally promoting a culture that considers failures as learning opportunities rather than arrest jokes, leadership has been able to cultivate resilience and encourage continuous improvement. This case study highlights the profound impact of the leadership style on innovation within the realm of the development of medical devices. Moving from a transformational transactional leadership style, the organization has not only rekindled its innovative practices but has also established a picture that has allowed prolonged growth and adaptability in response to the evolving market needs.

A predominant theme is the need for transformational leadership to catalyze innovation in medical device teams. Transformational leaders inspire and motivate employees through a shared vision, promoting an atmosphere of collaboration and creative problem solutions. Data from case studies revealed that these leaders effectively encouraged followers to exceed their interests, leading to significant innovations in product development processes. Besides, these leadership styles were associated with a strong cultural emphasis on learning and experimentation, which in turn encouraged continuous innovation (Prajogo and McDermott, 2005).

Evidence suggests that organizations that cultivate a culture that values feedback and iterative processes - elements of agile methodologies - reported higher instances of successful innovation. This points to the conclusion that an adaptive organizational culture, usually cultivated by support leadership, significantly increases the ability to respond to market needs and technological advances (Prajogo and McDermott, 2005; Elsbach and Stigliani, 2018).

Although some cases exhibited innovative advances under autocratic or transactional leadership styles, findings indicated that these approaches generally stifled creative contributions from lower organizational levels. Case studies illustrated that organizations with rigid hierarchies have faced challenges in innovation because of their inability to involve employees significantly in the process of ideation. These organizations struggled to cultivate an internal culture of innovation, limiting the full potential of various ideas that could promote medical advances (Sinclair, 2005).

On the other hand, leadership approaches that emphasized employee involvement and collaborative decision-making were associated with greater success in innovation. Case studies showed cases where leaders served as facilitators instead of authoritarian figures, promoting an inclusive culture that took advantage of a wide range of specializations. This collaborative environment allowed multifunctional teams to prosper. The importance of aligning the leadership vision with organizational values was a recurring theme. Leaders who effectively communicated their commitment to innovation and aligned it with major organizational goals were more successful in boosting initiatives that led to innovative medical devices. This alignment reflected a cohesive culture that not only adopted innovation but also integrated it as a strategic imperative.

## FUTURE RESEARCH DIRECTIONS AND GAPS IN THE LITERATURE

Based on the ideas collected from all these case studies, several emerging recommendations are correlated with effective leadership qualities with improved innovative results. First, the qualities of transformative leadership such as the outlining of vision and motivation were systematically associated with increased innovation. The leaders who present these traits create an environment where team members feel entitled to explore creative solutions without fear of failure. Consequently, organizations should prioritize the development and selection of managers who not only have strategic foresight but also demonstrate emotional intelligence, allowing them to connect and inspire their teams (Donate and Guadamillas, 2011). Training programs that focus on these attributes could facilitate a climate more favorable to innovation (Elsbach and Stigliani, 2018).

In addition, an opening to feedback and a culture of collaboration has emerged as vital components in successful case studies. The leaders who actively asked for the contributions of the team members and encouraged multidisciplinary collaboration have collected significant innovations. This suggests a need for organizations to cultivate a culture that embraces constructive criticism and interdisciplinary teamwork, thus improving collective problem-solving capacities.

Case studies have also stressed the importance of adaptability in leadership practices. The dynamic nature of the medical devices industry requires a flexible leadership approach, allowing managers to pivot in response to the evolution of market demands. Organizations should therefore invest in regular assessments and training of leadership that promote adaptive management strategies, helping managers remain reactive while stimulating innovation (Donate and Guadamillas, 2011).

In terms of challenges encountered, conflicting priorities between financial constraints and the continuity of innovative projects often hinder progress. Managers must navigate these challenges by promoting a balanced strategic perspective which explains both immediate financial realities and long-term creative aspirations. The implementation of adaptable resource allocation models can mitigate these pressures, allowing supported investments in innovative efforts, even with budget constrictions.

Furthermore, a culture which does not penalize failure but rather considers it as part of the learning process was a recurring theme among successful innovators. Managers must actively strengthen this state of mind, encouraging teams to consider setbacks as growth opportunities. Organizations can undertake initiatives that celebrate failure learning, thus normalizing risk-taking and creativity. This practice can involve narration sessions where team members share inspiring stories to overcome challenges (Sinclair, 2005).

It is also imperative to ensure the diversity of management teams because various perspectives stimulate richer discussions and more robust innovation strategies. Organizations should prioritize the recruitment and promotion of managers of various horizons, promoting an environment where various points of view are adopted and explored. Diversity initiatives not only support innovation directly but also improve organizational resilience to change and disturbances.

Finally, continuous learning and development opportunities play an important role in innovative success. Managers should defend a life culture throughout life, where continuous education is accessible to all team members, equipping them with the latest knowledge and skills of the industry necessary for the development of creative medical devices. Adaptation of training to respond to both technical skills and general skills can further improve the organization's overall adaptability.

The implications of these results underline the need for continuous research on leadership strategies that cause innovation in the medical devices industry. Future studies should analyze the longitudinal effects of various leadership approaches on innovation performance and consider the impact of various organizational cultures in different geographic and regulatory contexts.

## CONCLUSIONS

As a consequence of the implementation of these recommended leadership practices and cultural adjustments, organizations involved in the development of medical devices can create an ecosystem favorable to innovation, ultimately improving their competitive advantage and their response to market needs. The exploration of leadership styles and their influence on innovation in the development of medical devices reveal several critical results which have substantial implications for future leadership strategies in the industry. The case studies analyzed demonstrate that varied leadership styles - transformations, transactional and situational

- have undergone distinct effects on innovation processes, organizational cultures and the resulting challenges faced by medical devices.

A predominant theme is the distinct efficiency of transformational leadership in promoting an innovative environment. The leaders who adopt this style inspire not only their teams but also cultivate an atmosphere in which creativity and risk-taking are encouraged. Case studies indicate that transformational leaders play a central role in the alignment of team members around a shared vision, which is essential in the highly regulated and often resistant context of the medical devices industry. Such alignment can lead to an increase in employee commitment and a desire to adopt change, which is vital for innovative results.

On the other hand, the effectiveness of transactional leadership styles seems to be less conducive to innovation in this sector. Although transactional leaders can obtain short-term results through structured processes and reward-based systems, these approaches can inadvertently suffocate creativity and slow down the required adaptability in dynamic markets. Evidence shows that transactional leadership organizations may experience difficulties in cultivating innovative long-term practices because the emphasis on compliance and performance measures can overshadow the exploration of new ideas.

Moreover, the role of organizational culture is illustrated as an influential factor in the way in which leadership styles have expressed their effects on innovation. An organizational culture that prioritizes collaboration and open communication improves the capacities of transformational leaders to stimulate innovation, whereas cultures resistant to change can pose important challenges for any style of leadership. The results suggest that senior management should take deliberate measures to promote a culture that encourages experimentation and various perspectives because these elements are essential to overcome the challenges inherent in innovation in the development of medical devices.

In addition, the complexity of the regulatory environment specific to medical devices may present unique challenges that meet with leadership styles. Managers must strategically navigate these regulations while simultaneously promoting innovative ideas. Case studies highlight how managers who take advantage of collaborative and adaptive leadership styles can manage these challenges more effectively, suggesting a possible need for hybrid approaches that find adaptive and transformational qualities.

To summarize, the synthesis of these ideas reveals that effective leadership strategies, anchored in an understanding of leadership styles and organizational culture, are essential to promote innovation in the medical devices sector. The survey and continuous adaptation of these strategies will be essential as the industry evolves, highlighting the interdependence of leadership and innovation in the development complexities of medical devices.

## REFERENCES


Bass, B. M. (1999). Two decades of research and development in transformational leadership. *European Journal of Work and Organizational Psychology*, *8*(1), 9–32. DOI: 10.1080/135943299398410

Bass, B. M., & Avolio, B. J. (Eds.). (1994). *Improving organizational effectiveness through transformational leadership*. Sage Publications, Inc.

Bessant, J., & Tidd, J. (2013). *Managing Innovation* (5th ed.). John Wiley.

Buchanan, D., Fitzgerald, L., Ketley, D., Gollop, R., Jones, J. L., Lamont, S. S., Neath, A., & Whitby, E. (2005). No going back: A review of the literature on sustaining organizational change. *International Journal of Management Reviews*, *7*(3), 189–205. DOI: 10.1111/j.1468-2370.2005.00111.x

Çakar, N. D., & Ertürk, A. (2010). Comparing innovation capability of small and medium-sized enterprises: Examining the effects of organizational culture and empowerment. *Journal of Small Business Management*, *48*(3), 325–359. DOI: 10.1111/j.1540-627X.2010.00297.x

Chang, Y.-Y., Hodgkinson, I., Hughes, P., & Chang, C.-Y. (2019). The mediation between participative leadership and employee exploratory innovation: Examining intermediate knowledge mechanisms. *Leadership and Organization Development Journal*, *40*(3), 334–355. DOI: 10.1108/LODJ-07-2018-0245

Donate, M. J., & Guadamillas, F. (2011). Organizational factors to support knowledge management and innovation. *Journal of Knowledge Management*, *15*(6), 890–914. DOI: 10.1108/13673271111179271

Elsbach, K. D., & Stigliani, I. (2018). Design thinking and organizational culture: A review and framework for future research. *Journal of Management*, *44*(6), 2274–2306. DOI: 10.1177/0149206317744252

Hersey, P., & Blanchard, K. H. (1969). Life cycle theory of leadership. *Training and Development Journal*, *23*(5), 26–34.

Hickman, C. R., & Silva, M. A. (2018). *Creating excellence: Managing corporate culture, strategy, and change in the new age*. Routledge. DOI: 10.4324/9781351065306

Huey Yiing, L., & Ahmad, K. (2009). The moderating effects of organizational culture on the relationships between leadership behaviour and organizational commitment and between organizational commitment and job satisfaction and performance. *Leadership and Organization Development Journal*, *30*(1), 53–86. DOI: 10.1108/01437730910927106

Jung, D. I., Chow, C., & Wu, A. (2003). The role of transformational leadership in enhancing organizational innovation: Hypotheses and some preliminary findings. *The Leadership Quarterly*, *14*(4-5), 525–544. DOI: 10.1016/S1048-9843(03)00050-X

Jung, T., Scott, T., Davies, H. T., Bower, P., Whalley, D., McNally, R., & Mannion, R. (2009). Instruments for exploring organizational culture: A review of the literature. *Public Administration Review*, *69*(6), 1087–1096. DOI: 10.1111/j.1540-6210.2009.02066.x

Kirkpatrick, S. A., & Locke, E. A. (1996). Direct and indirect effects of three core charismatic leadership components on performance and attitudes. *The Journal of Applied Psychology*, *81*(1), 36–51. DOI: 10.1037/0021-9010.81.1.36

Lok, P., & Crawford, J. (2001). Antecedents of organizational commitment and the mediating role of job satisfaction. *Journal of Managerial Psychology*, *16*(8), 594–613. DOI: 10.1108/EUM0000000006302

Lok, P., & Crawford, J. (2004). The effect of organisational culture and leadership style on job satisfaction and organisational commitment: A cross-national comparison. *Journal of Management Development*, *23*(4), 321–338. DOI: 10.1108/02621710410529785

Lund, D. B. (2003). Organizational culture and job satisfaction. *Journal of Business and Industrial Marketing*, *18*(3), 219–236. DOI: 10.1108/0885862031047313

Martins, E. C., & Terblanche, F. (2003). Building organisational culture that stimulates creativity and innovation. *European Journal of Innovation Management*, *6*(1), 64–74. DOI: 10.1108/14601060310456337

Mohammad Mosadegh Rad, A. (2006). The impact of organizational culture on the successful implementation of total quality management. *The TQM Magazine*, *18*(6), 606–625. DOI: 10.1108/09544780610707101

Mohammad Mosadegh Rad, A., & Hossein Yarmohammadian, M. (2006). A study of relationship between managers' leadership style and employees' job satisfaction. *Leadership in Health Services*, *19*(2), 11–28. DOI: 10.1108/13660750610665008 PMID: 16875105

Mumford, M. D., Gibson, C., Giorgini, V., & Mecca, J. (2014). Leading for creativity: People, products, and systems.

O'Reilly, C. A.III, & Tushman, M. L. (2013). Organizational ambidexterity: Past, present, and future. *The Academy of Management Perspectives*, *27*(4), 324–338. DOI: 10.5465/amp.2013.0025

Oke, A., Munshi, N., & Walumbwa, F. O. (2009). The influence of leadership on innovation processes and activities. *Organizational Dynamics*, *38*(1), 64–72. DOI: 10.1016/j.orgdyn.2008.10.005

Prajogo, D. I., & McDermott, C. M. (2005). The relationship between total quality management practices and organizational culture. international Journal of operations & production management, 25(11), 1101-1122.

Schein, E. H. (2009). *The corporate culture survival guide* (Vol. 158). John Wiley & Sons.

Sinclair, A. (2005). *Doing leadership differently: Gender, power and sexuality in a changing business culture*. Melbourne Univ. Publishing.

Smith, J., Johnson, M., & Williams, A. (2019). Building Trust in e-Commerce: Exploring the Influence of Website Design Elements on Initial Trust Formation. [JOEUC]. *Journal of Organizational and End User Computing*, *31*, 52–72.

Somech, A. (2006). The effects of leadership style and team process on performance and innovation in functionally heterogeneous teams. *Journal of Management*, *32*(1), 132–157. DOI: 10.1177/0149206305277799

Sosik, J. J., & Godshalk, V. M. (2000). Leadership styles, mentoring functions received, and job-related stress: A conceptual model and preliminary study. *Journal of Organizational Behavior*, *21*(4), 365–390. DOI: 10.1002/(SICI)1099-1379(200006)21:4<365::AID-JOB14>3.0.CO;2-H

Tellis, G. J., Prabhu, J. C., & Chandy, R. K. (2009). Radical innovation across nations: The preeminence of corporate culture. *Journal of Marketing*, *73*(1), 3–23. DOI: 10.1509/jmkg.73.1.003

Tian, M., Deng, P., Zhang, Y., & Salmador, M. P. (2018). How does culture influence innovation? A systematic literature review. *Management Decision*, *56*(5), 1088–1107. DOI: 10.1108/MD-05-2017-0462

Weintraub, P., & McKee, M. (2019, March 1). Leadership for Innovation in Healthcare: An Exploration. *International Journal of Health Policy and Management*, *8*(3), 138–144. DOI: 10.15171/ijhpm.2018.122 PMID: 30980629

Yukl, G., & Mahsud, R. (2010). Why flexible and adaptive leadership is essential. *Consulting Psychology Journal*, *62*(2), 81–93. DOI: 10.1037/a0019835

# Compilation of References


Abbas, J., Al-Sulaiti, K., Lorente, D. B., Shah, S. A. R., & Shahzad, U. (2023). Reset the industry redux through corporate social responsibility: The COVID-19 tourism impact on hospitality firms through business model innovation. In Economic growth and environmental quality in a post-pandemic world (pp. 177-201). Routledge.

Abbas, J. (2024). Does the nexus of corporate social responsibility and green dynamic capabilities drive firms toward green technological innovation? The moderating role of green transformational leadership. *Technological Forecasting and Social Change*, *208*, 123698. DOI: 10.1016/j.techfore.2024.123698

Abdul-Azeez, O. Y., Nwabekee, U. S., Agu, E. E., & Ignatius, T. (2024). Strategic approaches to sustainability in multinational corporations: A comprehensive review. International Journal of Frontline Research in Science and Technology, 3(02), 038-054.

Abraham, N. (2020). Wonder VR: Interactive storytelling through VR 360 video with NHS patients living with dementia. *Contemporary Theatre Review*, *30*(4), 474–489. DOI: 10.1080/10486801.2020.1812591

Abrahams, T. O., Ewuga, S. K., Kaggwa, S., Uwaoma, P. U., Hassan, A. O., & Dawodu, S. O. (2024). Mastering compliance: A comprehensive review of regulatory frameworks in accounting and cybersecurity. *Computer Science & IT Investigation Journal*, *5*(1), 120–140.

Addo, M. K. (Ed.). (2024). *Human rights standards and the responsibility of transnational corporations*. Brill.

Adeniran, I. A., Abhulimen, A. O., Obiki-Osafiele, A. N., Osundare, O. S., Agu, E. E., & Efunniyi, C. P. (2024). Strategic risk management in financial institutions: Ensuring robust regulatory compliance. *Finance & Accounting Research Journal*, *6*(8), 1582–1596. DOI: 10.51594/farj.v6i8.1508

Agu, E. E., Iyelolu, T. V., Idemudia, C., & Ijomah, T. I. (2024). Exploring the relationship between sustainable business practices and increased brand loyalty. *International Journal of Management & Entrepreneurship Research*, *6*(8), 2463–2475. DOI: 10.51594/ijmer.v6i8.1365

Ahmad, M., Al-Amri, J. F., Subahi, A. F., Khatri, S., Seh, A. H., Nadeem, M., & Agrawal, A. (2021). Healthcare device security assessment through computational methodology. *Computer Systems Science and Engineering*, *41*, 811–828. DOI: 10.32604/csse.2022.020097

Ahn, J., Shamim, A., & Park, J. (2021). Impacts of cruise industry corporate social responsibility reputation on customers' loyalty: Mediating role of trust and identification. *International Journal of Hospitality Management*, *92*, 102706. DOI: 10.1016/j.ijhm.2020.102706

Alabdulatif, A., Khalil, I., & Rahman, M. S. (2022). Security of Blockchain and AI-Empowered Smart Healthcare: Application-Based Analysis. *Applied Sciences (Basel, Switzerland)*, *12*(21), 11039. DOI: 10.3390/app122111039

Algarni, A. (2020). A hybrid fuzzy rule-based multi-criteria framework for security assessment of medical device software. *Int. J. Intell. Eng. Syst.*, *13*, 51–62.

Alhakami, W., Baz, A., Alhakami, H., Ahmad, M., & Khan, R. A. (2021). Healthcare device security: Insights and implications. *Intelligent Automation & Soft Computing*, *27*(2), 409–424. DOI: 10.32604/iasc.2021.015351

Ali, S., Abdullah, , Armand, T. P. T., Athar, A., Hussain, A., Ali, M., Yaseen, M., Joo, M.-I., & Kim, H.-C. (2023). Metaverse in Healthcare Integrated with Explainable AI and Blockchain: Enabling Immersiveness, Ensuring Trust, and Providing Patient Data Security. *Sensors (Basel)*, *23*(2), 565. DOI: 10.3390/s23020565 PMID: 36679361

Allen, E. H., Haley, J. M., Aarons, J., & Lawrence, D. (2021). *Leveraging community expertise to advance health equity*. Urban Institute.

AlSaied, M., & McLaughlin, P. (2024). Organizational Culture Enabler and Inhibitor Dimensions for Ambidextrous Innovation. *Administrative Sciences, 14*(9), 207. DOI: 10.3390/admsci14090207

Alshukri, T., Seun Ojekemi, O., Öz, T., & Alzubi, A. (2024). The interplay of corporate social responsibility, innovation capability, organizational learning, and sustainable value creation: Does stakeholder engagement matter? *Sustainability (Basel), 16*(13), 5511. DOI: 10.3390/su16135511

Angerschmid, A., Zhou, J., Theuermann, K., Chen, F., & Holzinger, A. (2022). Fairness and Explanation in AI-Informed Decision Making. *Mach. Learn. Knowl. Extr., 4*(2), 556–579. DOI: 10.3390/make4020026

Ankaralı, Z. E., Abbasi, Q. H., Demir, A. F., Serpedin, E., Qaraqe, K., & Arslan, H. (2014, November). A comparative review on the security research for wireless implantable medical devices. In *Proc. 4th Int. Conf. Wireless Mobile Commun. Healthcare (Mobihealth)* (pp. 246-249).

Antonacopoulou, E. P., & Georgiadou, A. (2021). Leading through social distancing: The future of work, corporations and leadership from home. *Gender, Work and Organization, 28*(2), 749–767. DOI: 10.1111/gwao.12533

Appel, L., Kisonas, E., Appel, E., Klein, J., Bartlett, D., Rosenberg, J., & Smith, C. N. C. (2021). Administering virtual reality therapy to manage behavioral and psychological symptoms in patients with dementia admitted to an acute care hospital: Results of a pilot study. *JMIR Formative Research, 5*(2), e22406. Advance online publication. DOI: 10.2196/22406 PMID: 33533720

Avolio, B. J., & Gardner, W. L. (2005). Authentic leadership development: Getting to the root of positive forms of leadership. *The Leadership Quarterly, 16*(3), 315–338. DOI: 10.1016/j.leaqua.2005.03.001

Avotra, A. A. R. N., Chengang, Y., Wei, X., Ming, J., & Marcelline, T. R. S. (2021). Struggling with business corporate cynical impression? Powerful methods of CSR to enhance corporate image and consumer purchase intention. *Frontiers in Public Health*, *9*, 726727. DOI: 10.3389/fpubh.2021.726727 PMID: 34540793

Bajwa, J., Munir, U., Nori, A., & Williams, B. (2021). Artificial intelligence in healthcare: Transforming the practice of medicine. *Future Healthcare Journal*, *8*(2), e188–e194. DOI: 10.7861/fhj.2021-0095 PMID: 34286183

Basheer, S., & Reddy, T. P. (2008). The efficacy of Indian patent law: Ironing out the creases in Section 3 (d). *SCRIPTed, 5*, 232.

Bass, B. M. (1990). From transactional to transformational leadership: Learning to share the vision. *Organizational Dynamics*, *18*(3), 19–31. DOI: 10.1016/0090-2616(90)90061-S

Bass, B. M. (1999). Two decades of research and development in transformational leadership. *European Journal of Work and Organizational Psychology*, *8*(1), 9–32. DOI: 10.1080/135943299398410

Bass, B. M., & Avolio, B. J. (Eds.). (1994). *Improving organizational effectiveness through transformational leadership*. Sage Publications, Inc.

Bessant, J., & Tidd, J. (2013). *Managing Innovation* (5th ed.). John Wiley.

Biller-Andorno, N., Ferrario, A., Jöbges, S., Krones, T., Massini, F., Barth, P., Arampatzis, G., & Krauthammer, M. AI Support for Ethical Decision-Making around Resuscitation: Proceed with Care. Medrxiv (Cold Spring Harb. Lab.) 2020. preprint. DOI: 10.1101/2020.08.17.20171769

Boateng, A., Ameyaw, C., & Mensah, S. (2022). Assessment of systematic risk management practices on building construction projects in Ghana. *International Journal of Construction Management*, *22*(16), 3128–3136. DOI: 10.1080/15623599.2020.1842962

Bracci, E., & Tallaki, M. (2021). Resilience capacities and management control systems in public sector organisations. *Journal of Accounting & Organizational Change*, *17*(3), 332–351. DOI: 10.1108/JAOC-10-2019-0111

Buchanan, D., Fitzgerald, L., Ketley, D., Gollop, R., Jones, J. L., Lamont, S. S., Neath, A., & Whitby, E. (2005). No going back: A review of the literature on sustaining organizational change. *International Journal of Management Reviews*, *7*(3), 189–205. DOI: 10.1111/j.1468-2370.2005.00111.x

Buckley, M. (2004). Licensing intellectual property: Competition and definitions of abuse of a dominant position in United States and European Union. *Brooklyn Journal of International Law*, *29*, 797.

Burzyńska, O. (2024). Navigating branding frontiers: De-influencing, accessibility, and anti-greenwashing at Patagonia. [Master's thesis, Malmö University]. DiVA Portal.

Çakar, N. D., & Ertürk, A. (2010). Comparing innovation capability of small and medium-sized enterprises: Examining the effects of organizational culture and empowerment. *Journal of Small Business Management*, *48*(3), 325–359. DOI: 10.1111/j.1540-627X.2010.00297.x

Carroll, A. B. (2021). Corporate social responsibility: Perspectives on the CSR construct's development and future. *Business & Society*, *60*(6), 1258–1278. DOI: 10.1177/00076503211001765

Çelik, Ö., & Kaya, E. (2024). *Sağlık Hizmetlerinde Yapay Zeka ve Etik: Bir Bibliyometrik Analiz*. Süleyman Demirel Üniversitesi Vizyoner Dergisi., DOI: 10.21076/vizyoner.1455659

Cezarino, L. O., Liboni, L. B., Hunter, T., Pacheco, L. M., & Martins, F. P. (2022). Corporate social responsibility in emerging markets: Opportunities and challenges for sustainability integration. *Journal of Cleaner Production*, *362*, 132224. DOI: 10.1016/j.jclepro.2022.132224

Challoumis, C. (2024, October). Building a sustainable economy-how ai can optimize resource allocation. In *XVI International Scientific Conference* (pp. 190-224).

Chang, Y.-Y., Hodgkinson, I., Hughes, P., & Chang, C.-Y. (2019). The mediation between participative leadership and employee exploratory innovation: Examining intermediate knowledge mechanisms. *Leadership and Organization Development Journal*, *40*(3), 334–355. DOI: 10.1108/LODJ-07-2018-0245

Charpin, R., Powell, E. E., & Roth, A. V. (2021). The influence of perceived host country political risk on foreign subunits' supplier development strategies. *Journal of Operations Management*, *67*(3), 329–359. DOI: 10.1002/joom.1127

Chen, G., & Rodriguez-Villegas, E. System-level design trade-offs for truly wearable wireless medical devices. In *Proceedings of the Annual International Conference of the IEEE on Engineering in Medicine and Biology Society (EMBC)*, Buenos Aires, Argentina, 31 August–4 September 2010.

Chen, M., Gonzalez, S., Vasilakos, A., Cao, H., & Leung, V. (2010). Body Area Networks: A Survey. *Mobile Networks and Applications*, *16*(2), 171–193. DOI: 10.1007/s11036-010-0260-8

Chen, R. (2024). A investigation applying Rogers' innovation diffusion theory on the adoption process of new teaching methods in secondary education. *Investigation and Advances in Education*, *3*(2), 6–10.

Chen, R. C., & Hung, S. W. (2021). Exploring the impact of corporate social responsibility on real earning management and discretionary accruals. *Corporate Social Responsibility and Environmental Management*, *28*(1), 333–351. DOI: 10.1002/csr.2052

Civelek, M. E. (2018). Essentials of Structural Equation Modeling. In *Zea Books*. DOI: 10.13014/K2SJ1HR5

Competition Act, 2002, § 4, No. 12, Acts of Parliament, 2003 (India).

Conger, J. A., & Kanungo, R. N. (1998). *Charismatic leadership in organizations*. Sage.

Cortes, A. F., & Herrmann, P. (2021). Strategic leadership of innovation: A framework for future investigation. *International Journal of Management Reviews*, *23*(2), 224–243. DOI: 10.1111/ijmr.12246

Costa, J., & Fonseca, J. P. (2022). The impact of corporate social responsibility and innovative strategies on financial performance. *Risks*, *10*(5), 103. DOI: 10.3390/risks10050103

De, D., & Samuel, K. (2020). Evergreening of Patents: A Barrier to New Inventions. *Supremo Amicus*, *22*, 252.

Dey, N., Ashour, A. S., Shi, F., Fong, S. J., & Tavares, J. M. R. (2018). Medical cyber-physical systems: A survey. *Journal of Medical Systems*, *42*(4), 1–13. DOI: 10.1007/s10916-018-0921-x PMID: 29525900

Dinesan, A. (2022). Convergence of Competition Law and Patent Law: Dominant Position Monopoly and Evergreening of Patent. *Jus Corpus LJ*, *3*, 558.

Dohmen, A. E., Merrick, J. R., Saunders, L. W., Stank, T. P., & Goldsby, T. J. (2023). When preemptive risk mitigation is insufficient: The effectiveness of continuity and resilience techniques during COVID-19. *Production and Operations Management*, *32*(5), 1529–1549. DOI: 10.1111/poms.13677

Donate, M. J., & Guadamillas, F. (2011). Organizational factors to support knowledge management and innovation. *Journal of Knowledge Management*, *15*(6), 890–914. DOI: 10.1108/13673271111179271

Dorstewitz, P., & Lal, D. (2022). Re-imagining business agency through multi-agent cross-sector coalitions: Integrating CSR frameworks. *Philosophy of Management*, *21*(1), 87–103. DOI: 10.1007/s40926-021-00180-2 PMID: 34812263

Duan, J., Yao, D., Xu, Y., & Yu, L. (2022). Theory of self-cultivation manifested on Confucianism: A supplement to social exchange theory. *Chinese Management Studies*, *16*(1), 62–77. DOI: 10.1108/CMS-02-2020-0050

Dumitru Mircescu, G. (2023). Corporate Social Responsibility as a Strategic Tool: Impact on Stakeholder Perceptions and Organizational Performance. Case Study: The Pharma Industry. Ovidius University Annals, Series Economic Sciences, 23(1).

Eaton, L., Bridgman, T., & Cummings, S. (2024). Advancing the democratization of work: A new intellectual history of transformational leadership theory. *Leadership*, *20*(3), 125–143. DOI: 10.1177/17427150241232705

Elhoseny, M., Haseeb, K., Shah, A. A., Ahmad, I., Jan, Z., & Alghamdi, M. I. (2021). IoT Solution for AI-Enabled PRIVACY-PRESServing with Big Data Transferring: An Application for Healthcare Using Blockchain. *Energies*, *14*(17), 5364. DOI: 10.3390/en14175364

Elias, M. A., Faversani, L. A., Moreira, J. A. V., Masiero, A. V., & da Cunha, N. V. (2024). Inteligência artificial em saúde e implicações bioéticas: uma revisão sistemática. Revista Bioética, 31, e3542PT. https://doi.org/DOI: 10.1590/1983-803420233542EN

Elsbach, K. D., & Stigliani, I. (2018). Design thinking and organizational culture: A review and framework for future research. *Journal of Management*, *44*(6), 2274–2306. DOI: 10.1177/0149206317744252

Entine, J., Felipe, M. S. S., Groenewald, J.-H., Kershen, D. L., Lema, M., McHughen, A., Nepomuceno, A. L., Ohsawa, R., Ordonio, R. L., & Parrott, W. A. (2021). Regulatory styles for genome edited agricultural plants in select countries and jurisdictions around the world. *Transgenic Investigation*, *30*(4), 551–584. PMID: 33970411

European Commission. (2018). Artificial Intelligence for Europe. in *Communication from the commission to the european parliament, the european council, the council, the european economic and social committee and the committee of the regions* [Report]. https://eur-lex.europa.eu/legal-content/EN/TXT/PDF/?uri=CELEX:52018DC0237 item

F. Hoffmann-La Roche Ltd. & Anr. v. Cipla Ltd., 2008 (37) PTC 71 (Del HC).

Farmer, S. J., & Grund, M. (2008). Revision of the European Patent Convention & (and) Potential Impact on European Patent Practice. *AIPLA QJ, 36*, 419.

Feretzakis, G., Karlis, G., Loupelis, E., Kalles, D., Chatzikyriakou, R., Trakas, N., Karakou, E., Sakagianni, A., Tzelves, L., Petropoulou, S., Tika, A., Dalainas, I., & Kaldis, V. (2022). Using Machine Learning Techniques to Predict Hospital Admission at the Emergency Department. *Journal of Critical Care Medicine*, *8*(2), 107–116. DOI: 10.2478/jccm-2022-0003 PMID: 35950158

Flynn, A., Healy, D., Barry, M., Brennan, A., Redfern, S., Houghton, C., & Casey, D. (2022). Key stakeholders' experiences and perceptions of virtual reality for older adults living with dementia: Systematic review and thematic synthesis. *JMIR Serious Games*, *10*(4), e37228. Advance online publication. DOI: 10.2196/37228 PMID: 36563042

Formosa, P., Rogers, W., Bankins, S., Griep, Y., & Richards, D. (2022). Medical AI and Human Dignity: Contrasting Perceptions of Human and Artificially Intelligent (AI) Decision Making in Diagnostic and Medical Resource Allocation Contexts. *Computers in Human Behavior*, *133*, 107296. DOI: 10.1016/j.chb.2022.107296

Garattini, S., Natsis, Y., & Banzi, R. (2021). Pharmaceutical strategy for Europe: Reflections on public health-driven drug development, regulation, and policies. *Frontiers in Pharmacology*, *12*, 685604. DOI: 10.3389/fphar.2021.685604 PMID: 33995113

Garg, A. (2024). Emergency Services. In: Handbook on Hospital Planning & Designing. Springer, Singapore. https://doi.org/DOI: 10.1007/978-981-99-9001-6_12

Ghobakhloo, M., Iranmanesh, M., Morales, M. E., Nilashi, M., & Amran, A. (2023). Actions and approaches for enabling Industry 5.0-driven sustainable industrial transformation: A strategy roadmap. *Corporate Social Responsibility and Environmental Management*, *30*(3), 1473–1494. DOI: 10.1002/csr.2431

Goleman, D. (1998). What makes a leader? *Harvard Business Review, 76*(6), 93–102. PMID: 10187249

Goleman, D. (2000). *Leadership that gets results*. Harvard Business Review Press.

Gollakota, S., Hassanieh, H., Ransford, B., Katabi, D., & Fu, K. (2011, August). They can hear your heartbeats: Non-invasive security for implantable medical devices. In *Proceedings of the ACM SIGCOMM 2011 conference* (pp. 2-13).

Gomase, V., Priyadarshi, D., & Kathikar, P. (2023). Theories of Grant for Intellectual Property Rights. *Issue 3 Int'l JL Mgmt. &. Human., 6*, 1046.

Gomes, G., Paixão, H., & Luiza, M. (2024). Desafios do uso da inteligência artificial nos diagnósticos de saúde: Uma revisão integrativa. *Cadernos Ibero-americanos de Direito Sanitario = Cuadernos Iberoamericanos de Derecho Sanitario, 13*(2), 11–18. DOI: 10.17566/ciads.v13i2.1241

Grondys, K., Ślusarczyk, O., Hussain, H. I., & Androniceanu, A. (2021). Risk assessment of the SME sector operations during the COVID-19 pandemic. [PubMed]. *International Journal of Environmental Research and Public Health, 18*(8), 4183.

Gui, L., Lei, H., & Le, P. B. (2024). Fostering product and process innovation through transformational leadership and knowledge management capability: The moderating function of innovation culture. *European Journal of Innovation Management, 27*(1), 214–232. DOI: 10.1108/EJIM-02-2022-0063

Gupta, H., Kumar, A., & Wasan, P. (2021). Industry 4.0, cleaner production and circular economy: An integrative framework for evaluating ethical and sustainable business performance of manufacturing organizations. *Journal of Cleaner Production, 295*, 126253. DOI: 10.1016/j.jclepro.2021.126253

Gurgula, O. (2020). Strategic patenting by pharmaceutical companies–should competition law intervene? *IIC; International Review of Industrial Property and Copyright Law, 51*(9), 1062–1085. DOI: 10.1007/s40319-020-00985-0 PMID: 33132411

Guzzi, P. H., Defilippo, A., & Veltri, P. (2023). A novel Network Science Algorithm for Improving Triage of Patients. https://doi.org/https://doi.org/10.48550/arXiv.2310.05996Focustolearnmore DOI: 10.1109/BIBM58861.2023.10385396

Halperin, D., Heydt-Benjamin, T. S., Ransford, B., Clark, S. S., Defend, B., Morgan, W., . . . Maisel, W. H. (2008, May). Pacemakers and implantable cardiac defibrillators: Software radio attacks and zero-power defenses. In 2008 IEEE Symposium on Security and Privacy (sp 2008) (pp. 129-142). IEEE.

Hamadeh, W. A. (2024). Artificial intelligence in emergency medicine: A narrative review. *International Journal of Scientific Research*, *13*(09), 1–5. Advance online publication. DOI: 10.36106/ijsr/9024151

Hamwi, M., Lizarralde, I., & Legardeur, J. (2021). Demand response business model canvas: A tool for flexibility creation in the electricity markets. *Journal of Cleaner Production*, *282*, 124539. DOI: 10.1016/j.jclepro.2020.124539

Han, B. (2024). Retracted Article: Fostering sustainability: integrating social responsibility, green finance, and corporate performance. *Economic Change and Restructuring*, *57*(2), 64. DOI: 10.1007/s10644-024-09656-3

Hanna, S., Rolles, R., Molina-Markham, A., Poosankam, P., Blocki, J., Fu, K., & Song, D. (2011, August). Take Two Software Updates and See Me in the Morning: The Case for Software Security Evaluations of Medical Devices. In HealthSec.

Haque, S., Aziz, S., & Rahman, M. (2014). Review of Cyber-Physical System in Healthcare. *International Journal of Distributed Sensor Networks*, *2014*(4), 217415. DOI: 10.1155/2014/217415

Hasan, I., Singh, S., & Kashiramka, S. (2022). Does corporate social responsibility disclosure impact firm performance? An industry-wise analysis of Indian firms. *Environment, Development and Sustainability*, *24*(8), 10141–10181. DOI: 10.1007/s10668-021-01859-2

Haugan, G., & Eriksson, M. (2021). Health promotion in health care–vital theories and research.

Hersey, P., & Blanchard, K. H. (1969). Life cycle theory of leadership. *Training and Development Journal, 23*(5), 26–34.

Hickman, C. R., & Silva, M. A. (2018). *Creating excellence: Managing corporate culture, strategy, and change in the new age*. Routledge. DOI: 10.4324/9781351065306

Hopewell, S., McDonald, S., Clarke, M. J., & Egger, M. (2007). Grey literature in meta-analyses of randomized trials of health care interventions. In *Cochrane Database of Systematic Reviews* (Issue 2). John Wiley and Sons Ltd. https://doi.org/DOI: 10.1002/14651858.MR000010.pub3

House, R. J. (1977). A 1976 theory of charismatic leadership. In Hunt, J. G., & Larson, L. L. (Eds.), *Leadership: The cutting edge* (pp. 189–207). Southern Illinois University Press.

Huey Yiing, L., & Ahmad, K. (2009). The moderating effects of organizational culture on the relationships between leadership behaviour and organizational commitment and between organizational commitment and job satisfaction and performance. *Leadership and Organization Development Journal, 30*(1), 53–86. DOI: 10.1108/01437730910927106

Ion, L. M., Vodă, A. I., Butnaru, R. C., Butnaru, G. I., & Mircea Chirita, G. (2021). Effect of pharmaceutical companies' corporate reputation on drug prescribing intents in Romania. Economic research-. *Ekonomska Istrazivanja, 34*(1), 521–544. DOI: 10.1080/1331677X.2020.1798263

Ivascu, L., Ali, W., Khalid, R., & Raza, M. (2022). The impact of competitive strategies on performance of banking sector; the mediating role of corporate social responsibility and operational excellence. *Energies, 16*(1), 297. DOI: 10.3390/en16010297

Jayaratne, T. E. (2024). The value of quantitative methodology for feminist investigation 1. In *Theories of women's studies* (pp. 140–161). Routledge. DOI: 10.4324/9781003516392-10

Jung, D. I., Chow, C., & Wu, A. (2003). The role of transformational leadership in enhancing organizational innovation: Hypotheses and some preliminary findings. *The Leadership Quarterly*, *14*(4-5), 525–544. DOI: 10.1016/S1048-9843(03)00050-X

Jung, T., Scott, T., Davies, H. T., Bower, P., Whalley, D., McNally, R., & Mannion, R. (2009). Instruments for exploring organizational culture: A review of the literature. *Public Administration Review*, *69*(6), 1087–1096. DOI: 10.1111/j.1540-6210.2009.02066.x

Kachman, M. M., Brennan, I., Oskvarek, J. J., Waseem, T., & Pines, J. M. (2024). How artificial intelligence could transform emergency care. *The American Journal of Emergency Medicine*, *81*, 40–46. DOI: 10.1016/j.ajem.2024.04.024 PMID: 38663302

Kaittani, N. (2023). Corporate Social Responsibility: Where did it Originate From, How has it Evolved and Why is it Important?: a literature review of the history and evolution of CSR.

Kanade, T. M., Joseph, J., Ansari, S., Varghese, M. A. M., & Savale, T. (2024). Solid waste management for environmental sustainability and human health. *Journal of Informatics Education and Research*, *4*(1).

Kant, A. (2013). An attempt at quantification of 'efficacy' factors under Section 3 (d) of the Indian Patents Act.

Karwowski, M., & Raulinajtys-Grzybek, M. (2021). The application of corporate social responsibility (CSR) actions for mitigation of environmental, social, corporate governance (ESG) and reputational risk in integrated reports. *Corporate Social Responsibility and Environmental Management*, *28*(4), 1270–1284. DOI: 10.1002/csr.2137

Kavianpour, S., Shanmugam, B., Zolait, A., & Razaq, A. (2021). A Framework to Detect Cyber-attacks against Networked Medical Devices (Internet of Medical Things): An Attack-Surface-Reduction by Design Approach. *Int. J. Comput. Digit. Syst.*, *11*, 1–12.

Keshta, I. (2022). AI-Driven IoT for Smart Health Care: Security and Privacy Issues. *Informatics in Medicine Unlocked, 30*, 100903. DOI: 10.1016/j.imu.2022.100903

Khalid, N., Qayyum, A., Qayyum, A., Al-Fuqaha, A., & Qadir, J. (2023). Privacy-Preserving Artificial Intelligence in Healthcare: Techniques and Applications. *Computers in Biology and Medicine, 158*, 106848. DOI: 10.1016/j.compbiomed.2023.106848 PMID: 37044052

Khalifa, M., Albadawy, M., & Iqbal, U. (2024). Advancing clinical decision support: The role of artificial intelligence across six domains. In *Computer Methods and Programs in Biomedicine Update* (Vol. 5). Elsevier B.V., DOI: 10.1016/j.cmpbup.2024.100142

Khan, D., & Sharma, A. A. (2024, September 20). Competition Commission of India's jurisdiction across all sectoral boundaries. *SCC Online*. Retrieved from https://www.scconline.com/blog/post/2024/09/20/competition-commission-of-india-jurisdiction-across-all-sectoral-boundaries/

Khan, T., Emon, M. M. H., & Siam, S. A. J. (2024). Impact of Green Supply Chain Practices on Sustainable Development in Bangladesh. Available at *SSRN* 4958443.

Khattak, A., Tabash, M. I., Yousaf, Z., Radulescu, M., Nassani, A. A., & Haffar, M. (2022). Towards innovation sustainability of SMEs: Investigating the function of digital platforms, innovation culture and frugal innovation in emerging economies. *Journal of Entrepreneurship in Emerging Economies, 14*(5), 796–811. DOI: 10.1108/JEEE-08-2021-0318

Khorram-Manesh, A., Dulebenets, M. A., & Goniewicz, K. (2021). Implementing public health strategies—the need for educational initiatives: A systematic review. *International Journal of Environmental Research and Public Health, 18*(11), 5888. DOI: 10.3390/ijerph18115888 PMID: 34070882

Kim, J. H., Park, S., & Lim, H. (2021). Developing a virtual reality for people with dementia in nursing homes based on their psychological needs: A feasibility study. *BMC Geriatrics, 21*(1), 167. Advance online publication. DOI: 10.1186/s12877-021-02125-w PMID: 33678160

Kim, S. (2023). The COVID-19 pandemic and corporate social responsibility of Korean global firms: From the perspective of stakeholder theory. *Emerald Open Research, 1*(4). Advance online publication. DOI: 10.1108/EOR-04-2023-0013

Kirkpatrick, S. A., & Locke, E. A. (1996). Direct and indirect effects of three core charismatic leadership components on performance and attitudes. *The Journal of Applied Psychology, 81*(1), 36–51. DOI: 10.1037/0021-9010.81.1.36

Kolling, C., Ribeiro, J. L. D., & de Medeiros, J. F. (2022). Performance of the cosmetics industry from the perspective of Corporate Social Responsibility and Design for Sustainability. *Sustainable Production and Consumption, 30*, 171–185. DOI: 10.1016/j.spc.2021.12.002

Kotter, J. P. (1996). *Leading change*. Harvard Business School Press.

Kouzes, J. M., & Posner, B. Z. (2017). *The Leadership Challenge: How to Make Extraordinary Things Happen in Organizations* (6th ed.). Wiley.

Lazzini, A., Lazzini, S., & Balluchi, F. (2023). Social and moral accountability in action: the religious roots of corporate social responsibility in an Italian entrepreneurial family (1900–1950). Accounting History Review.

Lee, I., Sokolsky, O., Chen, S., Hatcliff, J., Jee, E., Kim, B., King, A., Mullen-Fortino, M., Park, S., & Roederer, A.. (2012). Challenges and research directions in medical cyber–physical systems. *Proceedings of the IEEE, 100*(1), 75–90. DOI: 10.1109/JPROC.2011.2165270

Lee, Y. J., & Cho, M. (2022). Socially stigmatized company's CSR efforts during the COVID-19 pandemic: The effects of CSR fit and perceived motives. *Public Relations Review, 48*(2), 102180. DOI: 10.1016/j.pubrev.2022.102180 PMID: 35368969

Liberati, A., Altman, D. G., Tetzlaff, J., Mulrow, C., Gøtzsche, P. C., Ioannidis, J. P. A., Clarke, M., Devereaux, P. J., Kleijnen, J., & Moher, D. (2009). The PRISMA statement for reporting systematic reviews and meta-analyses of studies that evaluate health care interventions: Explanation and elaboration. In *PLoS Medicine* (Vol. 6, Issue 7). https://doi.org/ DOI: 10.1371/journal.pmed.1000100

Lok, P., & Crawford, J. (2001). Antecedents of organizational commitment and the mediating role of job satisfaction. *Journal of Managerial Psychology*, *16*(8), 594–613. DOI: 10.1108/EUM0000000006302

Lok, P., & Crawford, J. (2004). The effect of organisational culture and leadership style on job satisfaction and organisational commitment: A cross-national comparison. *Journal of Management Development*, *23*(4), 321–338. DOI: 10.1108/02621710410529785

Lund, D. B. (2003). Organizational culture and job satisfaction. *Journal of Business and Industrial Marketing*, *18*(3), 219–236. DOI: 10.1108/0885862031047313

Lu, R. (2023). Set it in stone: Patagonia and the evolution toward stakeholder governance in social enterprise business structures. *Columbia Journal of Law and Social Problems*, *57*(4), 1–45.

Luyang, L. (2024). Brand management from the perspective of sustainable development: Responsibility marketing and social value creation. *Academic Journal of Business & Management*, *6*(1), 15–30.

Lv, Q., Jiang, J., Ma, S., Liu, L., Zhou, Z., Liu, L., Wang, X., & Bai, J. (2022). Catalytic pyrolysis of oil-based drill cuttings over metal oxides: The product properties and ecosystemal risk assessment of heavy metals in char. *Process Safety and Environmental Protection*, *159*, 354–361. DOI: 10.1016/j.psep.2021.12.063

Magalhães, M. E. A., Silva, C. V. L., da, , Oliveira, H. M., de, , Lima, A. B. R., de, , Flores, M. T. S., Leite, I. F., Silva, G. A., da, , Faria, I. A. F. K., de, , Cruz, A. N., da, , & Costa, J. H. (2024). The Use of Artificial Intelligence in Patient Triage in Emergency Departments: An Integrative Review. *Revista de Gestão Social e Ambiental, 18*(12), e010260. DOI: 10.24857/rgsa.v18n12-052

Mahato, R. (2022). "Artificial intelligence, what is it?" *in Outcomes of Best Practices in Classroom.* India. L' Ordine Nuovo Publication. pp. 197-202

Mahmood, S., Zaman, S., & Chaman, S. (2024). The Function of Transformational Leadership and Intellectual Capital to Augment Service Quality in Tourism Sector. *Pakistan Social Sciences Review, 8*(4), 515–635.

Martins, E. C., & Terblanche, F. (2003). Building organisational culture that stimulates creativity and innovation. *European Journal of Innovation Management, 6*(1), 64–74. DOI: 10.1108/14601060310456337

Matsutani, L., Rampasso, I. S., Serafim, M. P., Quelhas, O. L., Leal Filho, W., & Anholon, R. (2022). Critical analysis of corporate social responsibility projects developed by Brazilian companies: Providing new insights for debates. *Cleaner Engineering and Technology, 7*, 100412. DOI: 10.1016/j.clet.2022.100412

Maxwell, J. C. (2007). *The 21 Irrefutable Laws of Leadership: Follow Them and People Will Follow You.* HarperCollins.

McGowran, P., & Donovan, A. (2021). Assemblage theory and disaster risk management. *Progress in Human Geography, 45*(6), 1601–1624. DOI: 10.1177/03091325211003328

Metwally, A. B. M., Elsharkawy, A. A. M., & Salem, M. I. (2024). The impact of corporate social responsibility on operating cash flow opacity: The moderating role of tax avoidance. *Cogent Business & Management, 11*(1), 2390692. DOI: 10.1080/23311975.2024.2390692

Mitchell, R., & Chen, I. R. (2014). Behavior rule specification-based intrusion detection for safety critical medical cyber physical systems. *IEEE Transactions on Dependable and Secure Computing*, *12*(1), 16–30. DOI: 10.1109/TDSC.2014.2312327

Mohammad Mosadegh Rad, A. (2006). The impact of organizational culture on the successful implementation of total quality management. *The TQM Magazine*, *18*(6), 606–625. DOI: 10.1108/09544780610707101

Mohammad Mosadegh Rad, A., & Hossein Yarmohammadian, M. (2006). A study of relationship between managers' leadership style and employees' job satisfaction. *Leadership in Health Services*, *19*(2), 11–28. DOI: 10.1108/13660750610665008 PMID: 16875105

Morea, D., Fortunati, S., & Martiniello, L. (2021). Circular economy and corporate social responsibility: Towards an integrated strategic approach in the multinational cosmetics industry. *Journal of Cleaner Production*, *315*, 128232. DOI: 10.1016/j.jclepro.2021.128232

Morley, J., Machado, C., Burr, C., Cowls, J., Taddeo, M., & Floridi, L. (2019). The debate on the ethics of AI in health care: a reconstruction and critical review. Available at *SSRN* 3486518.

Mosaiyebzadeh, F., Pouriyeh, S., Parizi, R. M., Sheng, Q. Z., Han, M., Zhao, L., Sannino, G., Ranieri, C. M., Ueyama, J., & Batista, D. M. (2023). Privacy-Enhancing Technologies in Federated Learning for the Internet of Healthcare Things: A Survey. *Electronics (Basel)*, *12*(12), 2703. DOI: 10.3390/electronics12122703

Moslehpour, M., Chau, K. Y., Tu, Y. T., Nguyen, K. L., Barry, M., & Reddy, K. D. (2022). Impact of corporate sustainable practices, government initiative, technology usage, and organizational culture on automobile industry sustainable performance. *Environmental Science and Pollution Research International*, *29*(55), 83907–83920. DOI: 10.1007/s11356-022-21591-2 PMID: 35776298

Muhlfeit, J., & Costi, M. (2015). *The Positive Leader: How Energy and Happiness Fuel Top-Performing Teams*. Pearson.

Muleev, E. (2024). Orchestration of Marketplaces and Bureaucratic Knowledge Production in the Moscow Transportation Reform. *Urban Planning*, *9*(2).

Mumford, M. D., Gibson, C., Giorgini, V., & Mecca, J. (2014). Leading for creativity: People, products, and systems.

Munjal, K., & Bhatia, R. (2022). A Systematic Review of Homomorphic Encryption and Its Contributions in Healthcare Industry. *Complex & Intelligent Systems*, *9*(4), 3759–3786. DOI: 10.1007/s40747-022-00756-z PMID: 35531323

Murray, A., Kim, D., & Combs, J. (2023). The promise of a decentralized internet: What is Web3 and how can firms prepare? *Business Horizons*, *66*(2), 191–202. DOI: 10.1016/j.bushor.2022.06.002

Mysaka, H., Derun, I., & Skliaruk, I. (2021). The role of non-financial reporting in modern ecological problems updating and solving. *Journal of Environmental Management and Tourism*, *12*(1), 18–29. DOI: 10.14505/jemt.v12.1(49).02

Nabella, S. D., Rivaldo, Y., Kurniawan, R., Nurmayunita, N., Sari, D. P., Luran, M. F., Amirullah, A., Saputra, E. K., Rizki, M., Sova, M., Nurhayati, , & Wulandari, K. (2022). The Influence of Leadership and Organizational Culture Mediated by Organizational Climate on Governance at Senior High School in Batam City. *Journal of Educational and Social Research*, *12*(5), 119–130. DOI: 10.36941/jesr-2022-0127

Ning, Y., Teixayavong, S., Shang, Y., Savulescu, J., Nagaraj, V., Miao, D., Mertens, M., Ting, D. S. W., Ong, J. C. L., Liu, M., Cao, J., Dunn, M., Vaughan, R., Ong, M. E. H., Sung, J. J.-Y., Topol, E. J., & Liu, N. (2024, November). Generative artificial intelligence and ethical considerations in health care: A scoping review and ethics checklist. *The Lancet. Digital Health*, *6*(11), e848–e856. Advance online publication. DOI: 10.1016/S2589-7500(24)00143-2 PMID: 39294061

Niyommaneerat, W., Suwanteep, K., & Chavalparit, O. (2023). Sustainability indicators to achieve a circular economy: A case study of renewable energy and plastic waste recycling corporate social responsibility (CSR) projects in Thailand. *Journal of Cleaner Production, 391*, 136203. DOI: 10.1016/j.jclepro.2023.136203

Northouse, P. G. (2018). *Leadership: Theory and practice* (8th ed.). Sage.

Nunes, H. da C., Guimarães, R. M. C., & Dadalto, L. (2022). Desafios bioéticos do uso da inteligência artificial em hospitais. *Revista Bioética, 30*(1), 82–93. DOI: 10.1590/1983-80422022301509pt

Núnez, A.-G., Quiroz-Palma, P., Carmen Penadés, M., Parra, O., & Alvear, O. (2024). *Envisioning the Future of Emergency Management focused on Artificial Intelligence*.

O'Reilly, C. A.III, & Tushman, M. L. (2013). Organizational ambidexterity: Past, present, and future. *The Academy of Management Perspectives, 27*(4), 324–338. DOI: 10.5465/amp.2013.0025

Obeng, H. A., Arhinful, R., Mensah, L., & Owusu-Sarfo, J. S. (2024). Assessing the Influence of the Knowledge Management Cycle on Job Satisfaction and Organizational Culture Considering the Interplay of Employee Engagement. *Sustainability (Basel), 16*(20), 8728. DOI: 10.3390/su16208728

OECD. (2020). Abuse of dominance in digital markets (p. 7). *Organisation for Economic Co-operation and Development*. Retrieved from https://www.oecd.org/competition/globalforum/abuse-of-dominance-in-digital-markets.htm

Ogbu, A. D., Eyo-Udo, N. L., Adeyinka, M. A., Ozowe, W., & Ikevuje, A. H. (2023). A conceptual procurement model for sustainability and climate change mitigation in the oil, gas, and energy sectors. *World Journal of Advanced Research and Reviews, 20*(3), 1935–1952. DOI: 10.30574/wjarr.2023.20.3.2304

Oke, A., Munshi, N., & Walumbwa, F. O. (2009). The influence of leadership on innovation processes and activities. *Organizational Dynamics*, *38*(1), 64–72. DOI: 10.1016/j.orgdyn.2008.10.005

Okoye, C. C., Ofodile, O. C., Nifise, A. O. A., Odeyemi, O., & Tula, S. T. (2024). Climate risk assessment in petroleum operations: A review of CSR practices for sustainable Resilience in the United States and Africa. *GSC Advanced Research and Reviews*, *18*(2), 234–245. DOI: 10.30574/gscarr.2024.18.2.0060

Okoye, C. C., Ofodile, O. C., Tula, S. T., Nifise, A. O. A., Falaiye, T., Ejairu, E., & Addy, W. A. (2024). Risk management in international supply chains: A review with USA and African Cases. *Magna Scientia Advanced Investigation and Reviews*, *10*(1), 256–264. DOI: 10.30574/msarr.2024.10.1.0024

Olatunji, I. E., Rauch, J., Katzensteiner, M., & Khosla, M. (2022). A Review of Anonymization for Healthcare Data. *Big Data*. PMID: 35271377

Oliveira, J., Gamito, P., Souto, T., Conde, R., Ferreira, M., Corotnean, T., Fernandes, A., Silva, H., & Neto, T. (2021). Virtual reality-based cognitive stimulation on people with mild to moderate dementia due to Alzheimer's disease: A pilot randomized controlled trial. *International Journal of Environmental Research and Public Health*, *18*(10), 5290. Advance online publication. DOI: 10.3390/ijerph18105290 PMID: 34065698

Onu, P., Pradhan, A., & Mbohwa, C. (2024). Potential to use metaverse for future teaching and learning. *Education and Information Technologies*, *29*(7), 8893–8924. DOI: 10.1007/s10639-023-12167-9

Orozco, D. (2024). Innovation stakeholders: Developing a sustainable paradigm to integrate intellectual property and corporate social responsibility. *American Business Law Journal*, *61*(3), 211–237. DOI: 10.1111/ablj.12249

Oshioste, E. E., Okoye, C. C., & Udokwu, S. T. C. (2023). *The effectiveness of CSR in sustainable development: A case-study of Total's oil exploration activities in the Niger-Delta region. Economic Growth and Environment Sustainability*. EGNES.

Ozsoy, T. (2022). The influence of innovative organizational climate on staff job satisfaction. *Marketing i Menedžment Innovacij*, *2*, 9–16.

Page, M. J., McKenzie, J. E., Bossuyt, P. M., Boutron, I., Hoffmann, T. C., Mulrow, C. D., Shamseer, L., Tetzlaff, J. M., Akl, E. A., Brennan, S. E., Chou, R., Glanville, J., Grimshaw, J. M., Hróbjartsson, A., Lalu, M. M., Li, T., Loder, E. W., Mayo-Wilson, E., McDonald, S., & Moher, D. (2021). The PRISMA 2020 statement: An updated guideline for reporting systematic reviews. *BMJ (Clinical Research Ed.)*, *372*(71), n71. Advance online publication. DOI: 10.1136/bmj.n71 PMID: 33782057

Page, M. J., McKenzie, J. E., Bossuyt, P. M., Boutron, I., Hoffmann, T., Mulrow, C. D., Shamseer, L., Tetzlaff, J., Akl, E. A., & Brennan, S.. (2021). The PRISMA 2020 Statement: An Updated Guideline for Reporting Systematic Reviews. *BMJ (Clinical Research Ed.)*, *372*(71). PMID: 33782057

Pallathadka, H., & Pallathadka, L. K. (2022). Impact of CSR Practices on Firms' Goodwill: An Empirical Investigation. *Integrated Journal for Research in Arts and Humanities*, *2*(6), 239–246. DOI: 10.55544/ijrah.2.6.32

Panagopoulos, A., Minssen, T., Sideri, K., Yu, H., & Compagnucci, M. C. (2022). Incentivizing the Sharing of Healthcare Data in the AI Era. *Computer Law & Security Review*, *45*, 105670. DOI: 10.1016/j.clsr.2022.105670

Pelikánová, R. M., & Rubáček, F. (2022). Taxonomy for transparency in non-financial statements–clear duty with unclear sanction. *Danube*, *13*(3), 173–195. DOI: 10.2478/danb-2022-0011

Pereira, T., Morgado, J., Silva, F., Pelter, M. M., Dias, V., De Cássia Nogueira Barros, R., De Freitas, C., Negrão, E., De Lima, B. F., & Da Silva, M. C.. (2021). Sharing Biomedical Data: Strengthening AI Development in Healthcare. *Health Care*, *9*, 827. PMID: 34208830

Pfajfar, G., Shoham, A., Małecka, A., & Zalaznik, M. (2022). Value of corporate social responsibility for multiple stakeholders and social impact–Relationship marketing perspective. *Journal of Business Research*, *143*, 46–61. DOI: 10.1016/j.jbusres.2022.01.051

Phiri, A. K., Juba, O. O., Baladaniya, M., Regal, H. Y. A., & Nteziryayo, T. (2024). *Strategies for quality health standards*. Cari Journals USA LLC.

Prajogo, D. I., & McDermott, C. M. (2005). The relationship between total quality management practices and organizational culture. international Journal of operations & production management, 25(11), 1101-1122.

Prakash, S., Balaji, J. N., Joshi, A., & Surapaneni, K. M. (2022). Ethical Conundrums in the Application of Artificial Intelligence (AI) in Healthcare—A Scoping Review of Reviews. *Journal of Personalized Medicine, 12*(11), 1914. DOI: 10.3390/jpm12111914 PMID: 36422090

Prakhar, P. (2023). Interplay between Competition Law and IPR. *Issue 1 Indian JL & Legal Rsch., 5*, 1.

Presidência do Conselho de Ministros. (2023). "Decreto-Lei n.º 102/2023". *Diário da República,* 1ª série, 215 (novembro): 4-20. https://diariodarepublica.pt/dr/detalhe/decreto-lei/102-2023-223906278

Purwanda, E., & Achmad, W. (2022). Environmental concerns in the framework of general sustainable development and tourism sustainability. *Journal of Environmental Management & Tourism, 13*(7), 1911–1917. DOI: 10.14505/jemt.v13.7(63).11

Rabinowitz, J. (2018). *Protecting Patients with Cybersecurity*. Healthcare GLOBAL.

Ragavi, V., Santha Sheela, A. C., & Narayanan Kannaiyan, G. (2021). Impact of Artificial Intelligence in the field of Health Care. *Journal of Physics: Conference Series, 1831*(1), 012006. Advance online publication. DOI: 10.1088/1742-6596/1831/1/012006

Rahman, A., Hossain, M. S., Muhammad, G., Kundu, D., Debnath, T., Rahman, M. S., Khan, M. S. I., Tiwari, P., & Band, S. S. (2022). Federated Learning-Based AI Approaches in Smart Healthcare: Concepts, Taxonomies, Challenges and Open Issues. *Cluster Computing, 26*(4), 2271–2311. DOI: 10.1007/s10586-022-03658-4 PMID: 35996680

Rajput, S., Sharma, P. K., & Malviya, R. (2023). Artificial intelligence for emergency medical care. In *Health Care Science*. John Wiley and Sons Inc., DOI: 10.1002/hcs2.72

Ramos, A., Koesmono, T., Ellitan, L., & Otok, B. W. (2023). The Influence of Strategic Leadership, Organizational Learning, And Organizational Culture on Organizational Sustainability Through Organizational Citizenship Behavior in Timor-Leste National Police Using Structural Equation Modeling. *Fiscals and Business Quarterly Reviews, 6*(1).

Reddy, S., Allan, S., Coghlan, S., & Cooper, P. (2019). A Governance Model for the Application of AI in Health Care. *Journal of the American Medical Informatics Association : JAMIA, 27*(3), 491–497. DOI: 10.1093/jamia/ocz192 PMID: 31682262

Richardson, J. W., Smith, C., Curtis, S., Watson, S. E., Zhu, X., Barry, B. A., & Sharp, R. R. (2021). Patient Apprehensions about the Use of Artificial Intelligence in Healthcare. *NPJ Digital Medicine*, *4*(1), 140. DOI: 10.1038/s41746-021-00509-1 PMID: 34548621

Rinawiyanti, E. D., Huang, X., & As-Saber, S. (2021). Adopting management control systems through CSR strategic integration and investigating its impact on company performance: Evidence from Indonesia. *Corporate Governance (Bradford), 21*(3), 463–478. DOI: 10.1108/CG-04-2020-0150

Rini, S. (2023). Applying Indonesia Regulation on Fire Protection System at WTC 1 Building in Jakarta through Fire Risk Assessment (FRA). *E3S Web of Conferences, 388*, 1033.

Rivo-López, E., Villanueva-Villar, M., Michinel-Álvarez, M., & Reyes-Santías, F. (2021). Corporate social responsibility and family business in the time of COVID-19: Changing strategy? *Sustainability (Basel), 13*(4), 2041. DOI: 10.3390/su13042041

Rolls, J. (2024). The transformational leader: The wellspring of the learning organization. In *Learning organizations* (pp. 101–110). Productivity Press. DOI: 10.4324/9781003578840-8

Rondon, L. P., Babun, L., Aris, A., Akkaya, K., & Uluagac, A. S. (2022). Survey on enterprise Internet-of-Things systems (E-IoT): A security perspective. *Ad Hoc Networks*, *125*, 102728. DOI: 10.1016/j.adhoc.2021.102728

Rostami, M., Burleson, W., Koushanfar, F., & Juels, A. (2013, May). Balancing security and utility in medical devices? In *Proceedings of the 50th annual design automation conference* (pp. 1-6).

Rushanan, M., Rubin, A. D., Kune, D. F., & Swanson, C. M. (2014, May). Sok: Security and privacy in implantable medical devices and body area networks. In 2014 IEEE symposium on security and privacy (pp. 524-539). IEEE.

Saaiq, M., & Ashraf, B. (2017). *Modifying "Pico" Question into "Picos" Model for More Robust and Reproducible Presentation of the Methodology Employed in A Scientific Study*. www.wjps.ir

Saks, A. M. (2022). Caring human resources management and staff engagement. *Human Resource Management Review*, *32*(3), 100835. DOI: 10.1016/j.hrmr.2021.100835

Santos, H., & Alves Lopes, A. (2024). A inteligência artificial nas ciências da saúde: Oportunidades, desafios e perspetivas futuras. *Revista Científica Internacional RevSALUS*, *6*(1), 1–9. DOI: 10.51126/revsalus.v6i1.653

Savage, T. S. (2011, April). The implications of RoHS on active implantable medical devices. In *2011 International Reliability Physics Symposium* (pp. 3B-1). IEEE.

Schein, E. H. (2009). *The corporate culture survival guide* (Vol. 158). John Wiley & Sons.

Scott, L. V. (2024). Leadership for a living planet: Strategies for integrating sustainability and profit. tredition.

Senyapar, H. N. (2024). Healthcare Branding and Reputation Management Strategies for Organizational Success. *Technium Soc. Sci. J.*, *55*, 26.

Shaikh, E. (2024). Strategies and approaches of corporate social responsibility toward multinational enterprises. *Advances in Logistics, Operations, and Management Science, 12*(3), 45–62. DOI: 10.4018/979-8-3693-0363-4

Shamir, B., House, R. J., & Arthur, M. B. (1993). The motivational effects of charismatic leadership: A self-concept based theory. *Organization Science, 4*(4), 577–594. DOI: 10.1287/orsc.4.4.577

Shaw, J., Ali, J., Atuire, C. A., Cheah, P. Y., Español, A. G., Gichoya, J. W., Hunt, A., Jjingo, D., Littler, K., Paolotti, D., & Vayena, E. (2024). Research ethics and artificial intelligence for global health: Perspectives from the global forum on bioethics in research. *BMC Medical Ethics, 25*(1), 46. Advance online publication. DOI: 10.1186/s12910-024-01044-w PMID: 38637857

Sheehy, L., Bouchard, S., Kakkar, A., El Hakim, R., Lhoest, J., & Frank, A. (2024). Development and initial testing of an artificial intelligence-based virtual reality companion for people living with dementia in long-term care. *Journal of Clinical Medicine, 13*(18), 5574. Advance online publication. DOI: 10.3390/jcm13185574 PMID: 39337060

Shinde, R., Patil, S., Kotecha, K., & Ruikar, K. (2021). Blockchain for Securing AI Applications and Open Innovations. *Journal of Open Innovation, 7*(3), 189. DOI: 10.3390/joitmc7030189

Sinclair, A. (2005). *Doing leadership differently: Gender, power and sexuality in a changing business culture*. Melbourne Univ. Publishing.

Singh, B., Rahim, M. A. B. U., Hussain, S., Rizwan, M. A., & Zhao, J. (2023, October 1). AI Ethics in Healthcare - A Survey. IEEE Xplore. DOI: 10.1109/QRS-C60940.2023.00086

Singh, K. (2023). Impact of Patent (Amendment) Act, 2005 on Indian pharmaceutical industry. [JIPR]. *Journal of Intellectual Property Rights, 27*(6), 397–414.

Siripipatthanakul, S., & Sixl-Daniell, K. (2021). A Review Article Branding Dental Clinic Through Corporate Social Responsibility (CSR). *International of Trend in Scientific Research and Development, 5*(5), 866–876.

Siswadi, Y., Jufrizen, J., Saripuddin, J., Farisi, S., & Sari, M. (2023). Organizational Culture and Organizational Citizenship Behavior: The Mediating Function of Learning Firms and Organizational Commitment. *Jurnal Riset Bisnis Dan Manajemen, 16*(1), 73–82. DOI: 10.23969/jrbm.v16i1.7184

Sivagourounadin, K., Ravichandran, M., & Rajendran, P. (2021). National guidelines for gene therapy product (2019): A road-map to gene therapy products development and clinical trials. *Perspectives in Clinical Research, 12*(3), 118–125. DOI: 10.4103/picr.PICR_189_20 PMID: 34386375

Sjödin, D., Parida, V., & Visnjic, I. (2022). How can large manufacturers digitalize their business models? A framework for orchestrating industrial ecosystems. *California Management Review, 64*(3), 49–77. DOI: 10.1177/00081256211059140

Smith, J., Johnson, M., & Williams, A. (2019). Building Trust in e-Commerce: Exploring the Influence of Website Design Elements on Initial Trust Formation. [JOEUC]. *Journal of Organizational and End User Computing, 31*, 52–72.

Somech, A. (2006). The effects of leadership style and team process on performance and innovation in functionally heterogeneous teams. *Journal of Management, 32*(1), 132–157. DOI: 10.1177/0149206305277799

Sosik, J. J., & Godshalk, V. M. (2000). Leadership styles, mentoring functions received, and job-related stress: A conceptual model and preliminary study. *Journal of Organizational Behavior, 21*(4), 365–390. DOI: 10.1002/(SICI)1099-1379(200006)21:4<365::AID-JOB14>3.0.CO;2-H

Srivastava, A. (2019). Patent and competition interface: Issues and challenges in India. *International Journal of Social Science and Economic Research, 4*(2), 1521–1527.

Stasolla, F., Di Gioia, M., Messina, I., Treglia, F., Passaro, A., Zullo, A., & Dragone, M. (2024). Assessing and recovering Alzheimer's disease: A comparative analysis of standard neuropsychological approaches and virtual reality interventions with the use of digital storytelling. *Frontiers in Psychology*, *15*, 1406167. Advance online publication. DOI: 10.3389/fpsyg.2024.1406167 PMID: 39114597

Student, S. K. (2023). Business and Health Communication Strategies in Healthcare Organizations for Corporate Social Responsibility (CSR) and the Role of Ethics in Healthcare Organizations (Master's thesis, Georgetown University).

Tagde, P., Tagde, S., Bhattacharya, T., Tagde, P., Chopra, H., Akter, R., Kaushik, D., & Rahman, M. H. (2021). Blockchain and Artificial Intelligence Technology in E-Health. *Environmental Science and Pollution Research International*, *28*(38), 52810–52831. DOI: 10.1007/s11356-021-16223-0 PMID: 34476701

Tang, Y., Akram, A., Cioca, L. I., Shah, S. G. M., & Qureshi, M. A. A. (2021). Whether an innovation act as a catalytic moderator between corporate social responsibility performance and stated owned and non-state owned enterprises' performance or not? An evidence from Pakistani listed firms. *Corporate Social Responsibility and Environmental Management*, *28*(3), 1127–1141. DOI: 10.1002/csr.2112

Tang, Y., Liu, H., & Wu, L. (2024). Fostering new product development through social media tools within an emerging digital world. *Technology Analysis and Strategic Management*, *36*(6), 1220–1233. DOI: 10.1080/09537325.2022.2088344

Telefonaktiebolaget LM Ericsson (PUBL) v. Competition Commission of India & Anr.

Tellis, G. J., Prabhu, J. C., & Chandy, R. K. (2009). Radical innovation across nations: The preeminence of corporate culture. *Journal of Marketing*, *73*(1), 3–23. DOI: 10.1509/jmkg.73.1.003

Temsah, M.-H., Jamal, A., Alhasan, K., Temsah, A. A., & Malki, K. H. (2024). OpenAI o1-Preview vs. ChatGPT in Healthcare: A New Frontier in Medical AI Reasoning. *Cureus*. Advance online publication. DOI: 10.7759/cureus.70640 PMID: 39359332

Thusini, S., Soukup, T., & Henderson, C. (2024). What influences perceptions about the concept of return on investment from healthcare quality improvement programmes? An institutional theory perspective. *International Journal of Health Governance*, *29*(3), 213–228. DOI: 10.1108/IJHG-04-2024-0045

Tian, M., Deng, P., Zhang, Y., & Salmador, M. P. (2018). How does culture influence innovation? A systematic literature review. *Management Decision*, *56*(5), 1088–1107. DOI: 10.1108/MD-05-2017-0462

Tony Mon George v. Deputy Controller of Patents & Designs, 2023:MHC:5451.

Tornini, V. A., Politi, S. P., Bruce, L., & Latham, S. R. (2023). Maximizing biomedical research impacts through bioethical considerations. *Disease Models & Mechanisms*, *16*(4), dmm050046. Advance online publication. DOI: 10.1242/dmm.050046 PMID: 37092345

Tran, N. T. (2022). Impact of corporate social responsibility on customer loyalty: Evidence from the Vietnamese jewellery industry. *Cogent Business & Management*, *9*(1), 2025675. DOI: 10.1080/23311975.2022.2025675

Tyler, B. B., Lahneman, B., Cerrato, D., Cruz, A. D., Beukel, K., Spielmann, N., & Minciullo, M. (2024). Environmental practice adoption in SMEs: The effects of firm proactive orientation and regulatory pressure. *Journal of Small Business Management*, *62*(5), 2211–2246. DOI: 10.1080/00472778.2023.2218435

Ucaryilmaz Deibel, T. (2022). Corporate social responsibility in the legal framework of global value chains. *Law and Development Review*, *15*(2), 329–356. DOI: 10.1515/ldr-2021-0098

Vaas, L. (2013). Doctors disabled wireless in Dick Cheney's pacemaker to thwart hacking. nakedsecurity by sophos, 22.

Vandemeulebroucke, T. (2024). The ethics of artificial intelligence systems in healthcare and medicine: From a local to a global perspective, and back. *Pflügers Archiv*. Advance online publication. DOI: 10.1007/s00424-024-02984-3 PMID: 38969841

Vázquez-Maguirre, M., & Benito, A. E. (2022). Impact or outputs? Exploring multinational's CSR activities in Mexico. *Sustainability (Basel), 14*(7), 4140. DOI: 10.3390/su14074140

Vora, K., & Schaeffer, M. (2017). A platform approach to securing your medical devices. White Paper. Renesas Electronics, 5, 2017.

Vrabcová, P., & Urbancová, H. (2021). Approaches of selected organisations in the Czech Republic to promoting the concept of sustainable development and corporate social responsibility. Agricultural Economics/Zemědělská Ekonomika, 67(7).

Walden, A., & Feliciano, L. (2022). A virtual reality intervention to reduce dementia-related agitation using single-case design. *Clinical Gerontologist, 45*(4), 1044–1054. DOI: 10.1080/07317115.2021.1954121 PMID: 34346857

Walumbwa, F. O., Avolio, B. J., Gardner, W. L., Wernsing, T. S., & Peterson, S. J. (2008). Authentic leadership: Development and validation of a theory-based measure. *Journal of Management, 34*(1), 89–126. DOI: 10.1177/0149206307308913

Wang, C., Zhang, J., Lassi, N., & Zhang, X. (2022). Privacy Protection in Using Artificial Intelligence for Healthcare: Chinese Regulation in Comparative Perspective. *Health Care, 10*, 1878. PMID: 36292325

Wartini, S., Prananta, W., Febriatmoko, B., & Putri, P. I. (2024). Theory of Resource-Based View (RBV): Integrated Framework of Distinctive Capability in University Performance. *Media Ekonomi Dan Manajemen, 39*(2), 334–349. DOI: 10.56444/mem.v39i2.4891

Weintraub, P., & McKee, M. (2019, March 1). Leadership for Innovation in Healthcare: An Exploration. *International Journal of Health Policy and Management*, *8*(3), 138–144. DOI: 10.15171/ijhpm.2018.122 PMID: 30980629

Wen, J., Yan, H., Wang, S., Xu, J., & Zhou, Z. (2024). The effectiveness of nursing interventions for elderly dementia patients based on virtual reality technology: A systematic review and meta-analysis. *Ageing Research Reviews*, *93*, 102135. Advance online publication. DOI: 10.1016/j.arr.2023.102135 PMID: 37995900

Wickert, C. (2021). Corporate Social Responsibility Research in the Journal of Management Studies: A Shift from a Business-Centric to a Society-Centric Focus. *Journal of Management Studies*, *58*(8). Advance online publication. DOI: 10.1111/joms.12775

Wirba, A. V. (2024). Corporate social responsibility (CSR): The role of government in promoting CSR. *Journal of the Knowledge Economy*, *15*(2), 7428–7454. DOI: 10.1007/s13132-023-01185-0

Wolniak, R., Wyszomirski, A., Olkiewicz, M., & Olkiewicz, A. (2021). Environmental corporate social responsibility activities in heating industry: Case study. *Energies*, *14*(7), 1930.

Xu, J., Glicksberg, B. S., Su, C., Walker, P. B., Bian, J., & Wang, F. (2020). Federated Learning for Healthcare Informatics. *Journal of Healthcare Informatics Research*, *5*(1), 1–19. DOI: 10.1007/s41666-020-00082-4 PMID: 33204939

Yaqoob, T., Abbas, H., & Atiquzzaman, M. (2019). Security vulnerabilities, attacks, countermeasures, and regulations of networked medical devices—A review. *IEEE Communications Surveys and Tutorials*, *21*(4), 3723–3768. DOI: 10.1109/COMST.2019.2914094

Ye, J., & Dela, E. (2023). The effect of green investment and green financing on sustainable business performance of foreign chemical industries operating in Indonesia: The mediating role of corporate social responsibility. *Sustainability (Basel)*, *15*(14), 11218. DOI: 10.3390/su151411218

Yuen, K. F., Cai, L., Qi, G., & Wang, X. (2021). Dimensions influencing autonomous vehicle adoption: An application of the technology acceptance model and innovation diffusion theory. *Technology Analysis and Strategic Management*, *33*(5), 505–519. DOI: 10.1080/09537325.2020.1826423

Yukl, G., & Mahsud, R. (2010). Why flexible and adaptive leadership is essential. *Consulting Psychology Journal*, *62*(2), 81–93. DOI: 10.1037/a0019835

Zaidi, S. Y. A., Waqas, M., Mahmood, F., Bint Raza, S., & Rehman, I. U. (2023). Is Seth Leadership a Quagmire? Depicting Its Characteristics Through the Subordinates Perspectives Form Pakistani Construction Companies. *Journal of Investigation & Reviews in Social Sciences Pakistan*, *6*(2), 2266–2281.

Zarifis, A., Kawalek, P., & Azadegan, A. (2020). Evaluating If Trust and Personal Information Privacy Concerns Are Barriers to Using Health Insurance That Explicitly Utilizes AI. *Journal of Internet Commerce*, *20*(1), 66–83. DOI: 10.1080/15332861.2020.1832817

Zeltiņa, J. (2019). Effectiveness of Article 102 of the Treaty on the Functioning of the European Union (TFEU) in regulating markets.

# About The Contributors

**Ricardo Marcão**, PhD, MBA, PMP, is a globally recognized expert in Project Management, Finance, and Strategy, currently serving as a Senior International Project Manager at SIBS, a leader in the Payments and Banking industry. With deep experience across sectors like Pharma and MedTech, IT, and Professional Services, Ricardo's unique expertise spans Grand Strategy, Democracy, and International Relations, positioning him as a thought leader in driving innovation, governance, and strategic transformation on a global scale. As the coordinator of several advanced programs at ISLA Santarém, including the Masters in Business Administration and Post-Graduations in Project Management, Quality Management, and Diplomacy and Financial-Economic Management, Ricardo shapes the next generation of business leaders through a strategic lens that integrates organizational management with international relations and democratic governance. A distinguished international speaker and academic, Ricardo plays a key role in fostering transatlantic relations between the US and Europe, contributing to global discourse on strategy, leadership, and governance. His active involvement with SCIP Portugal, APMP in NYC, PMI Portugal, and PMI South Florida underscores his commitment to strategic intelligence, project management excellence, and international cooperation.

**Vasco Santos** holds a PhD in Business Sciences with specialization in Marketing (Fernando Pessoa University, Portugal), a PhD in Tourism (Seville University, Spain), a Post-Doc in Innovation Management applied to Sustainable Luxury Tourism (Aveiro University, Portugal), an

Habilitation in Management (European University, Portugal), an MSc in Marketing and Tourism Promotion, and a BA in Hospitality Management (Higher School of Tourism and Maritime Technology, Polytechnic of Leiria). Lecturer at the Polytechnic University of Tomar. Lecturer at the Higher Institute of Management and Administrationof Santarém. Full researcher in GOVCOPP (Competitiveness, Innovation and Sustainability Research Group), University of Aveiro. Effective and founding member of PNT - National Tourism Platform. Author of several scientific papers and book chapters. Research areas: tourism, marketing, employer branding and management.

**Stéphanie Monteiro** is a Senior Quality Engineer at Nemotec, specializing in medical devices. She holds an MSc in Biomedical Technology and is a PhD researcher in Biomedical Engineering, focusing on medical devices and simulator development. Stéphanie has extensive expertise in quality management, medical devices, medical prototypes, and the pharmaceutical industry. She is a Certified Six Sigma Black Belt™ and has significant experience as a CSV Engineer and QA Technical Specialist, focusing on quality systems and continuous improvement. Additionally, she is affiliated with the Institute for Systems and Robotics (ISR-Lisboa), where she contributes as a Medical Devices Researcher, advancing innovation in healthcare technology.

***

**Gonçalo Rodrigues Brás** has been contributing to academia as a visiting professor and research fellow at various higher education institutions in Portugal since 2006. With a diverse professional background in consultancy, banking, and accounting, he brings a wealth of practical experience to his academic pursuits. Gonçalo earned his PhD in Business Management from the University of Coimbra in 2016. As an economist with a specialisation in econometric modelling, his research now focuses on sustainable development, responsible innovation, and public policy and administration. Alongside his academic work, his contributions to Portuguese newspapers have made him a significant voice, especially in the field of public economics.

**Sandra Mariya Koshi** is an LLM student specializing in Intellectual Property and Trade Law at Christ Deemed to be University. She is particularly interested in the nuances of intellectual property rights and their intersection with competition law, international trade, and emerging technologies.

**Isabel Reis,** Associate Professor at ISLA Santarém, teaching subjects such as Knowledge and Innovation Management, Change Management, People Management, Performance Management, among others. Member of scientific and pedagogical councils, Specialist Professor in Management and Administration, Master in Entrepreneurship and Innovation Management and PhD in Management, with a thesis on Employer Branding in the Digital Age. Coordinator of HRM master's program at the same Institution as well as head to Inclusion & Interculturality area. Since ever passionate about people management. Extensive experience in HR techniques and management. Researcher concerned with Talent Management issues, focused on attracting talent, and communicating with the new work generations.

# Index

## A



## B



## C



## D



## E



## F



## H



## I

## V



## W

www.ingramcontent.com/pod-product-compliance
Lightning Source LLC
LaVergne TN
LVHW082051011026
849162LV00019B/494